ASPECTS OF BLOOMSBURY

Also by S. P. Rosenbaum

*VICTORIAN BLOOMSBURY: The Early Literary History of the Bloomsbury Group, Volume 1

*EDWARDIAN BLOOMSBURY: The Early Literary History of the Bloomsbury Group, Volume 2

A BLOOMSBURY GROUP READER

VIRGINIA WOOLF'S WOMEN & FICTION: The Manuscript Versions of *A Room of One's Own*

THE BLOOMSBURY GROUP: A Collection of Memoirs and Commentary (*revised edition*)

* *From the same publishers*

Aspects of Bloomsbury

Studies in Modern English Literary
and Intellectual History

S. P. Rosenbaum

First published in Great Britain 1998 by
MACMILLAN PRESS LTD
Houndmills, Basingstoke, Hampshire RG21 6XS and London
Companies and representatives throughout the world

A catalogue record for this book is available from the British Library.

ISBN 0–333–72042–3

 First published in the United States of America 1998 by
ST. MARTIN'S PRESS, INC.,
Scholarly and Reference Division,
175 Fifth Avenue, New York, N.Y. 10010

ISBN 0–312–21305–0

Library of Congress Cataloging-in-Publication Data
Rosenbaum, S. P. (Stanford Patrick), 1929–
Aspects of Bloomsbury : studies in modern English literary and
intellectual history / S.P. Rosenbaum.
p. cm.
Includes bibliographical references and index.
ISBN 0–312–21305–0 (cloth)
1. English literature—20th century—History and criticism.
2. Bloomsbury (London, England)—Intellectual life—20th century.
3. Great Britain—Intellectual life—20th century. 4. Bloomsbury
group. I. Title.
PR478.B46R66 1998
820.9'00912—dc21   97–41112
                                                        CIP

© S. P. Rosenbaum 1998

All rights reserved. No reproduction, copy or transmission of this publication may be made without written permission.

No paragraph of this publication may be reproduced, copied or transmitted save with written permission or in accordance with the provisions of the Copyright, Designs and Patents Act 1988, or under the terms of any licence permitting limited copying issued by the Copyright Licensing Agency, 90 Tottenham Court Road, London W1P 9HE.

Any person who does any unauthorised act in relation to this publication may be liable to criminal prosecution and civil claims for damages.

The author has asserted his right to be identified as the author of this work in accordance with the Copyright, Designs and Patents Act 1988.

This book is printed on paper suitable for recycling and made from fully managed and sustained forest sources.

10 9 8 7 6 5 4 3 2 1
07 06 05 04 03 02 01 00 99 98

Printed and bound in Great Britain by
Antony Rowe Ltd, Chippenham, Wiltshire

To the Memory of
Max Black
and
Quentin Bell

Elders and Betters

'Everything is what it is, and not another thing' – Bishop Butler
(Epigraph to G. E. Moore's *Principia Ethica*)

'Only connect ...'
(Epigraph to E. M. Forster's *Howards End*)

Contents

Preface		x
1	The Philosophical Realism of Virginia Woolf	1
2	Bertrand Russell: The Logic of a Literary Symbol	37
3	Bloomsbury Letters	60
4	Keynes, Lawrence and Cambridge Revisited	68
5	E. M. Forster's *Aspects of the Novel* and Literary History	84
6	Towards the Literary History of *A Room of One's Own*	110
7	Leonard and Virginia Woolf at the Hogarth Press	142
8	Wittgenstein in Bloomsbury	161
Notes		190
Index of Names		209

Preface

The studies collected in *Aspects of Bloomsbury* have been published over the past twenty-five years. The subtitle, reused epigraphs, and first two essays reflect the focus of this collection on the interrelations of modern English literature and British philosophy out of which developed my interest in the literary history of Bloomsbury. The rest of the studies are offshoots of that history that I began in 1987 with *Victorian Bloomsbury* and continued in 1994 with *Edwardian Bloomsbury*. (*Georgian Bloomsbury* should appear before the next millennium and subsequent volumes in its first decade.) Some of the material here will be used in the volumes to come but little has been incorporated in those already published. Other essays I have written on Bloomsbury's intellectual backgrounds, the Group's early poetry, E. M. Forster's Edwardian novels, Virginia Woolf's beginnings and Lytton Strachey's Indian dissertation have become chapters and are not reprinted here. Also not included are the introductions to Virginia Woolf's unknown essays and stories that I discovered during the course of my research and which have now been incorporated in editions of those works.

In a collection such as this some repetition is inevitable. Repetition can be meaningful, however, and I have not attempted to remove it. In three of the essays, for example, there are discussions of the brilliant late essay 'My Early Beliefs' that Keynes wrote for Bloomsbury's Memoir Club. Here the repetition is justified by the number of commentators who have taken the memoir as the last word on Bloomsbury's beliefs when it was really only the first. The original principal members of that collectivity of loving friends and relations known as the Bloomsbury Group may also be worth listing here again. They included the sisters Virginia Woolf and Vanessa Bell, their husbands and companions Leonard Woolf, Clive Bell, Duncan Grant and Roger Fry as well as those friends from Cambridge Lytton Strachey, John Maynard Keynes, E. M. Forster, Desmond MacCarthy and his wife Molly. Other more obscure names could be added, but the limits of the Group cannot be properly stretched to encompass any friend of the friends.

Interest in Bloomsbury has developed enormously over the past quarter century; much of it remains biographically driven, though without the Group's works there would be little interest in their lives. The literary history of the Bloomsbury Group is devoted, however, to the analysis and comparison of the Group's interrelated writings in chronological sequence, and that concern is present as well in most of the essays collected here. But no systematic explanation of historical influence is assumed or implied. The approaches of these studies are, in accordance with Bloomsbury's own ideas, eclectic. They attempt to provide aspects or, as Wittgenstein called them in his notes on Frazer's *The Golden Bough*, hypothetical links that are intended only to bring attention to connections between the facts (see below, p. 161).

I have not tried to revise these essays beyond correcting errors, altering an awkward word or phrase, making the spelling uniform, updating references to previously unpublished sources, and occasionally omitting a passage that now seems wrong-headed. Details of changes together with information about the occasions for which these studies were done is given in the notes at the end of the volume.

I have acknowledged in other places the many individuals and institutions that have made my work possible over the years, but I must thank Andrew McNeillie here for suggesting a title for the collection. My deepest debts are indicated in the dedication. What I owe Naomi Black is beyond acknowledgement.

S. P. R.

Toronto
January 1998

1 The Philosophical Realism of Virginia Woolf

> 'Why dont you contribute to the Queen's dolls House, Virginia?' 'Is there a W. C. in it, Vita?' 'You're a bit hoity toity, Virginia.' Well, I was educated in the old Cambridge School. 'Ever heard of Moore?' 'George Moore the novelist?' 'My dear Vita, we start at different ends.'
> (Conversation with Vita Sackville-West reported by Virginia Woolf in a letter to Clive Bell, 23 January 1924)[1]

During the past thirty or forty years a number of studies have found the fiction of Virginia Woolf to be philosophically significant, though she has seldom been called outright a philosophical novelist. Perhaps the tendency to identify the philosophical novel with the novel of ideas is the reason why critics appear to be reluctant to think about her in those terms. That there were other ways of using philosophy in fiction besides the novel of ideas is clearly implied by Virginia Woolf in her essay on George Meredith. She complained that his teaching was obtrusive in his fiction,

> and when philosophy is not consumed in a novel, when we can underline this phrase with a pencil, and cut out that exhortation with a pair of scissors and paste the whole into a system, it is safe to say that there is something wrong with the philosophy or with the novel or with both (I, 230).[2]

These remarks were not written by someone hostile or even indifferent to philosophy and its importance for fiction. They suggest, on the contrary, that Virginia Woolf had her own ideas about the nature of philosophy as well as the novel. This essay is an attempt to examine some of those ideas and the ways in which they are 'consumed' in her fiction.

I

If many critics have agreed that Virginia Woolf's novels have philosophical meanings of one kind or another, they have disagreed as to what the philosophy actually is. Bergsonism, empiricism, idealism and existentialism have all been brought to bear on her work but with unconvincing results.[3] The publication of John Maynard Keynes's *Two Memoirs* in 1949 introduced a different and more important philosophical dimension to the interpretation of Virginia Woolf. Keynes does not mention her specifically in his second memoir, entitled 'My Early Beliefs', but his brilliant, partial generalisations cover the impact of G. E. Moore's ethics and personality on himself, his friends and their circle, which of course included Virginia Woolf. Keynes discusses how he and his friends accepted Moore's 'religion' as set forth in *Principia Ethica*. It consisted of 'timeless, passionate states of contemplation and communion', the greatest of which were, according to Moore, 'certain states of consciousness, which may be roughly described as the pleasures of human intercourse and the enjoyment of beautiful objects'. Moore himself, says Keynes, was 'a puritan and a precisian', but his followers ignored his morals, his concern with the relation of ethics to conduct. Keynes marvelled that Moore was so oblivious to the life of action, that the basic intuitions of his ethics were so limited, and that his influence on them was so much of a piece with Edwardian individualism.[4]

Keynes's account, which has been cited by friend and foe alike in discussions of the importance of *Principia Ethica* for the Bloomsbury Group,[5] was authoritatively challenged and modified in 1960 by Leonard Woolf's first volume of autobiography, *Sowing*. Woolf found Keynes 'quite wrong' in saying that Moore's disciples separated his morals and religion or that Moore ignored action for contemplation.[6] The details of the disagreement, together with memoirs and interpretations by Clive Bell, Desmond MacCarthy, Bertrand Russell and others, need not be gone into here. The point is that in assessing Moore's influence on his Cambridge circle, it is not sufficient to rely on Keynes's memoir. Leonard Woolf's account is also indispensable.

Virginia Woolf once wrote to a critic that she had no training in philosophy; such knowledge of it as she possessed came 'simply from listening to people talking...'.[7] In addition to her father, those people included a brother, a brother-in-law, a husband and at least one close friend, all of whom had seriously concerned themselves with philosophy at Cambridge, and all of whom, with the exception of Leslie Stephen, had come under the influence of G. E. Moore and to a lesser extent Bertrand Russell and J. McT. E. McTaggart. Leonard Woolf has well described how he and a number of friends – including Roger Fry – were 'permanently inoculated with Moore and Moorism', and through them, others who were not at Cambridge or did not belong to the Apostles – Vanessa and Virginia Stephen, Clive Bell, Duncan Grant – were also

> deeply affected by the astringent influence of Moore and the purification of that divinely cathartic question... 'What do you mean by that?' Artistically the purification can, I think, be traced in the clarity, light, absence of humbug in Virginia's literary style and perhaps in Vanessa's painting.
> ... The colour of our minds and thought had been given to us by the climate of Cambridge and Moore's philosophy.... But we had no common theory, system, or principles which we wanted to convert the world to....[8]

To this revealing assertion of G. E. Moore's importance for Virginia Woolf can now be added the information that she read Moore himself carefully. In August 1908, when she was twenty-seven years old and at work on *The Voyage Out*, Virginia Stephen wrote to Saxon Sydney Turner that she was making headway with Moore and what must have been *Principia Ethica*, 'though I have to crawl over the same page a number of times, till I almost see my own tracks'. To her brother-in-law Clive Bell she wrote in the same month,

> I split my head over Moore every night, feeling ideas travelling to the remotest parts of my brain, and setting up a feeble disturbance hardly to be called thought. It is almost a physical feeling, as though some little coil of brain unvisited by any blood so far, and pale as wax, had got a little life into it at last; but had not strength to keep it. I have a very clear notion which parts of my brain think.

Finally, on 29 August she wrote to her sister,

> I finished Moore last night; he has a fine flare of arrogance at the end – and no wonder. I am not so dumb foundered as I was; but

the more I understand, the more I admire. He is so humane in spite of his desire to know the truth....⁹

Leonard Woolf's statements along with these letters show the extent to which Virginia Woolf was educated, as she said to Vita Sackville-West, in 'the old Cambridge school' where one George Moore was not to be confused with another. And it would seem reasonable that an examination of the philosophical bases of her fiction should begin for once at the same end that she did. Philosophically, G. E. Moore influenced Virginia Woolf more than anyone else, but in addition to this direct influence on her and her circle Moore's philosophy is also *representative* of the intellectual milieu in which Virginia Woolf was born and bred. Many of the ideals and ideas in or underneath Virginia Woolf's novels were shared by Moore with such diverse persons as Leslie Stephen, McTaggart, Roger Fry, Lowes Dickinson and Bertrand Russell. Candour, clarity, analysis, art, love, logic and common sense are among the more important features of a family resemblance among these men, though they did not value all of these things equally.

In his 'Reply to My Critics' written at the end of his career, Moore divided his responses into three categories that reflect the nature of his achievement. They were sense-perception, ethics and philosophic method.[10] It is not possible to examine in the space that I have here the way these divisions correspond to Moore's significance for Virginia Woolf, and I have had to select what seems to me to be the most important of them, namely sense-perception. Moore's ethics, though of crucial significance in Virginia Woolf's art and life, depend fundamentally on his epistemology. Similarly, in her fiction ethical assumptions rest on epistemological ones.

II

The term 'blue' is easy enough to distinguish, but the other element which I have called 'consciousness' – that which sensation of blue has in common with sensation of green – is extremely difficult to fix. That many people fail to distinguish it at all is sufficiently shown by the fact that there are materialists. And, in general, that which makes the sensation of blue a mental fact seems to escape us: it seems, if I may use a metaphor, to be transparent – we look through it and see nothing but the blue;

we may be convinced that there *is something* but *what* it is no philosopher, I think, has yet clearly recognised.[11]

This passage from G. E. Moore's famous 'The Refutation of Idealism', which he published at the age of thirty in 1903 – in the same year as *Principia Ethica* – illustrates the relevance of Moore's epistemology for Virginia Woolf's fiction. But first the general context of the quotation needs to be understood. When Moore came up to Cambridge he was apparently a Lucretian materialist.[12] Under the influence of McTaggart he became an idealist. But already in the early idealist essays that he published before the turn of the century Moore was distinguishing between mind and ideas, 'and this was the beginning, I think, of certain tendencies in me which have led some people to call me a "Realist"....'.[13] In 'The Refutation of Idealism', Moore as a modern philosophical realist criticised not the idealists' contention that reality was spiritual (he said he devoutly hoped it was) but their central assumption that everything was mental because to be is to be perceived. Moore argued that the assumption is contradictory: it affirms that 'being' is identical with 'being perceived', and at the same time it distinguishes between them in making the statement. If a colour and the perception of a colour were identical, then the statement that a colour was being perceived would be the same as a statement saying that a colour is a colour. Moore concluded that we must distinguish between consciousness and the objects of consciousness that exist independently of it, and thus he maintained the position of modern – as opposed to medieval – philosophical realism. He is not a materialist here because he asserts the non-material reality of consciousness; he is not an idealist because he asserts the separate reality of material objects. Throughout his earlier philosophy Moore's most basic point is the distinction between the act and the object of consciousness. Or as Russell summarised it, 'What I think at first chiefly interested Moore was the independence of fact from knowledge and the rejection of the whole Kantian apparatus of *a priori* intuitions and categories, moulding experience but not the outer world.'[14]

In later years Moore came to think little of 'The Refutation of Idealism', but he did not alter his assumption of the basic dualism of consciousness and its objects. Much of his work in epistemology was spent in struggling with the nature of those objects. He had almost nothing to say, however, about the act itself, the nature of consciousness, apart from the passage just quoted and a later description of it in the same essay as 'diaphanous'.[15] Nevertheless, Moore is, along with William James and Bergson, a philosopher of consciousness. The very ideals of his ethics are states of consciousness. But it is the epistemological dualism, with its distinction of fact from knowing, that becomes a basic philosophical presupposition of Virginia Woolf's criticism and fiction.

The significance of Moore's realism for Virginia Woolf's critical theory can be seen in her well-known essay, 'Modern Fiction', which she first published in 1919. In attacking literary materialists, as she called Bennett, Wells and Galsworthy, Virginia Woolf uses the same distinction that Moore did in refuting philosophical materialists. By attending only to material reality both overlook that other reality that Moore called 'transparent' and 'diaphanous' and that Virginia Woolf described as 'a luminous halo, a semi-transparent envelope'. The literary materialists have also ignored the life of consciousness; they have attended to the fabric of things instead of recording 'the atoms as they fall upon the mind in the order in which they fall... the pattern, however disconnected and incoherent in appearance, which each sight or incident scores upon the consciousness' (II, 106–7). These familiar words have misled several critics into describing Virginia Woolf as an empiricist. One says he does not wish to get involved in philosophical distinctions yet finds it 'worth insisting that Mrs. Woolf was of all writers the least justified in using the word "materialist" as a term of abuse' because her own view of consciousness 'is in fact an expression of pure, crude, mechanical Lockean materialism'.[16] It is worth getting involved in philosophical distinctions when they are muddled, however, and when the writer's work is partly misconceived as a result. Materialism and empiricism are being confused here. Furthermore, neither was maintained by Virginia Woolf or G. E. Moore. Moore might be thought of as belonging to a broadly conceived empirical tradition in his approach to knowledge and in his concern with sense data; but in his insistence that consciousness included more than just sensory experience and in his refusal to accept sceptical conclusions that conflicted with common sense Moore was not an empiricist.[17] In 'The Refutation of Idealism' Moore rejected alike both the psychologism of empiricism and the subjectivity of idealism. In these ideas the representativeness of Moore's thought can be seen. In a very general way he is in the same philosophical tradition as Leslie Stephen; his criticism of materialism Moore could have adopted from McTaggart. But in his epistemological realism the influence on Virginia Woolf seems to have been direct. Through his ideas it should be clear that her emphasis on consciousness and her critique of literary materialists are no more an indication that Virginia Woolf is an idealist than her concern with sense impressions makes her an empiricist or materialist. For her and for Moore the most accurate and useful philosophical classification here is realism.

The significance of G. E. Moore's epistemology for Virginia Woolf's fiction can be seen most clearly to begin with in the experimental stories and sketches published in *Monday or Tuesday*. How Moore's realism helped her to write about the life of consciousness that the Edwardian materialistic novelists had neglected appears in them and in the novels that followed. Even the slightest pieces in the collection, the two impressionistic sketches called 'Blue and Green', appear to be exercises in the rendering of consciousness. In the passage quoted above Moore described consciousness as 'that which sensation of blue has in common with sensation of green'; by juxtaposing the descriptions of a series of blue and then green impressions, Virginia Woolf implies consciousness (which Moore said was so difficult to fix) through what the two sets of impressions have in common. Most of the stories in *Monday or Tuesday* are studies of the way consciousness combines with what it perceives to produce those states of mind that Virginia Woolf felt fiction should be about. The combining sometimes brings in the question of what is truth. Moore's realism involved a correspondence rather than an idealistic coherence theory of truth, and while Virginia Woolf was not directly concerned with anything so abstruse, we shall see later in her novels that truth is to be found in both the correspondence of the deliverances of consciousness with external reality and the coherence of mystical moments. Virginia Woolf's first published story, 'The Mark on the Wall', shows very well how Moore's philosophical realism together with the correspondence theory of truth underlies her early fiction. It is not a difficult story and yet it and 'An Unwritten Novel' have frequently been misunderstood. 'The Mark on the Wall' consists of a narrator sitting in a chair wondering what a certain mark on the wall is, and engaging in various reveries that start from the possibility that the mark is one thing or another. Only at the end of the story does the narrator learn from another character that the mark is a snail. The reveries, or trains of thought as they are called in the story, are represented by a technique that Virginia Woolf said in her diary allowed 'one thing [to] open out of another' (p. 23)[18] and that her commentators have described as the stream of consciousness technique. It is undoubtedly too late in the day to protest against a label that is indiscriminately affixed to such different writers as Joyce, Faulkner and Virginia Woolf, but it may still be worth noting what Virginia Woolf herself meant by the phrase. In her essay 'Middlebrow' she refers parenthetically to 'lapsing into that stream which people call, so oddly, consciousness, and gathering wool from the sheep...' (II, 202). This kind of stream is not represented in her fiction. What is called her stream of consciousness technique resembles, say, Joyce's, only in its depiction of internal, subjective awareness and in the representation of thoughts and feelings as opening out of one another. In these sequences she never abandons punctuation or syntax and rarely tries to represent the subconscious. They are usually presented in the third person – 'one', not 'I', is her favourite pronoun – and the most accurate description of them is that Virginia Woolf used in her diary when she referred to her technique in *To the Lighthouse* as 'oratio obliqua' (p. 100). Her technique in *The Waves* she described as 'soliloquies' (p. 159). The sequences she represents in these novels and in her short stories owe more to Locke and Sterne than they do to Freud, though Virginia Woolf does not engage in the empiricists' atomisation of experience that William James was criticising in his famous phrase. It is more useful on the whole to think of Virginia Woolf's representations of consciousness in terms of states rather than streams. In these states, consciousness is not chopped up but represented as organic wholes in G. E. Moore's sense of the term meaning a whole that has no regular relation to the sum of its parts.[19] William James also used the images of a halo and a penumbra to illustrate his conception of consciousness, both of which give a better general notion of consciousness as Moore and Virginia Woolf conceived of it than a stream.

In 'The Mark on the Wall' the technique and content of the trains of thought started by the mark have led to misinterpretations of their function. The story presents not merely these ideas but also the ludicrous discrepancy between them and their cause, between the ranging speculations and the mark that the narrator cannot be bothered to identify. A recent critic is as wide of the mark as the narrator when he reads this and other stories as an 'assertion of subjectivity or idealism'[20] in which the snail is unimportant and the ideas all important. There is no denying the significance in Virginia

Woolf's subsequent work of such ideas as the masculine conception of reality, the mysteriousness of life, or the impersonal world that exists apart from us, but these ideas and the methods by which they are presented must be seen in the context of the story. The point of view in the story, the personality of the narrator who speculates on the impossibility of knowing anything because she cannot be troubled to stand up and see just what exactly is the mark on the wall, is an element in the story that should not be overlooked. Sanity and sense involve the interrelations of thought *and* external reality, of consciousness *and* the objects of consciousness. In 'An Unwritten Novel' there is the same silly discrepancy between the trains of thought and their cause, between imagined and actual reality. And there is the same plunging from ridiculing to being ridiculous in the narrator's sequence of ideas. There is also the same deflating revelation at the end of the true nature of external reality.

A number of the stories in *Monday or Tuesday* could be described as epistemological tales. Moore's dualistic theory of perception underlies their representation of the acts and objects of consciousness. In stories like 'The Mark on the Wall' and 'An Unwritten Novel', as well as in essays like 'Modern Fiction', Virginia Woolf is exploring the world through these assumptions and criticising views of reality that ignore or minimise either half of the dualism.

III

In Virginia Woolf's first two novels, *The Voyage Out* and *Night and Day*, G. E. Moore's ethics appear in various interesting guises,[21] but his epistemology is only latent. Not until the experiments of *Monday or Tuesday* that led to *Jacob's Room*, the third and most epistemological of her novels, does Moore's realism become crucial for Virginia Woolf's art. A key to *Jacob's Room* can be found again in the essay 'Modern Fiction' where Virginia Woolf maintained that if a writer were free to

> base his work upon his own feeling and not upon convention, there would be no plot, no comedy, no tragedy, no love interest or catastrophe in the accepted style... (II, 106)

There is little or no plot, comedy, tragedy or love interest in *Jacob's Room*. The catastrophe of Jacob's death is not even given.

Jacob's Room is an anti-novel. Echoes of *Tristram Shandy* can be heard in the visits of Captain Barfoot to the widowed Mrs Flanders. Jacob's name – Jacob means supplanter – alludes not only to the famous place where so many of his generation were buried but also to that celebrated heroine of another eighteenth-century novel that Virginia Woolf described in 1919 as 'indisputably great': *Moll Flanders* (I, 63). 'The Fortunes and Misfortunes of the Famous Moll Flanders' are replaced by a modern quest for Jacob himself. The direction of the quest follows Jacob's education into the ways of mind and matter. The title names a room, not an occupant. At the beginning Archer is calling '"Ja–cob! Ja–cob!"' (p. 6). At the end Bonamy cries '"Jacob! Jacob!"' (p. 176). Other characters call him throughout the novel. Everyone who loves Jacob seems to lose him at one time or another; the shifting dislocations of time and especially place help to convey this absence or remoteness. On one level *Jacob's Room* is an author in search of her character. The quest is also elegiac because Jacob resembles Virginia Woolf's brother Thoby who died at twenty-six. Epistemologically, the novel is a quest for the nature of consciousness. Is not the task of the novelist, Virginia Woolf asked in 'Modern Fiction', 'to convey this varying, this unknown and uncircumscribed spirit' (II, 106) that is consciousness? But what *is* consciousness and how can the novelist convey it? These questions to which *Jacob's Room* is addressed are distinct because Virginia Woolf does not present a narrator introspecting his own consciousness. She wanted to avoid what, in a diary entry made before the beginning of her third novel, she called 'the damned egotistical self' that spoiled the work of James Joyce and Dorothy Richardson for her. She wanted a technique instead that would 'enclose the human heart' but without also enclosing the scaffolding and bricks of the materialistic novelists; all was to be 'crepuscular, but the heart, the passion, humour, everything as bright as fire in the mist' (p. 23). When she went on in this entry to note that the theme of her new novel 'is a blank to me', Virginia Woolf was closer than she realized to what *Jacob's Room* is all about.

Twice in *Jacob's Room*, once as Jacob is going up to Cambridge and then after his return from Greece, the narrator observes in the identical words, 'It is no use trying to sum people up. One must follow hints, not exactly what is said, nor yet entirely what is done' (pp. 29, 153). People cannot be summed up in *Jacob's Room* because people are not sums but Moorean organic unities that may be better or worse, greater or less, than the sums of their parts. 'Of all futile occupations', the narrator observes, 'this of cataloguing features is the worst. One word is sufficient. But if one cannot find it?' (p. 69). Thus do problems in epistemology become problems in poetics for Virginia Woolf. Nor is there any essence of character, any 'unseizable force' that novelists never catch; this crude vitalism of cabinet and club men who say character-drawing is a frivolous art 'enclosing vacancy' allows them to contemplate with equanimity the destruction of lives such as Jacob's (pp. 154–5). Though he may not be knowable, Jacob is killable. Another reason why people cannot be summed up is the translucent character of consciousness.

One of the ways that Virginia Woolf describes consciousness throughout her work is in metaphors of translucence. It is a halo, a semi-transparent envelope, a mist, through which light is dispersed. In *Jacob's Room* consciousness is referred to once as a darkening glass: 'We start out transparent, and then the cloud thickens. All history backs our pane of glass. To escape is vain' (p. 47). The sorrow of human experience is what darkens us. The translucence of consciousness keeps us from comprehending our own as well as other people's; we can never be sure their consciousnesses respond in the same way as ours do. Uncertainties and inconsistencies in the point of view of the novel somewhat obscure this in *Jacob's Room*. At one point the narrator says 'Whether we know what was in his mind is another question' (p. 93), yet there are places in the novel – at King's College Chapel, at the Parthenon – where we are unambiguously presented with the contents of Jacob's mind. These occasional inside views do not seriously detract from the difficulties that the narrator presents of understanding another person's mind.

In 1905 Moore published a long and difficult paper entitled 'The Nature and Reality of Objects of Perception', which caused considerable excitement among such friends as Keynes and Strachey.[22] Starting with the assumption that 'there is a sense in which no man can observe the perceptions, feelings or thoughts of any other man', Moore tried to answer the question '*What* reason do my observations give me for believing that any other person has any particular perceptions or beliefs?' His answer involved the postulation of 'sense-contents' (later called sense-data) that Moore argued were independent of our private perceptions of them.[23] Moore's question, if not exactly his answer, underlies the quest for Jacob's consciousness. We can describe what Jacob looks like and how he acts, yet 'there remains over something which can never be conveyed to a second person save by Jacob himself.... Even the exact words get the wrong accent on them.... What remains is mostly a matter of guess work. Yet over him we hang vibrating' (pp. 71–2). Why we have to hang vibrating is explained a page or so before in a passage that eloquently summarises the epistemological and the elegaic aspects of the quest:

> In any case life is but a procession of shadows, and God knows why it is that we embrace them so eagerly, and see them depart with such anguish, being shadows. And why, if this and much more than this is true, why are we yet surprised in the window corner by a sudden vision that the young man in the chair is of all things in the world the most real, the most solid, the best known to us – why indeed? For the moment after we know nothing about him.
>
> Such is the manner of our seeing. Such the conditions of our love. (pp. 70–1)

What can the novelist do with these conditions of perception and love? The answer is in the novel's title. We must attend not merely to what Jacob says and does but also to what he perceives. We must go to Jacob's room.

Jacob's room represents what he perceives in two ways. First, it is his immediate environment. From his rooms in Cambridge, London, Patras, we follow hints about his thoughts and feelings by becoming conscious of what he has been conscious of. Second, Jacob's room is symbolic of his consciousness itself. Critics have noted Virginia Woolf's use of windows as epistemological symbols;[24] the rooms from which one looks out through these windows are often symbolic of a consciousness perceiving external reality. Twice the word 'room' appears in titles of her works. In *A Room of One's Own* Virginia Woolf argued that to be a good writer one had to have an independent consciousness of one's own in order to attend to worthwhile ends and not be distracted by goods that were only means to these ends.[25] The two meanings of room as symbol of consciousness are not completely separable, of course. The symbolic room often includes objects of perception inside or outside itself; mere consciousness is as difficult to fix as Moore said it was. But both meanings are consistent with Moore's realism. Jacob's rooms are symbols of the acts and the objects, the form and the content, of consciousness.

Jacob's rooms are also where epistemology and poetics come together again. On the first page of the notebook in which Virginia Woolf wrote *Jacob's Room* (she had the title from the start), she asked and then answered, 'Yet what about form? Let us suppose that the Room will hold it together.'[26]

The dualistic realism that is the principal philosophical presupposition underlying *Jacob's Room* can also be seen in the novel's concern with mind and body. Jacob's education makes him aware, through such different people as Cambridge dons and London prostitutes, of the indispensable value of mind, but the discussion of all this belongs to the examination of Moore's ethical influence on Virginia Woolf. Epistemologically, the dualism of mind and body in the novel is unmistakable in *Jacob's Room*'s pervasive concern with death. Jacob's consciousness is so difficult to apprehend not only because of its unity, translucence and privacy, but also because of its transience. The room as symbolic of consciousness and the objects of consciousness is so appropriate here because the room can be emptied, as the title suggests, leaving only the objects. The question asked of Jacob's father – described on his tombstone as a merchant of the city because, though he had only been one for three months, he had to be called something – is a question that haunts the narrator and the novel: 'Had he then been nothing?' The question applies to Jacob as well, as does the reply: 'An unanswerable question, since even if it weren't the habit of the undertaker to close the eyes, the light so soon goes out of them' (p. 14). *Jacob's Room* is finally a novel about the perception of mortality. It tries to present how we perceive what it is that dies, and in doing this the novel again assumes the rudiments of a realistic theory of perception. Consciousness dies; things like rooms and shoes endure. Death as an ultimate problem in epistemology was not, however, a concern of Moore's. His few published remarks on immortality show that he did not believe in it and found attempts such as McTaggart's to theorise about it incomprehensible.[27] There are no whispers of immortality in *Jacob's Room* either.[28] The quest for the mysterious and transient consciousness of another is bewildering if not futile, and these are the conditions of our love and our perceiving. The only epistemological certainty concerning death seems to be the way that the thoughts and facts of death can alter our perceptions of external reality. At the beginning of the novel Mrs Flanders's tears make the bay she sees quiver, and the original last line of the novel describing her in *Jacob's Room* was, 'The room waved behind her tears.'[29] In Virginia Woolf's third novel a tear is an epistemological thing.

IV

The rooms of *Mrs. Dalloway* like those of *Jacob* are symbolic. Clarissa's attic bedroom represents her virginal perceptions and reactions to certain things. When Septimus Smith's consciousness is about to be invaded by a soul-forcing doctor, he throws himself out of his room to death. And there is the old lady living across from Clarissa. Two-thirds of the way through *Mrs. Dalloway*, the heroine stands at her drawing-room window watching the lady and brooding over her daughter's somewhat fanatical tutor and an old lover just back from India:

> Why creeds and prayers and mackintoshes? when, thought Clarissa, that's the miracle, that's the mystery; that old lady, she meant, whom she could see going from chest of drawers to dressing-table. She could still see her. And the supreme mystery which Kilman might say she had solved, or Peter might say he had solved, but Clarissa didn't believe either of them had the ghost of an idea of solving, was simply this: here was one room; there another. Did religion solve that, or love? (pp. 140–1)

E. M. Forster has quoted this passage to illustrate how wrong it is to describe Virginia Woolf's work in terms of 'mysticism, unity beneath multiplicity, twin souls...', and he concludes, 'As far as her work has a message, it seems to be contained in the above paragraph. Here is one room, there another.'[30] Forster's comments, made when *Mrs. Dalloway* was Virginia Woolf's latest novel, are as relevant to his own work as to his friend's. Both staunchly represent in their fiction the marvellous, irreducible otherness of people, the plurality of souls, the obduracy of matter. Both are philosophical realists, and there is something of the mystic in each as well. Ignoring either aspect results in misinterpretation, though in fact it is the realistic assumptions that are most often overlooked.

How Virginia Woolf contrives to base a novel on both mysticism and philosophical realism can be seen in the climax of *Mrs. Dalloway* when there recurs the scene that Forster called the embodiment of Virginia Woolf's message. Just before the scene Mrs Dalloway hears of Septimus Smith's suicide. She goes into a little room away from the party and thinks,

> A thing there was that mattered; a thing, wreathed about with chatter, defaced, obscured in her own life, let drop every day in corruption, lies, chatter. This he had preserved. Death was defiance. Death was an attempt to communicate, people feeling the impossibility of reaching the centre which, mystically, evaded them; closeness drew apart; rapture faded; one was alone. There was an embrace in death. (p. 202)

This nearly mystical response to the suicide is anticipated earlier in the novel when Clarissa is thinking about her own inadequacies; they are presented as sexual but the experience described is not to be confined to that. 'She could see what she lacked. It was not beauty; it was not mind. It was something central which permeated; something warm which broke up surfaces and rippled the cold contact of man and woman, or of women together.' Sometimes she could yield to the charm of a woman: 'Then, for that moment, she had seen an illumination; a match burning in a crocus; an inner meaning almost expressed. But the close withdrew; the hard softened. It was over – the moment' (p. 36). Something that mattered; a mystical centre of some kind, momentary in duration and ecstatic in character – this becomes familiar in Virginia Woolf's work from *Mrs. Dalloway* onward. (The mystical moments of *Night and Day* are somewhat different.) In *Mrs. Dalloway*, however, the experience is tied to the separate lives of other people in their rooms. This clearly appears in the climactic scene of the novel when Mrs Dalloway draws the curtains apart and sees again the old lady in her room across the street; Mrs Dalloway's thoughts here recapitulate the novel's themes:

> It was fascinating, with people still laughing and shouting in the drawing-room, to watch that old woman, quite quietly, going to bed alone. She pulled the blind now. The clock began striking. The young man had killed himself; but she did not pity him; with the clock striking the hour, one, two, three, she did not pity him, with all this going on. There! the old lady had put out her light! the whole house was dark now with this going on, she repeated,

and the words came to her, Fear no more the heat of the sun. She must go back to them. But what an extraordinary night! She felt somehow very like him – the young man who had killed himself. She felt glad that he had done it; thrown it away while they went on living. The clock was striking. The leaden circles dissolved in the air. But she must go back. She must assemble. She must find Sally and Peter. And she came in from the little room. (pp. 204–5)

Just what other rooms and their occupants have to do with the mystical experience of closeness in Virginia Woolf's art can be seen in Moore's and Russell's early philosophical realism; other people and the mystical centre are both independent of our consciousness of them. Mystically, Virginia Woolf could be described as extroverted rather than introverted,[31] and her realistic epistemology is consistent with this.

In addition to the mysticism of *Mrs. Dalloway* there are two other major differences in the treatment of consciousness between it and *Jacob's Room*. First, instead of a quest for the consciousness of the central character there is postulated representation of different people's consciousnesses. This is not simply a change in point of view. Both novels contain limited and omniscient narration, but in *Mrs. Dalloway* there is a change in emphasis from the outside observer-narrator to the private consciousness of Clarissa Dalloway, Septimus Smith, Peter Walsh and others. (The observer also remains, as can be seen in the scathing description of the Bradshaws.) The second major difference between the two novels comes out of the first. Between the distinct, directly represented minds in *Mrs. Dalloway* there are crucial connections and disconnections. Through these relations Virginia Woolf is able to maintain her realistic outlook while confining her narration principally to individual subjective awarenesses. What the characters are conscious *of*, what they perceive in common, binds them and the novel together. Virginia Woolf touched on both these differences when she asked herself in her notes for the novel, 'whether the inside of the mind in both Mrs. D. and S. S. can be made luminous – that is to say the stuff of the book – lights on it coming from external sources.'[32] The degree to which she succeeded in *Mrs. Dalloway* measures the degree to which she met Arnold Bennett's criticism that it was all very well to attack Edwardian materialism but her own approach had not managed to create character.[33] The quest for

Jacob's consciousness left little time for any other characters in the novel, and one result is that our understanding of Jacob's own perceptions of others is limited by the little we know about those people. Virginia Woolf's well-known reply to Bennett, which she wrote while at work on *Mrs. Dalloway*, accepts his premise that novels are written to create character but complains that it is *his* characters who are not real enough.

> In one day thousands of ideas have coursed through your brains; thousands of emotions have met, collided, and disappeared in astonishing disorder. Nevertheless, you allow the writers to palm off upon you a version of all this, an image of Mrs. Brown, which has no likeness to that surprising apparition whatsoever. (I, 336)

That surprising apparition, Mrs Dalloway, is Virginia Woolf's Mrs Brown. *Jacob's Room* ends with empty shoes in a tenantless room; the last line of *Mrs. Dalloway* is 'For there she was.'

Yet in representing the consciousness of several characters rather than concentrating on the pursuit of one, Virginia Woolf does not forsake the privacy of consciousness that so interested her in *Jacob's Room*. *Mrs. Dalloway* is organised around private souls. Even the culminating party is a collection of individuals essentially alone. Each central consciousness is isolated with his own frigidity, madness or sentimentality that others can perceive but not alter. Septimus and Clarissa are linked in their isolating inability to love, though they feel more intensely than the other characters. They are consoled somewhat in their awareness of the isolation of others and in the value in their own integrity that must be protected from the soul-forcers, be they lovers or psychiatrists. But these essentially ethical matters cannot be discussed here apart from noting that the change from one consciousness to several makes personal relations and thus ethics much more important for Virginia Woolf's fourth novel than for her third.

Individual consciousnesses in *Mrs. Dalloway* relate to one another directly through their perceptions of one another and indirectly through their perceptions of their common environment. The direct relations develop from scattered encounters at the beginning of the novel to the party at the end. The general effect is similar to that in *The Years* where everything is described as coming over again yet differently. Consciousnesses are indirectly related to one another in

Mrs. Dalloway by a web of their perceptions. The warp and the woof of this web are their various perceptions of space and of time. The image of a web is actually used in the novel to describe Lady Bruton's consciousness, a thread of which attaches to her luncheon guests after they leave; it stretches and finally snaps when she sleeps (p. 124). A few pages later the web reappears with Richard Dalloway: 'And as a single spider's thread after wavering here and there attaches itself to the point of a leaf, so Richard's mind, recovering from its lethargy, set now on his wife...' (p. 126). The spatial perceptions that link consciousnesses are often of an external event that provides a transition in the novel from one mind to another. The prime minister's car, the airplane, the pattern of clouds are some of the examples that London provides. The pervasiveness of London in Mrs. Dalloway comes from Virginia Woolf's concern with her characters' awareness of their environment; a city is a very convenient setting in which to represent shared objects of perception and different responses to them. A skywriting advertisement for toffee is a thing of exquisite beauty for the insane Septimus. But perception is not merely a relative matter in the novel, and even Septimus knows at times his madness from his sanity: 'He began, very cautiously, to open his eyes, to see whether a gramophone was really there. But real things – real things were too exciting. He must be cautious' (p. 156).

One of the ways that Clarissa Dalloway thinks of herself is as a mist spread out between her friends (pp. 11–12). Peter Walsh recalls her idea that

> to know her, or any one, one must seek out the people who completed them; even the places.... It ended in a transcendental theory which, with her horror of death, allowed her to believe, or say that she believed (for all her scepticism), that since our apparitions, the part of us which appears, are so momentary compared with the other, the unseen part of us, which spreads wide, the unseen might survive, be recovered somehow attached to this person or that, or even haunting certain places, after death. Perhaps – perhaps. (p. 168)[34]

Clarissa's is a theory of perception as well as immortality. Its translucent metaphor of consciousness and its epistemological dualism are familiar features of Virginia Woolf's representations of perception. Less familiar is the notion of consciousness being defined or completed by what it is conscious of – a notion that in *Mrs. Dalloway* suggests how individual consciousnesses are related to one another through their perceptions of a common environment. The temporal perceptions of the characters illustrate this very clearly. One of Virginia Woolf's working titles for the novel was 'The Hours'. Views of time appear in the 'timeless' yet transitory moments of joy and despair that the central characters experience in the hours struck off on the bells of London's clocks, in the passage of a single day during which the forward action of the novel is set, and in the patterns of the lives of Clarissa, Septimus and Peter. These different uses of time are interrelated variously; the moment, for example, is connected with death through the recurring quotation from *Othello*, 'if it were now to die 'twere now to be most happy'. But there is no one unifying theme or theory of time in *Mrs. Dalloway*. Time as moment, hour, day or life is a condition of existence.

The uses of time in *Mrs. Dalloway* are worth belabouring a little because they have often been taken as philosophically very important – the philosophy being Bergson's. Time in Virginia Woolf's fiction ought not to be reduced to a dichotomy of scientific time and *durée réelle*. Mind time in *Mrs. Dalloway* is synchronised with clock time; the bells of the clocks fit naturally into the rhythm of the heroine's life, even coinciding with her final insights. Only the clocks of Harley Street are appropriately 'shredding and slicing, dividing and subdividing' (p. 113). The exaltation of the moment is a static not a dynamic experience; the consciousness of time is sequential, spatialised. All of which Bergson said it should not be. Time in *Mrs. Dalloway* does not so much flow as spread; rather than a river it is a sea in which the characters live like fish and experience in their different places the rippling circles of the hours. One of the most extraordinary things about *Mrs. Dalloway* is the water imagery in which Virginia Woolf describes the London existences of her characters. Even the function of time past in *Mrs. Dalloway* is part of the novel's philosophical realism that presents time as something that is experienced by consciousnesses, something that is outside themselves and that they share in the perception of. A number of critics have taken, as indications of a theory of memory similar to Bergson's, the tunnels of time that Virginia Woolf said in her diary she was digging out behind her characters when she needed their pasts (p. 61). That they are not can be seen in the acute criticism of Bergson's theory that Bertrand Russell made in 1912:

The whole of Bergson's theory of duration and time rests throughout on the elementary confusion between the present occurrence of a recollection and the past occurrence which is recollected.... What Bergson gives is an account of the difference between perception and recollection – both *present* facts – and what he believes himself to have given is an account of the difference between the present and the past.[35]

The consciousnesses of Clarissa and Peter move from perception to recollection and back again, but all the action of the novel is in the present. Through both perception and recollection Clarissa observes not only the pattern of her own life but also Peter's and even Sally Seaton's. The tunnels of time like the clocks of London are part of the novel's web of perceptions.

V

A discussion of the epistemology of *Mrs. Dalloway* is an incomplete way of approaching that novel because so many of its philosophical concerns are also ethical. This is true as well of Virginia Woolf's most overtly philosophical novel, *To the Lighthouse*. Yet here too philosophical realism shapes the novel. In Virginia Woolf's fifth novel we have for the first and last time a major character who *is* a philosopher. Despite this fact the philosophy in the novel has been overlooked because *To the Lighthouse* is also Virginia Woolf's most autobiographical novel. Mr Ramsay has been recognised as a philosopher only insofar as Leslie Stephen was one. With the evidence of Virginia Woolf's diary and Stephen's own 'sentimental autobiography'[36] it is as certain as these things ever are that Mr Ramsay is a close portrait of the author's father, just as Mrs Ramsay is modelled on her mother. One of the uses of biography in the study of fiction is the emphasis it can give to dissimilarities; with Mr Ramsay the ways in which he differs from Leslie Stephen are as interesting as the ways in which he resembles him. Leslie Stephen appeared once before in Virginia Woolf's fiction as the classical scholarly Ridley Ambrose in *The Voyage Out*. Both could pass as good likenesses of Leslie Stephen – except for the significant difference of their occupations. Leslie Stephen's achievements were those of a historian of thought, a biographer, an editor, a literary critic and a moral philosopher. Mr Ramsay is none of these. He resembles

Leslie Stephen in his sentimentality, his sense of failure, his implicitly agnostic stoicism, and in what his daughter once in an essay called his 'intemperate candour' (II, 48). But as close as he comes to the pursuits of the author of *English Thought in the Eighteenth Century* is when he has promised 'to talk "some nonsense" to the young men of Cardiff about Locke, Hume, Berkeley and the causes of the French Revolution' (p. 73). Philosophically, Leslie Stephen's major work was an amalgam of Darwin and Mill entitled *The Science of Ethics*. Moore's demolition of Spencer's ethics in *Principia Ethica* destroyed it too. Nothing of *The Science of Ethics* survives in *To the Lighthouse* except maybe the faint echo of utilitarianism in Mr Ramsay's thoughts on Shakespeare and the average man (p. 70). Furthermore, Leslie Stephen does not appear to have been very interested in Mr Ramsay's philosophical preoccupations. He was not an epistemologist and no one could call him 'the greatest metaphysician of the time' (p. 62).

Once Lily Briscoe asked Andrew Ramsay what his father's books were about.

> 'Subject and object and the nature of reality', Andrew had said. And when she said Heavens, she had no notion what that meant. 'Think of a kitchen table then', he told her, 'when you're not there.' (p. 40)

Brief, vague and fanciful as it is, this is an account not of Leslie Stephen's empiricism but of G. E. Moore's realism, where kitchen tables exist apart from our perceptions of them. 'The Refutation of Idealism' is on this very subject. It even has an example of a table existing in space. And certain features of Ramsay's career resembles Moore's. Mr Ramsay is described by Mr Bankes as ' "one of those men who do their best work before they are forty" '; his definite contribution had been a little book when he was twenty-five, and 'what came after was more or less amplification, repetition' (p. 41). Moore was thirty when *Principia Ethica* appeared, and his subsequent career was an anticlimax for some of his friends. Ramsay also suggests Moore rather than Stephen in his method of thought. His attempts 'to arrive at a perfectly clear understanding of the problem' (p. 56) are like the method of no philosopher Virginia Woolf read or knew of so much as Moore. These similarities between Moore and Ramsay have perhaps been obscured by the recurrent misunderstanding of the symbolisation of Mr Ramsay's thinking in the letters of the alphabet of thought. When she describes Mr Ramsay's futile struggle to get from Q to R, Virginia Woolf is not displaying what has been called 'some cerebral etiolation' in the portrait of a philosopher who '"thinks" with the most helpless particularity'.[37] She is doing the opposite. By representing Mr Ramsay's thinking as proceeding in the very general form of conventional logical symbols, Virginia Woolf is wittily extending the standard letters used to symbolise the conditional type of argument, If P then Q. Mr Ramsay on the frontiers of thought is struggling to get from Q to R. As E. M. Forster remarked about a scene in *Jacob's Room*, Virginia Woolf is describing not what the character is thinking of but something rarer: the process of thought itself.[38]

In certain respects, of course, Ramsay resembles G. E. Moore because Moore and Stephen belong to that general philosophical orientation inadequately described as Cambridge Rationalism. A discussion of Mr Ramsay's ethical convictions could show the extent to which Moore and Stephen agree and disagree, but this is unimportant here because the significance of Mr Ramsay's philosophy is his realism rather than his ethics. Moore's ethics did not accompany his epistemology into Mr Ramsay's thought; *Principia Ethica* is fundamental to the novel as a whole rather than to the part that is Mr Ramsay's moral thought. Just what the philosophical importance of Mr Ramsay is can be seen in the dichotomies running throughout *To the Lighthouse*. Mr and Mrs Ramsay can be viewed as embodying not only the masculine and feminine principles but also reason and intuition, analysis and synthesis, farsightedness and nearsightedness, thought and action, truth and beauty, perhaps even realism and idealism in some sense or other. These poles are not simply positive and negative values. Mr Ramsay's logic is a counterweight to his wife's instinct; she must yield to his truth and he pay homage to her beauty. Beneath the dichotomies is love, the fundamental value of the novel that they share and in which their differences are resolved at the end of the first part of *To the Lighthouse*. The Ramsays are individuals as well as a couple, and both have the capacity to lose their personalities in something outside themselves. The lighthouse symbolises and is a symbol for both. Its strokes of light bring Mrs Ramsay from a 'wedge-shaped core of darkness' (p. 99) into ecstasy; its physical isolation and purpose imply Mr Ramsay, who is described as being 'out thus on a spit of land which the sea is slowly eating away.... marking the channel out there in the floods alone' (pp. 71–2).

Autobiographically, the truism that *To the Lighthouse* offers is that Virginia Woolf was the daughter of Julia *and* Leslie Stephen. If *Mrs. Dalloway* can be regarded as Virginia Woolf's *Ulysses*, *To the Lighthouse* is her *À la recherche du temps perdu*. She wanted a new name for the kind of book she was writing after *Mrs. Dalloway* and thought of calling it an elegy, according to her diary (p. 80). Love and death are its main concerns, though in ways quite different from the elegiac *Jacob's Room*. Philosophically, the novel displays the indispensableness – as well as the incompleteness – of philosophical realism, and this is brought out by the third major character in the novel, Lily Briscoe. For all its dualisms, *To the Lighthouse* is also a novel of triads. It is emphatically divided into three parts, being the only novel of Virginia Woolf's with a table of contents and named rather than simply numbered sections. Even the lighthouse has three flashes. Set against the antitheses that include the different consciousnesses of Mr and Mrs Ramsay is the ultimate extinction of consciousness presented in the second part of the novel. In the third part Lily Briscoe struggles to harmonise the Ramsays' dichotomies through her own love and art. She finally balances Mr Ramsay's philosophy with what Mrs Ramsay has taught her. Form is finally combined with colour in her vision, and thus she is able to resolve at the end the last dichotomy of the novel, that of time and space.

In calling the first section of the novel 'The Window' Virginia Woolf indicates once more her concerns with the innerness and outerness of perception. Behind the window sits Mrs Ramsay on whose consciousness much of this section is focused. Outside, in front of the window, Mr Ramsay paces among the objects of perception. The inner-outer dualism is also represented, as in *Mrs. Dalloway*, by relating perceivers through their perceptions. The beam of the lighthouse functions in a similar way to the bell of Big Ben. Erich Auerbach has been one of the few critics to recognise that Virginia Woolf's 'multipersonal' rather than 'unipersonal' method places her work in the broad tradition of literary realism by virtue of the way it investigates objective reality.[39] Here is one point at which literary and philosophical realism touch. The most memorable use of this 'multipersonal' method so far in her fiction is to be found in the dinner party of *To the Lighthouse*. By moving from one person's private state of consciousness to another while still maintaining the public conversations, Virginia Woolf is able to juxtapose the different awarenesses without sacrificing the realities of the party. The Boeuf en Daube is as real as the subjective anxieties of its eaters. 'Subject and object and the nature of reality' is the philosophical basis of the party; the nature of reality appears not only in the individual awarenesses and what they are aware of but also more generally in the dualism that is symbolised throughout the novel in images of light and water. The lighthouse surrounded by the sea is an unmistakable example, but not only the lighthouse. When the candles are lit at the party, the characters become aware of the contrast of 'order and dry land' inside, and 'outside, a reflection in which things wavered and vanished, waterily'. They were all 'conscious of making a party together in a hollow, on an island; had their common cause against that fluidity out there' (pp. 151–2). Later in the party Mrs Ramsay feels 'there is a coherence in things, a stability; something, she meant, is immune from change, and shines out... in the face of the flowing, the fleeting, the spectral...' (p. 163). The light of consciousness can transcend the fluidity of matter, for a while anyway.

In the second section of *To the Lighthouse* the dualisms are extended beyond modes of perception, beyond mind and matter, to the poles of the human and the non-human. For all its obscure lyricism, 'Time Passes' is still the most sustained impersonal meditation on man and nature, on consciousness and its non-conscious environment, anywhere in Virginia Woolf's fiction. Amid the passing of time, the deaths of the old and the young, we are presented with the ineluctable separateness of nature from human consciousness of it. The difference between the human and the non-human pervades the whole section, even though 'the pool of time' that the house of the Ramsays is temporarily rescued from by Mrs McNab eventually includes people together with things.

> Did Nature supplement what man advanced? Did she complete what he began? With equal complacence she saw his misery, condoned his meanness, and acquiesced in his torture. That dream, then, of sharing, completing, finding in solitude on the beach an answer, was but a reflection in a mirror?... (pp. 207–8)

But if nature is independent of man, he is not independent of her, for nature's moods affect him and at times 'it was impossible to resist the strange intimation... that good triumphs, happiness

The Philosophical Realism of Virginia Woolf

prevails, order rules; or to resist the extraordinary stimulus to range hither and thither in search of some absolute good...' (p. 205). In other words, the nature of reality is such that objects are not dependent upon subjects but subjects are affected, at least, by their objects. This abstract conclusion is born out in the different perceptions of the Ramsays in 'The Window'. Mr Ramsay insists on the contingent nature of reality: the facts of weather cannot be changed by human wishes. Mrs Ramsay's mystical experience is, however, an inner state brought about by an outer reality.

The best commentary on 'Time Passes' is the last section of the novel, 'The Lighthouse'. Through the double action of Mr Ramsay's ritual journey to the lighthouse and Lily's painted vision, the oppositions between kinds of consciousness and between consciousness and temporal nature are brought together. Mr Ramsay completes the action of the novel's title and receives his children's love, as he received his wife's at the end of part one. Lily is finally able to paint her post-impressionist, non-representational balancing of coloured shapes. The trains of thought and feeling that accompany the creating of this picture involve philosophy in important ways. The stages of what could be called Lily's philosophical painting are worth looking at closely.

As Mr Ramsay and the two children go down to the boat Lily recalls her symbol for him and his philosophy:

> The kitchen table was something visionary, austere; something bare, hard, not ornamental. There was no colour to it; it was all edges and angles; it was uncompromisingly plain.

Mr Ramsay, Lily feels, had concentrated on this table until he 'partook of this unornamented beauty which so deeply impressed her' (pp. 240–1). Next, Lily faces her canvas and confronts 'this formidable ancient enemy of hers – this other thing, this truth, this reality, which suddenly laid hands on her, emerged stark at the back of appearances and commanded her attention'. Then doing what the Ramsays in their different ways have done, she exchanges 'the fluidity of life for the concentration of painting' (p. 245). Finally, when Lily asks the question of herself, 'What is the meaning of life?' the first stage in the thinking that accompanies her philosophical painting is reached. The answer has frequently been cited as one of the central passages in Virginia Woolf's fiction:

The great revelation had never come. The great revelation perhaps never did come. Instead there were little daily miracles, illuminations, matches struck unexpectedly in the dark; here was one.... Mrs. Ramsay saying 'Life stand still here'; Mrs. Ramsay making of the moment something permanent (as in another sphere Lily herself tried to make of the moment something permanent) – this was of the nature of a revelation. In the midst of chaos there was shape; this eternal passing and flowing... was struck into stability. Life stand still here, Mrs. Ramsay said. 'Mrs. Ramsay! Mrs. Ramsay!' she repeated. She owed this revelation to her (pp. 249–50).

In addition to the connections between art and ethics that it suggests, this revelation is very significant in *To the Lighthouse* not so much because of its novelty – something quite like it had been said in *Night and Day* and *Mrs. Dalloway* – as because of its incompleteness. Moments of illumination are no longer enough. As Lily struggles with her painting, 'tunnelling her way into her picture, into the past' (p. 267), thinking of love and of death, Lily repeats her question about the meaning of life:

What was it then? What did it mean? Could things thrust their hands up and grip one; could the blade cut; the fist grasp? Was there no safety? No learning by heart of the ways of the world? No guide, no shelter, but all was miracle, and leaping from the pinnacle of a tower into the air?

If, she goes on silently addressing the old poet Carmichael (according to Ramsay he might have been a great philosopher), the two of them could demand an explanation of why life was so inexplicable, then the space of her canvas would fill and Mrs Ramsay would return (p. 277). But without an explanation Mrs Ramsay's teaching is not enough; a life of matches struck in the dark is a life mainly spent in the dark. 'The waters of annihilation' (p. 278) that Lily feels she has stepped off into with these questions are like those Mr Ramsay and his children sail over to reach that tower symbolising miraculous insight in the midst of water – but from which one leaps when the miracle ends.

No explanations come, and Lily struggles with her painting, thinking of Mr Ramsay sailing farther away to the lighthouse. 'For whatever reason she could not achieve that razor edge of balance between two opposite forces; Mr. Ramsay and the picture; which was necessary' (p. 296). Something is missing from the design, just as something is missing from Mrs Ramsay's moments of illumination. Lily continues to recall the events of ten years ago: the marriage of the Ramsays was 'no monotony of bliss – she with her impulses and quicknesses; he with his shudders and glooms' (p. 305). Then Lily's concentration on her painting suddenly returns as something flutters at the window, Mrs Ramsay's window. Lily now attains the final stage of her thought and her painting:

> One wanted, she thought, dipping her brush deliberately, to be on a level with ordinary experience, to feel simply that's a chair, that's a table, and yet at the same time, It's a miracle, it's an ecstasy. The problem might be solved after all.

But then something moves at the window; a wave of white goes over the pane.

> 'Mrs. Ramsay! Mrs. Ramsay!' she cried, feeling the old horror come back – to want and want and not to have. Could she inflict that still? And then, quietly, as if she refrained, that too became part of ordinary experience, was on a level with the chair, with the table. Mrs. Ramsay – it was part of her perfect goodness to Lily – sat there quite simply, in the chair....

Lily's response is to walk to the edge of the lawn and look out over the bay: 'Where was that boat now? Mr. Ramsay? She wanted him' (pp. 309–10). Lily realises he must have reached the lighthouse. She can now draw the line at the centre of her balanced picture. The painting and the novel are finished.

What completes Lily's vision and brings about the reappearance of Mrs Ramsay is Mr Ramsay's philosophy. It is only when Lily is able to combine Mr Ramsay's epistemology of ordinary experience and Mrs Ramsay's illuminations that her problem is solved, the Ramsays balanced, time and space reconciled, the picture finished. The kitchen table when you are not there provides the commonsense ground, the safety, for miracles of illumination. Mr Ramsay's realism, when recalled by Lily, results in the most unreal return of Mrs Ramsay – but a return, it should be remembered, that is also dependent upon the supreme values of *Principia Ethica*, art and love.

VI

Of the extended piece of fiction that she wrote between *To the Lighthouse* and *The Waves*, Virginia Woolf said in her diary that, among other things, *Orlando* taught her 'how to keep the realities at bay' (p. 136). The plural is not to be confused with the singular here; the realities were to be kept at bay so that reality would have more scope. 'Philosophic words, if one has not been educated at a university, are apt to play one false', Virginia Woolf half-mockingly noted in *A Room of One's Own*. She knew very well that a great deal of G. E. Moore's work had shown how such words played philosophers false. *A Room of One's Own* was written right after *Orlando* and provides a kind of commentary on it in the way that *Three Guineas* comments on *The Years*. After her remark about philosophic words, Virginia Woolf went on,

> What is meant by 'reality'? It would seem to be something very erratic, very undependable – now to be found in a dusty road, now in a scrap of newspaper in the street, now a daffodil in the sun. It lights up a group in a room and stamps some casual saying. It overwhelms one walking home beneath the stars and makes the silent world more real than the world of speech – and then there it is again in an omnibus in the uproar of Piccadilly. Sometimes, too, it seems to dwell in shapes too far away for us to discern what their nature is. But whatever it touches, it fixes and makes permanent. That is what remains over when the skin of the day has been cast into the hedge; that is what is left of past time and of our loves and hates (pp. 165–6).

To live 'in the presence of reality' she concludes one must be independent, one must have a room and all that it symbolises of one's own. Reality here approaches the Ideal in *Principia Ethica* through the exaltation of shared and recollected moments of insight and illumination. In *Orlando* some of Moore's ethical ideas are explored and occasionally satirised; his epistemology is playfully distorted through the manner with which Virginia Woolf fends off the realities by separating consciousness from sexual and temporal realities. Orlando's metamorphosis and immortality allow her an impossible variety of states of consciousness. Virginia Woolf's notion of the androgynous mind, as developed in *A Room of One's Own*, appears to be based on a theory of mind that postulates changing states of mind rather than a single form of mental being. In *Orlando* these states are manifested in one's different selves; identity depends on a master conscious self which paradoxically assumes control only when one becomes unselfconscious. The distinction here between consciousness and self-consciousness, between awareness and self, becomes very important in *The Waves*. In *Orlando*, however, it serves as mainly a comic examination of the possibilities of the androgynous mind when attached to a body that has an androgynous past.

Yet time is as important as sex in *Orlando*. The absence of death in *Orlando* removes the mainspring of Virginia Woolf's preoccupation with time in her fiction, and her interest in the remembrance of things past and in the difference between change and our awareness of it becomes correspondingly emphasised. With three hundred years to draw on, Orlando has a rich store of recollection with which to back her perceptions. The distinction in *Orlando* between mind and clock time is, again, the distinction between consciousness of change and change itself. When Virginia Woolf writes of how an hour once lodged in 'the queer element of the human spirit' may be stretched to days or shrunk to a second, she is assuming a dualism of the act and objects of perception in order even to describe what she calls 'this extraordinary discrepancy between time on the clock and time in the mind' (p. 91).

Time in *The Waves* appears both within and without 'the queer element of the human spirit' that consciousness is for Virginia Woolf. As the dust jacket of the first English edition of the novel puts it,

> In Mrs. Woolf's new novel each character speaks in soliloquy against the background of the sea. Several lives thus appear as in a pageant detached from the framework of daily life, but they change and grow old as time goes on. In the end one of the characters sums up the effect of their lives as a whole.

Enough is known from Leonard Woolf's autobiographies about the operations of the Hogarth Press to make it more than likely that the person who wrote this account of *The Waves* was either the author or her husband. It is a just summary, and in using dramatic terms such as 'pageant' and 'soliloquy' it points up the drama of consciousness that the novel presents. *The Waves* is the culmination of Virginia Woolf's progress that began more than ten years before when she called upon novelists to exclude the extraneous and convey the semi-transparent envelope of consciousness.[40] This novel is her own fulfilment of a prophecy about the future of the novel that she wrote after *To the Lighthouse*. In 'The Narrow Bridge of Art' she wrote that the novel to come,

> will give, as poetry does, the outline rather than the detail. It will make little use of the marvellous fact-recording power.... It will have little kinship with the sociological novel or the novel of environment. With these limitations it will express the feeling and ideas of the characters closely and vividly, but from a different angle. It will resemble poetry in this that it will give not only or mainly people's relations to each other and their activities together, as the novel has hitherto done, but it will give the relation of the mind to general ideas and its soliloquy in solitude (II, 224–5).

All of this is done in *The Waves* through the form of six soliloquising consciousnesses that are preoccupied, at various periods in their lives, with their individual awareness of both outer and inner reality. The six are concerned not only with the impingement of others and the sea on their consciousnesses but also with their individual identities, their separate developing selves that are distinguishable from their consciousnesses. The philosophical realism of *The Waves* is, in short, both external and internal.

The external is the familiar dualism of consciousness and external reality, and nowhere in her fiction is this made more explicit than in the soliloquies and their lyrical, stage-direction settings of the sea – settings that Virginia Woolf described in her diary as 'insensitive nature' (p. 153). The same dualism underlies what the author once saw as the essential conflict of the novel: Bernard's final speech was, again according to her diary, to show 'the theme effort, effort, dominates: not the waves: and personality: and defiance...' (p. 162). Human consciousness is confronted with its impending extinction by the natural. The brevity of life is symbolised by the one day of consciousness that the rising and setting sun of the intervals represents as the duration of the six lives. Death has returned from its holiday in *Orlando*. Halfway through dinner at Hampton Court, the six – their egotism blunted by food and wine – share an experience of momentary extinction in which, as Louis says, ' "Our separate drops are dissolved; we are extinct, lost in the abysses of time, in the darkness."'' But when Bernard cries '"Fight!"'' and Neville says '"Oppose ourselves to this illimitable chaos"'', time returns with their consciousness of it, and the six move to a very different kind of moment in which they become one conscious life, a six-sided flower, as they did when they last dined with Percival. This moment is opposed to the non-consciousness of the natural order. '"Let it blaze against the yew trees"'' says Bernard. '"One life. There. It is over. Gone out"'' (pp. 159–62). The same dualism with the same urgency of conscious effort and the same inevitable result occurs at the end of the novel. Bernard flings himself, unvanquished, unyielding, against death – but the last line of the novel is '*The Waves broke on the shore*' (p. 211).

Almost paradoxically there is something of a dualism in the extrovertive mysticism of *The Waves*. Bernard's mystical experience of a 'Fin in a waste of waters' (pp. 134–5) and Rhoda's losses of identity both parallel strikingly the remarks on her mystical experiences that Virginia Woolf made in her diary on 30 September 1926 (pp. 101–2). In all these experiences something – it is called 'reality' in her diary – lies outside rather than within one's consciousness. This 'reality' attracts consciousness, as it were, until at the height of the experience the awareness of everything else except it is lost. Even here, however, there seems to be a distinction between the awareness and what one is aware of. This seems to be true, at any rate, of Bernard's experience when he sees something essential, something that is described as making Tahiti possible, out in the midst of 'a waste of waters'.

The internal philosophical realism of *The Waves* is a less familiar feature of Virginia Woolf's fiction than the external, but in this novel it is at least as important. G. E. Moore's argument for the logical independence of what is perceived from the action of perceiving can be applied to distinguish self from consciousness of self. Moore criticised the idealists in 'The Refutation of Idealism' for denying the possibility of self-consciousness:

> I think it may be seen that if the object of an Idealist's sensation were, as he supposes, *not* the object but merely the content of that sensation, if, that is to say, it really were an inseparable aspect of his experience, each Idealist could never be aware either of himself or of any other real thing.... The fact is, on his own theory, that himself and that other person are in reality mere *contents* of an awareness, which is aware *of* nothing whatever.[41]

In *The Waves* internal perceptions are no more mere contents of awareness than external perceptions. To be self-conscious is to be aware of something independent of consciousness. The meditations of the soliloquising consciousnesses on their identities illustrate how basic this distinction is to *The Waves*. It can be seen in the uniform way in which the different consciousnesses speak, because consciousness lies too deep for the tears of personality and style. The effect of a monotone in the soliloquies helps to represent the existence of an awareness separate from the six highly individualised personalities of the novel. It is this awareness, common to the six characters, that is present when they are able at the two dinners to separate themselves from their egos and commune for a moment as one consciousness, one life. At these moments the novel is fully a drama of consciousness as well as consciousnesses.

At the centre of the one life that the six petals momentarily at least arrange themselves around is the impressive but illusive figure of Percival. He closely resembles Jacob Flanders, and behind both is Thoby Stephen. (When she finished *The Waves* Virginia Woolf wondered in her diary [p. 169] if she could put 'Julian Thoby Stephen 1881–1906' on the first page of the novel.) Looking back to *Jacob's Room* we can see other significant similarities and differences. *Jacob's Room* is a quest for consciousness itself; *The Waves* is an exploration of *self-*consciousness. The earlier work tries to determine what Jacob was and what he was conscious of, the later novel tries to show what Percival meant to his friends and how he existed in their consciousnesses. If *Jacob's Room* is about the problem of other minds, *The Waves* is about the problem of our own. These different aims require different forms for each novel, but not different epistemologies. All of this can be illustrated in the preoccupations of the six characters with apprehending their developing identities.

Bernard, the most inclusive and various of the six, is continually thinking about his different selves. At college Bernard notes, ' "The complexity of things becomes more close.... What am I? I ask. This? No, I am that" ' (p. 54). After an orgy of self-consciousness accompanying his engagement, Bernard ceases to be himself for a while and is caught up in the lives of others – but only for a while. The description of his returning identity diagramatically separates consciousness and the objects of consciousness:

'Yet behold, it returns. One cannot extinguish that persistent smell. It steals in through some crack in the structure – one's identity. I am not part of the street – no, I observe the street. One splits off, therefore.' (p. 82)

Unlike Louis's or Rhoda's, Bernard's identity also depends upon other people's identities. Louis is obsessively self-aware; with his success in business comes a new self that he affirms as he signs his name again and again and thinks how he must concentrate his consciousness on what he is now and not be distracted by his imagination or the uncommercial world around him. Only when past inferiorities have been completely shed will he be free to write his poetry. In her solitude Rhoda is even more insecure than Louis, but her identity is something that she is always losing. As a young girl she is conscious that,

> 'I have no face. Other people have faces; Susan and Jinny have faces; they are here. Their world is the real world. The things they lift are heavy.' (pp. 30–1)

Her solitude torments her and yet she would have nothing else. Her final comment on consciousness without a self is suicide. Louis and Rhoda resemble each other – they are lovers for a time – in their isolated awareness of their uncertain identities; with both the independence of self from awareness is manifest. Jinny and Neville also resemble each other in the ways they fix their identities on love. Neville's homosexuality is more tormented than Jinny's heterosexuality, however. Susan invests her identity in nature and motherhood, yet as with all the others she too perceives the difference between her awareness and this self. On her farm she asks,

> 'But who am I, who lean on this gate and watch my setter nose in a circle? I think sometimes (I am not twenty yet) I am not a woman, but the light that falls on this gate, on this ground.' (pp. 70–1).

It is Percival, says Louis, '"who makes us aware that these attempts to say, 'I am this, I am that,' which we make, coming together, like separated parts of one body and soul, are false"' (p. 98). Fear and vanity motivate the attempts, but still the communion of the six selfless, merged consciousnesses is inevitably transitory. The loss and recovery of self is also the crucial experience in Bernard's long summing-up that appears almost as an epilogue to the drama of consciousness. Bernard's purpose in his final soliloquy is to explain the meaning of his life, but his inclusiveness and the way in which the six lives have been experienced as one enable him, in the words of the dust jacket, to summarise 'the effect of their lives as a whole'. As with the rest of *The Waves*, the explanation is not so much in social, religious, psychological or even moral terms as it is in perceptual ones. Bernard's explanation consists of a review of the principal perceptions of his life. His identity as a child developed from the 'arrows of sensation' that struck his unprotected consciousness. ' "A shell forms upon the soft soul, nacreous, shiny, upon which sensations tap their beaks in vain" ' (p. 181). Another epistemological symbol used by Bernard and illustrative of his philosophical realism is a tree: ' "The mind grows rings; the identity becomes robust; pain is absorbed in growth" ' (pp. 182–3). Growth teaches the independence of nature from mind – if only in death. Percival's death shows to Bernard the realities of the world outside one's consciousness; experiencing the first morning that the dead Percival would not know leads Bernard ' "to see things without attachment, from the outside, and to realise their beauty in itself – how strange!" ' (p. 187). The sources of ethical and aesthetic value in the realism of *The Waves* appear here.

After the Hampton Court reunion and communion, Bernard suffers an appalling experience. He addressed his self and nothing happened. He is conscious, but of nothing. There is not even the fin in the waste of waters, as there was when he realised he had lost his youth and shed one of his 'life-skins' (p. 134). He realises he is a man without a self. Earlier in his life Bernard had noticed the expression of old men in clubs – ' "they had given up calling for a self who does not come" ' – and now that he is old, it happens to him. In this crisis Bernard is reduced to mere consciousness:

> 'So the landscape returned to me; so I saw fields rolling in waves of colour beneath me, but now with this difference; I saw but was not seen. I walked unshadowed; I came unheralded.... Thin as a ghost, leaving no trace where I trod, perceiving merely, I walked alone in a new world...'. (p. 203)

This experience is the background to Bernard's final dinner with an acquaintance. During it Bernard becomes aware first of his mere physical self and then of the immense receptivity of his being. In the midst of this celebration of himself, Bernard sees what he is reflected in his companion's eyes. His physical self-awareness returns with a sickening blow reminiscent of his collision with the pillar box after his engagement. Insensitive matter, the enemy of consciousness, has to be confronted once more; the wave has tumbled over him again, scattering the contents of consciousness. The struggle must begin yet again, and as Bernard begins it, things gradually come together. Consciousness of self, of others, of external reality all fuse and he can conclude to his companion, ' "I regain the sense of the complexity and the reality and the struggle, for which I thank you"' (p. 208). This is the meaning of his life.

The three things that Bernard regains his sense of at the end of *The Waves* summarise Virginia Woolf's philosophy in the novel. The complexity entailed in the perception of the individual's changing identity, the reality that in various ways is independent of one's awareness, and the struggle that the individual must make against the extinguishing chaos of external non-conscious nature – all are central philosophical matters in the novel. There are others as well, such as the supreme values of artistic beauty and love, that derive from consciousness and fit into the perspectives of philosophical realism.

One of Virginia Woolf's contemporaries who had also read some G. E. Moore and was probably aware of his influence on the Bloomsbury Group seems to have recognised some of these perspectives in *The Waves*. In the introduction to his play, appositely titled *Fighting the Waves*, William Butler Yeats observed the year after *The Waves* was published that,

> certain typical books – *Ulysses*, Virginia Woolf's *The Waves*, Mr. Ezra Pound's *Draft of XXX Cantos* – suggest a philosophy like that of the *Samkara* school of ancient India, mental and physical objects alike material, a deluge of experience breaking over us and within us, melting limits whether of line or tint; man no hard bright mirror dawdling by the dry sticks of a hedge, but a swimmer, or rather the waves themselves.[42]

Shortly before the publication of *The Waves* Yeats had written that 'The romantic movement seems related to the idealist philosophy; the naturalistic movement, Stendhal's mirror dawdling down a lane, to Locke's mechanical philosophy,...' and the work of Joyce, Pound and Proust to 'that form of the new realist philosophy which thinks that the secondary and primary qualities alike are independent of consciousness...'.[43] Yeats has a footnote at this point citing Moore's 'The Refutation of Idealism' as a source of this philosophy. Without going into Yeats's extraordinary reading of Moore and Russell or being put off by Yeats's finding realism under the beds of Joyce, Pound, Proust and Virginia Woolf (he may have been only responding to the fact that none of them was a romantic idealist or mechanical empiricist), we can recognise that Yeats was right about the philosophical presuppositions of *The Waves*.

VII

In her last two novels Virginia Woolf is less preoccupied with consciousness and perception than in her four preceding ones. *The Years* and *Between the Acts* are closer to *The Voyage Out* and *Night and Day* in the kinds of life they represent. In each the content of consciousness is more important than the act; literary realism is more evident in them than philosophical realism. *The Years* and *Between the Acts* share the same philosophical assumptions with the more epistemological works in Virginia Woolf's canon but they are not about perception in the same way that her middle novels are. The remarkable otherness of people's consciousnesses and the spatial, temporal relations their perceptions have in common, the need to combine miracles of intuition with realities of ordinary experience, the drama of transient consciousness that is both a struggle for identity and against enduring, non-conscious nature – these are the epistemological concerns of *Monday or Tuesday*, *Jacob's Room*, *Mrs. Dalloway*, *To the Lighthouse* and *The Waves*. The stories and novels are not, of course, reducible merely to accounts of sense-perception. Yet if her assumptions about consciousness and its relations to external and internal reality are ignored, we may well misconceive the art and the values of Virginia Woolf's fiction.

2 Bertrand Russell: The Logic of a Literary Symbol

Once when he was still a philosopher, T. S. Eliot took his friend Ezra Pound to a meeting of the Aristotelian Society. Pound absorbed as much of the discussion as he could take and then retired outside with Eliot where they encountered G. R. S. Mead. Mead expressed surprise at finding Pound there, and many years later Pound recalled how Eliot had replied 'with perfect decorum and suavity... "Oh, he's not here as a phil-*os*-opher;/ He's here as an an-thro-pologist."'[1]

I can neither participate in Russell's centenary rituals as a philosopher nor observe them as an anthropologist. I am here rather as a literary historian interested in the interrelations of modern English literature and British philosophy. This may well strike many philosophers, literary critics and even anthropologists as a curious preoccupation, for it is widely assumed that there are none. I have tried elsewhere to illustrate some of the connections that have existed between British philosophy and English literature.[2] On the occasion of the centenary of the most celebrated British philosopher of the past hundred years, I would like to look at one particular aspect of Russell's relevance to English literature, and that is the symbolic significance that he has been given in a number of literary works.

This is by no means the only connection that can be made between Russell and his native literature, though I believe it is the most interesting. Russell has testified how important English literature was for him.[3] Unlike so many other English philosophers of the time, he was not schooled in the classics. The influence of the early and prolonged study of Greek and Latin literature on modern analytic philosophy has not yet, as far as I know, been studied; when it is, the importance of translation for conceptual analysis may emerge along with at least a partial explanation of why so many philosophers – though again Russell is an exception – have become deadened to literature. Russell's literary education consisted largely of unsupervised reading of English, European and American writers. He is reputed to have memorised all of

Shakespeare's sonnets;[4] the romantic poet-radicals Blake, Shelley and Whitman were deeply admired by him, as were the works of such diverse writers as Milton, Gibbon and Carlyle. Gilbert Murray and Joseph Conrad affected Russell strongly through both their friendship and their literary work. Despite all these influences, the nature of Russell's achievement in philosophy is such that English literature is largely irrelevant to it.

So remote has English literature become for modern symbolic logic that I suspect the identity of *Waverley* and perhaps Scott himself will have to be explained by some teachers of logic before they can proceed with Russell's theory of descriptions and his famous conundrum of what exactly George IV meant when he asked if Sir Walter Scott were the author of *Waverley*. Gray's *Elegy* possibly offers fewer difficulties for the student of logic seeking to comprehend

> ' The meaning of the first line of Gray's Elegy' is the same as 'The meaning of "The curfew tolls the knell of parting day"' and is not the same as 'The meaning of "the first line of Gray's Elegy"'.[5]

Russell once used a more apt illustration from English literature. He invoked Laurence Sterne's *Tristram Shandy* to exemplify a paradox of Cantor's that is the converse of Zeno's paradox of Achilles and the tortoise. After Tristram Shandy had taken two years to chronicle the first two days of his life, he realised that as his life went on he would be farther and farther away from the end of his life's history. Russell argued, however, that 'if he had lived for ever, and had not wearied of his task, then, even if his life had continued as eventfully as it began, no part of his biography would have remained unwritten in all time'. This paradoxical proposition rests on the fact that the number of days is not greater than the number of years. One must choose between Achilles and Tristram Shandy; either Achilles will never catch the tortoise or Tristram will leave no part of his infinitely regressive autobiography unwritten. In the face of such a dilemma Russell cheerfully admitted that common sense ought to commit suicide.[6] Russell came later to have more respect for common sense than he showed in 1902, but the chief irony here is that Russell should have derived his paradox from a work that satirises the absurdities to which man's thinking can lead him. Sterne grounded his satire in Locke's empiricism; it allowed him to illustrate the comic possibilities of such doctrines as the association of ideas and the subjectivity of time. Russell used Sterne's hero to reveal the unreasonable behaviour of infinite numbers. The aims of Russell and Sterne are very different here. By formally proving an absurd state of affairs Russell reveals a limitation of Sterne's empiricism, and yet Russell also seems in a way to be admitting the absurdity of what he is proving by the use of Tristram Shandy to do it.

Russell's moral and social philosophy has quite likely been shaped to some extent by the various writers he was devoted to. Yet such influences are practically impossible to determine with any precision or usefulness because, unlike his more technical philosophy, Russell's ideas here are not of sufficient originality. Russell's quick and wide receptivity to the ideas of his time makes the sources of his thought difficult to gauge with any definiteness. Similar difficulties occur in the attempt to determine the influence of Russell's ideas on his contemporaries. He received the Nobel literary prize for the works of philosophy he addressed to the general public – thus keeping alive, in the words of the committee's presentation, 'the interest in general philosophy'.[7] This kind of interest is almost impossible to isolate in particular cases, however.[8] Russell's most widely read piece of writing used to be 'A Free Man's Worship', but the essay is so derivative in content and style that it would be foolish to seek for its particular influence on modern literature.[9] Russell's work in epistemology, on the other hand, might have had discoverable literary implications – as G. E. Moore's did for the Bloomsbury Group – but perhaps because of Moore's influence, Russell's work actually had no literary impact.

Russell does deserve a place in the canon of English literature as a master of expository prose. (Though as a writer of fiction he merits the oblivion that an injudicious admirer has recently tried to dispel by publishing what he calls *The Collected Stories of Bertrand Russell*.) It would certainly be worthwhile to analyse the development of Russell's various prose styles and the very different purposes that they served. But aside from his considerable attainment as a stylist, Russell's relation to English literature appears most significantly in the ways he was used as a character in fiction and poetry. For the writers who were his contemporaries, Russell's ideas were essentially inseparable from the extraordinary personality that expressed them. The greatest symbolic logician of his time was himself turned into something of a literary symbol. What I would like to examine here is how this was done.

It should come as no surprise to readers of Russell that the literary mode in which he has been most often represented is the ironic. Russell's marvellous wit would seem almost to require this. His own excursions into fiction have almost always been in this mode, and they have often taken the shape of that satirical form of irony that Northrop Frye has identified as the anatomy. The anatomy, according to Frye, 'deals less with people as such than with mental attitudes. Pedants, bigots, cranks, *parvenus*, virtuosi, enthusiasts, rapacious and incompetent professional men of all kinds, are handled in terms of their occupational approach to life as distinct from their social behaviour'. The anatomy is further characterised by Frye as having 'a great variety of subject-matter and a strong interest in ideas. In shorter forms it often has a *cena* or symposium setting and verse interludes.' *The Life and Opinions of Tristram Shandy, Gentleman*, Burton's *Anatomy of Melancholy*, Swift's *Gulliver's Travels*, Thomas Love Peacock's novels, Lewis Carroll's Alice books, Butler's Erewhon books are other great examples in English of this kind of satire.[10] Russell modelled his first extended piece of fiction, 'The Perplexities of John Forstice', on W. H. Mallock's *The New Republic: or Culture, Faith and Philosophy in an English Country House*,[11] a Victorian anatomy that owes much to Peacock's novels. In 'The Perplexities of John Forstice', and again in the stories of *Satan in the Suburbs* and *Nightmares of Eminent Persons*, Russell presents in one frame or another a collection of ironically articulated and heavily moralised intellectual attitudes.

The anatomy is the form of the very first piece of published fiction (the term seems scarcely adequate) in which Russell had a hand[12] – a work that can also be considered as the first fictional representation of Russell. Philip Jourdain's *The Philosophy of Mr. B*rtr*nd R*ss*ll* is so curious and apparently obscure in its intent that one of Russell's bibliographers felt it necessary to warn his readers, 'This book is intended as a joke.'[13] The book is purportedly a manuscript of the late Mr B*rtr*nd R*ss*ll that was saved from the fire along with his interleaved *Prayer-Book of Free Man's Worship* when 'a body of eager champions of the Sacredness of Personal Property' burnt his house down. Mr R*ss*ll himself met his end following the advice given by William James to get in touch with reality, 'and in July 1911 was torn to pieces by Anti-Suffragists....'[14] The work itself consists of forty-three very short chapters that develop philosophical jokes such as Tristram Shandy's paradox. One chapter on the hierarchy of jokes, for instance, tells of the Oxford don who reduced all jokes to thirty-seven primitive proto-Aryan types. 'When any proposition was propounded to him, he would reflect and afterwards pronounce on the question as to whether the proposition was a joke or not.' The question then arises as to the category of this anecdote; if it is a joke, then 'we must conclude that there is at least one joke which is not proto-Aryan; and, in fact, is of a higher type'. The chapter goes on to describe the misadventures of this second-order joke among archetypal humourless Scotchmen, misadventures that yield jokes of the third and even fourth order; the appreciation of these and higher orders requires 'sound logical training, ... while jokes of transfinite order presumably only excite the inaudible laughter of the gods'.[15] This chapter, of course, is a spoof of Russell's theory of types. The Mr Russell of 'On Denoting' is nevertheless not to be confused with Mr R*ss*ll. Jourdain admits that there is an unusual case of influence here. Mr R*ss*ll has derived from Mr Bertrand Russell his views, the organisation of his book, and even his style, which fortunately – again according to Jourdain – 'reminds us more of Mr. Russell's later clear and charming subtleties than his earlier brilliant and no less subtle obscurities'.[16]

Jourdain's collection of the wit and wisdom of Mr R*ss*ll is a slight anatomical *jeu d'esprit*, yet it embodies several striking features that will recur in the symbolising of Bertrand Russell. First of all there is the explicit connection of Russell with Lewis Carroll. *The Philosophy of Mr. B*rtr*nd R*ss*ll* has twenty appendices made up of apposite quotations from Lewis Carroll's work. Russell's treatment of non-existent entities, for example, is described as the position of the White Knight in *Through the Looking-Glass*, who, when Alice said 'I see nobody on the road', replied fretfully, 'I only wish *I* had such eyes....'[17] The genius with which Lewis Carroll anatomised conceptual confusions and hypocrisies, the brilliance of his puns and paradoxes, has endeared him to modern British philosophers more perhaps than any other writer of English literature. Russell recalled being brought up on the first editions of *Alice in Wonderland* and *Through the Looking-Glass* and learning them by heart at an early age.[18] (Once Russell even wrote a short satire on communism and Catholicism entitled 'The Prelate and the Commissar';[19] they treat the workers just as the Walrus and the Carpenter treat the oysters.) As mathematical logicians with a fondness for witty logical and linguistic puzzles, Lewis Carroll and Bertrand Russell had more than a few things in common, and the association of Russell with Lewis Carroll has been helped by Lewis Carroll's illustrator; Tenniel's prescient drawings of the Mad Hatter bear a surprising resemblance to photographs of Russell as a young man. But if Lewis Carroll did not invent Bertrand Russell, he at least created a world that the various symbolic representations of Russell have found congenial. It is a world in which characters appear absurd because of their preconceived ideas and their resulting behaviour; but their absurdity does not prevent them from being mercilessly shrewd in pointing out the follies and ambiguities of others. Russell and the Mad Hatter are both ridiculous and ridiculing. Each serves both as a butt and as a vehicle for satire.

This double function in the characters of Lewis Carroll and in the literary symbolic uses of Bertrand Russell coincides with the role of the disguises or metamorphoses in each. Jourdain's satire creates a *doppelgänger* for Russell, who, like the inhabitants of wonderland, pokes, and is a figure of, fun. In Mr R*ss*ll can also be seen faint traces of some superhuman being. Like Dionysus, he is torn to pieces – though his destroyers are not suffragette maenads but 'anti-suffragists' who tear apart a kind of Apollo. Mr R*ss*ll is certainly more Apollonian than Dionysian when he writes in Jourdain's collection, 'Those people who think that it is more godlike to seem to turn water into wine than to seem to turn wine into water surprise me.'[20] For some lovers of philosophy, the art of turning wine into water may not be a bad description of what ordinary language philosophy does.

The symbolic associations of Russell with Apollo are best represented in English literature by the young philosophy student and poet T. S. Eliot, who studied symbolic logic with Russell at Harvard just before the First World War. Eliot's complex and changing relationship with Russell is an important context for his depiction of Russell in the poem 'Mr. Apollinax'. Eliot and Russell grew so antipathetic to each other that Russell asserted with characteristic flatness in his autobiography 'the suggestion sometimes made...that one of us influenced the other is without foundation'.[21] This may be an accurate statement of Eliot's impact on Russell but it hardly carries the same authority as a statement about Russell's importance for Eliot. There is a foundation for considering Russell's influence on Eliot, and it consists of philosophical, personal and poetic elements. Eliot had a high opinion of Russell's work in logic, though he was unable to understand its importance when he wrote his thesis on F. H. Bradley in 1916. By 1920, however, Eliot was comparing Russell and Bradley as follows: 'Certain works of philosophy can be called works of art: much of Aristotle and Plato, Spinoza, parts of Hume, Mr. Bradley's *Principles of Logic*, Mr. Russell's essay on "Denoting": clear and beautifully formed thought.' Bergson, whom Eliot admired before encountering Russell, comes off badly in comparison with these touchstones.[22] The mixture of metaphysics and style that was F. H. Bradley's influence on Eliot has been recognised, but the extent to which Russell's earlier philosophical work impressed Eliot is still ignored. Here, for example, is Eliot's comparison of Russell and Bradley in a little known review of *Mysticism and Logic* that Eliot did for *The Nation* in 1918:

> In those essays which are most philosophical...Mr. Russell reaches the level of the very best philosophical prose in the language. The only contemporary writer who can even approach him is Mr. Bradley.... His hardness is of the surface, and conceals an affinity to Walter Pater. But Mr. Russell's hardness is from within. His style has perfect lucidity; it neither increases nor dissimulates the difficulty of the subject.

Thanks to Russell, Eliot continues, English philosophy will be finally liberated from German influence: 'His victory has been largely due to the possession of a science which most admirers of German philosophy in this country but imperfectly understood, but in the end will be due to his style, a style which this science has trained.'[23]

Russell's personal involvement with Eliot began at Harvard. 'My pupil Eliot was there –' Russell wrote to Lady Ottoline Morrell of a weekend spent at the country house of B. A. G. Fuller, 'the only one who is civilized, and he is ultra-civilized, knows his classics very well, is familiar with all French literature from Villon to Vildrach, and is altogether impeccable in his taste but has no vigour or life – or enthusiasm. He is going to Oxford where I expect he will be very happy.'[24] Contrary to Russell's sardonic prediction Eliot was not happy at Oxford. He came to London, made a disastrous marriage, was introduced by Russell to Lady Ottoline Morrell's circle and from there to the Bloomsbury Group. Russell helped Eliot financially in various ways, and became intimately if obscurely involved in Eliot's marital difficulties. Eliot's mother had hopes, as she wrote to Russell, that 'your influence in every way will confirm my son in his choice of Philosophy as a life work....I have absolute faith in his Philosophy but not in the vers libres.'[25] But it was not to be. The surviving letters that Eliot wrote to Russell from time to time up through 1925 reveal an intense, almost dependent, admiration for Russell.[26] With Eliot's conversion in 1927 and Russell's emergence as a popular iconoclastic moralist, the relationship ceased. Eliot continued to think highly of Russell's work in mathematical logic and epistemology, but such things as *Why I Am Not a Christian* irritated him.[27]

The first draft of 'Mr. Apollinax' was written at Oxford in 1915.[28] The occasion for the poem may well have been the country-house weekend at Fuller's that Russell described to Lady Ottoline Morrell. The Greek epigraph comes from Lucian and sets the tone of the poem; roughly translated, it reads 'What originality. By Hercules what paradoxes! What an ingenious man.' Thus the note of the paradoxer is struck again, and again the mode is ironic, with the satire directed not only at Mr. Apollinax – whose name means Apollo's offspring – but also at those wasteland figures who cannot cope with him.

The twenty-two line poem depicts one Mr Apollinax who talks and laughs his way through garden parties on a visit to the United States. Priapus, the old man of the sea, centaurs are all invoked to describe the contrast of his vitality with the sterility of his hosts Mrs Phlaccus and Professor Channing-Cheetah. Eliot's symbolising of Russell in the poem displays several characteristics that accrue to Russell in his various literary incarnations. Here again is the laughing philosopher – one of the most familiar premises in the logic of Russell as a symbol. But the laughter of Mr Apollinax differs from the laughter of Mr R*ss*ll as the wasteland differs from wonderland. Mr Apollinax's laughter is part of his sexual imagery, and it clearly differentiates him from Lewis Carroll's pre-pubescent characters. In 'Mr. Apollinax' and other works using Russell, the laughing philosopher is also a lecherous one, and not always a shy lecher at that, as he is in the poem. The futility of his bewildered hosts is shared with other figures in *Prufrock and Other Observations*, the book of poems that included 'Mr. Apollinax'. But Mr Apollinax himself resembles neither J. Alfred Prufrock nor his opposite, the sensual apelike Sweeney. Mr Apollinax's talk is both dry *and* passionate. The connection here between intellectuality and sexuality will frequently recur in representations of Russell. Eliot calls Russell the son of the sun, but the behaviour he describes is Dionysian. The poet has it both ways, in keeping with Russell's almost infinite variety. He takes Mr Apollinax through an extraordinary series of transformations: he is Priapus and a foetus, a bodiless head and a centaur, Fragilion (whoever he is) and, most significant of all, Proteus, the multiform old man of the sea. Such metamorphoses brilliantly embody the protean logic of Bertrand Russell as a literary symbol. In this poem and elsewhere it is, of course, a comic logic. Mr Apollinax's seaweed laurels, his pointed ears,[29] the decapitated effect, the gaping foetal laughter (whatever *that* is) are all part of Eliot's satiric treatment. But there is something else as well. For all his fun, Mr Apollinax is somewhat sinister. His submarine laughter bubbles about the 'worried bodies of drowned men'. 'Worried' is an unusual word here, meaning, presumably (as in *The Waste Land*) the way the current picks their bones in whispers; but it also suggests the anxiety that the supernatural Mr Apollinax gives rise to in mere mortals. Originally Eliot had written 'desperate bodies'. Death by water in 'Mr. Apollinax' is not the same as death by water in *The Waste Land*.[30]

While T. S. Eliot was putting Russell into his poetry as 'Mr Apollinax', D. H. Lawrence was using him as a minor character in his great novel *Women in Love*. All the characters in that novel appear to be modelled on people Lawrence knew, including himself. Russell's appearance there resembles his other literary symbolisations. Sir Joshua Malleson – Lawrence appears to have rather crudely borrowed the last name from Russell's current mistress[31] – is an 'elderly sociologist', 'a learned dry Baronet of fifty, who was always making witticisms and laughing at them heartily in a harsh horse-laugh...'.[32] Birkin, the Lawrentian hero, encounters Sir Joshua at yet another futile country house. Lawrence's novel of ideas uses this setting to present, in a brief anatomy, the ideas, personalities and behaviour of Sir Joshua and others as additional examples of the disintegrating English life that *Women in Love* depicts. The talk at this only faintly disguised description of Lady Ottoline Morrell's Garsington is smart and wearying for all except Sir Joshua, who talks endlessly. The hardness that Eliot saw under the surface in Russell's philosophical work is reflected in Lawrence's description of Malleson as possessing a 'mental fibre ... so tough as to be insentient...'. He has an 'eighteenth-century appearance', but he also somehow looks like a great lizard from a primeval world. But this harshly yet somehow mincingly laughing and endlessly talking lizard-like pre-romantic sociologist lacks the sexual aura of Mr Apollinax. In an impromptu swimming party at which others are dressed in bathing suits or brightly coloured scarves, Sir Joshua turns up in an overcoat. His body is described by different characters as being stiff and little, having 'thick, crude shoulders', and looking like a flat bottle containing tabloids of knowledge that yield liberty. Nor does Sir Joshua's talk appear to be as interesting as Mr Apollinax's. He refutes Birkin's notion that all knowledge is of the past by the counter-example of our knowledge of the laws of gravity, and later in a discussion about equality he maintains the familiar idea of social equality against arguments for spiritual equality or for a state organised by occupations. Birkin is not having any of these ideas, however, and argues, though not with Sir Joshua, for what seems to be an equality of importance, as it were, rather than opportunity: everyone is to have a share of the world's goods so that he will leave others alone.

The symbolic lineaments of Lawrence's sketch of Russell in *Women in Love* are an addition to the logic of Russell as a literary symbol, though not an especially illuminating one. Lawrence comes closer than any other writer to making Russell into the stereotyped intellectual of the anatomy genre. Sir Joshua Malleson is actually more interesting because of his origin than because of his presence in Lawrence's novel. The encounter of Russell and Lawrence is itself provocatively symbolic, and their year of friendship and quarrels ought not to be reduced as it has been by various of their partisans, to a thought–feeling dichotomy. Lawrence repeatedly insisted that 'the two ways of knowing, for man, are knowing in terms of apartness, which is mental, rational, scientific, and knowing in terms of togetherness, which is religious and poetic'.[33] Russell's well-known essay on mysticism and logic is an attempt to reconcile these same ways of knowing, and throughout most of his career Russell maintained with Hume that reason is and ought to be the slave of the passions. Yet the opposition between Russell and Lawrence was deep. They came to disagree about everything from ethics and politics to epistemology and metaphysics. Given their utterly different backgrounds and abilities, the wonder is that they engaged each other at all. Yet they did, and their affinities as well as their differences are part of what Michael L. Ross has called the mythology of their friendship.[34] The myth is embodied, as Ross has shown, in Lawrence's superb story, 'The Blind Man'. Here for the first time the literary symbolisation of Russell is not satiric, though the story is very ironic. To see this we must first know something about the friendship of Russell and Lawrence.

The facts of the relationship are fairly simple. Russell was a fellow of the Royal Society, the co-author of *Principia Mathematica* and a lecturer at Cambridge. His first marriage had failed and he was now in love with Lady Ottoline Morrell. Lawrence was one of three young geniuses, all in their twenties, that Russell in his forties had become intensely involved with, intellectually and personally. The resemblance of Russell's relationship with Lawrence to his relationships with Ludwig Wittgenstein and T. S. Eliot must be left to Russell's biographers, however, as must the parallels between Russell's admiration for Lawrence and for Joseph Conrad. At the time he met Russell, Lawrence had published, in addition to poems and short stories, three novels, the last of which was *Sons and Lovers*. And he had recently been forced into bankruptcy by his wife's former husband. Lawrence and Russell were introduced to each other by Lady Ottoline Morrell early in 1915. Their shared hatred of England's involvement in the First World War was the original basis of their coming together, and they were deeply impressed with each other. The relationship survived a singularly inauspicious visit of Lawrence's to meet Russell's friends at Cambridge. Lawrence was now writing what he called his philosophy, and asking Russell's help with it. His long essay 'The Crown' probably contains the gist of the philosophy; it is best read as a rhetorical meditation on *The Rainbow*, which he had recently finished. The essay is difficult to summarise, but some notion of its orientation can be seen in Lawrence's conclusion that the function of art is to represent the equilibrium of the eternities of matter and spirit through 'the revelation of a pure, an absolute relation between the two eternities'.[35] Russell wrote to Lady Ottoline Morrell, 'I can't make head or tail of Lawrence's philosophy. I dread talking to him about it. It is not sympathetic to me.'[36] This is hardly a surprising response from a philosopher who at this time considered philosophy's primary function to be criticism. Yet for a while Russell came to accept and even be moved by Lawrence's philosophy. Russell even helped Lawrence's thinking by introducing him to the pre-Socratic philosophers.

'The Crown' may also include some of the things that Lawrence intended to include in the joint lectures that he and Russell were planning to give in June. Russell was to lecture on ethics, Lawrence on immortality. Russell produced an outline of the lectures he intended to give – they turned out to be on the philosophy of social reconstruction – and Lawrence annotated the typescript vigorously.³⁷ He agreed with what Russell had to say about the evils of wealth, the dangers of subjectivism and the causes of war, but he disagreed basically with Russell's conceptions of morality, the state and religion.³⁸ Russell took umbrage at Lawrence's criticisms and his hectoring, schoolmaster tone. The idea of the joint lectures was abandoned, but Lawrence's criticisms had their impact on what became Russell's first widely popular book, *Principles of Social Reconstruction*.³⁹ The relationship between Lawrence and Russell continued along until Russell sent an essay for a magazine Lawrence was starting. Entitled 'The Danger to Civilization', it argues that our wonderful civilisation was in danger of being destroyed if the war continued. The evils of the civilisation that produced the war are ignored in the essay. It was unwise of Russell to expect that Lawrence would be interested in such an approach, especially after his criticisms of Russell's philosophy of social reconstruction. Yet the violence of Lawrence's response is startling. His letter to Russell ended, 'The enemy of all mankind, you are, full of the lust of enmity. It is *not* the hatred of falsehood which inspires you. It is the hatred of people, of flesh and blood. It is a perverted, mental blood-lust. Why don't you own it. Let us become strangers again, I think it is better.'⁴⁰ Russell's reaction is also surprising. 'I was inclined to believe that he had some insight denied to me', he wrote some forty years later in the harsh portrait of Lawrence he did for the BBC, and then incorporated into his autobiography, 'and when he said my pacifism was rooted in blood-lust I supposed he must be right. For twenty-four hours I thought that I was not fit to live and contemplated suicide. But at the end of that time, a healthier reaction set in, and I decided to have done with such morbidness.' Russell conceded, however, that he had received from Lawrence 'a vivifying dose of unreason'.⁴¹

Despite Lawrence's letter, the relationship continued for another six months or so. In November 1915, Lawrence admitted revealingly to Russell that 'my quarrelling with you was largely a quarrelling with something in *myself*, something I was struggling away from in myself'.⁴² And in December he wrote a famous letter to Russell about ways of knowing. Lawrence argued there was another way of knowing besides mental consciousness:

> there is blood-consciousness which exists in us independently of the ordinary mental consciousness which depends on the eye as its source or connector. There is the blood-consciousness, with

the sexual connection holding the same relation as the eye, in seeing, holds to the mental consciousness.

The tragedy of our life is that mental consciousness tyrannises over blood-consciousness.[43] Russell claimed in his account of Lawrence that this mystical philosophy of blood-consciousness led straight to Auschwitz.[44] It leads much more directly to 'The Blind Man'.

Lawrence finished 'The Blind Man' shortly after Armistice Day. It describes an afternoon and evening in the life of Maurice Previn, a country gentleman who has been totally blinded in the war and now spends his time working on his farm. His pregnant wife Isabel and Maurice himself alternate in their blind, unspeakable intimacy between deep, fulfilling joy, and black, panicky despair. A childhood friend of Isabel's, disliked by Maurice and not seen by Isabel since her husband's going off to war, has been invited to visit them. The story is essentially about the relationship that the blind man establishes with his wife's friend. In his name, his appearance, his intelligence and his relationship to Previn, this character seems partly a symbolic representation of Bertrand Russell and partly of James Barrie. Bertie Reid is a Scottish barrister, 'a little dark man, with a very big forehead, thin, wispy hair, and sad, large eyes. His expression was inordinately sad – almost funny. He had odd, short legs.' Maurice Previn, by contrast, is powerful, massive, slow. His mind too is slow but his feelings are quick and acute, so that, in Lawrence's words, 'he was just the opposite to Bertie, whose mind was much quicker than his emotions, which were not so very fine'. Maurice's blindness has led to a new way of consciousness for him:

> It was a pleasure to him to rock thus through a world of things, carried on the flood in a sort of blood-prescience. He did not think much or trouble much.... He did not try to remember, to visualize. He did not want to. The new way of consciousness substituted itself to him.[45]

Among the most brilliant parts of Lawrence's short story are the descriptions of Maurice embodying this new consciousness, particularly in the two barn scenes with his wife and then with Bertie.

Maurice's blindness is compared with Bertie Reid's

> incurable weakness, which made him unable ever to enter into close contact of any sort.... He could not marry, could not

approach women physically. He wanted to do so. But he could not.... Hence he was a brilliant and successful barrister, also *littérateur* of high repute, a rich man, and a great social success. At the centre he felt himself neuter, nothing.

This description seems to fit Barrie more than Russell; but the missing sexual premise that recurs in the various literary representations of Russell is also an aspect of Lawrence's dramatising the essential failure of both blood-consciousness and mental consciousness when they are separated from each other. Previn's loss of mental consciousness is symbolised by his blindness, while the symbolism of Reid's loss of blood-consciousness is his impotence.

'... I've done "The Blind Man" – the end queer and ironical', Lawrence wrote to Katherine Mansfield in November 1918. 'I realize *how* many people are just rotten at the quick.'[47] Katherine Mansfield knew Russell well at this time and might be expected to recognise him in the story and perhaps even agree with Lawrence's judgement. But the ironical ending that Lawrence refers to is perhaps also a comment on his own deficiencies – insofar as Maurice is a self-portrait. In the barn scene at the end of the story Maurice feels Bertie's head and face with 'a strong, naked hand', and he asks Bertie to touch his scar and disfigured eye sockets. Bertie is filled with revulsion while Previn is 'filled with hot, poignant love, the passion of friendship'. 'Oh, my God', he says to Bertie, 'We shall know each other now, shan't we?' When Isabel joins them she finds her husband standing like a colossus, exulting in their friendship, but watching Bertie 'she knew that he had one desire – to escape from this intimacy, this friendship, which had been thrust upon him. He could not bear it that he had been touched by the blind man, his insane reserve broken in. He was like a mollusc whose shell is broken.'[48] These are the last words of the story.

Maurice Previn and Bertie Reid do not, in fact, know each other. But naturally the blind man cannot see this. His blood-consciousness misapprehends their relationship. 'I suppose we're all deficient somewhere',[49] Bertie says in the course of the story, and the ending bears this out. An ideal of friendship in which each man, through his heightened, one-sided consciousness, complements the other's deficiency is pathetically impossible.

Lawrence never really understood what Russell was trying to do in philosophy, and Russell – especially in his bitter recollection of Lawrence – shows no comprehension of what Lawrence accomplished as an artist. When each man dabbled in the other's field, the results were usually awful; it would be cruel to have to choose between Lawrence's philosophy and Russell's fiction. And yet their brief friendship affected the life and work of each. Lawrence's genius for conveying states of subconscious feeling makes 'The Blind Man' a finer story than a somewhat diagrammatic analysis of it may suggest. The symbolism of light and darkness, vision and blindness, is, as Ross has shown, fundamental to Lawrence's work at this juncture in his career. The story is also a crucial demonstration and qualification of what blood-consciousness meant to Lawrence. What 'The Blind Man' shows us about the literary symbolisation of Russell is the association of him, once again, with light and vision. But the double source and the demands of Lawrence's story deny to this symbolic characterization sexuality and humour. Bertie Reid is smaller than life, an impotent lawyer in no way dangerous or divine, whose brilliance is never displayed. Though something of a sadly ridiculous figure, he never ridicules. One reason why this account of Russell differs from other representations of Russell is that Lawrence's intention in 'The Blind Man' is not satiric. In order to describe an encounter between a man of light and a man of darkness, both seriously deficient, Lawrence reduced the complex versatility of both Russell and himself. What he achieved has an extraordinary symbolic intensity, including ironies that are deeper than those a satire could have attained.

In certain respects the caricature of Russell as Sir Joshua Malleson in *Women in Love* is more realistic than the fuller treatment of Russell in 'The Blind Man'. Neither is anything like a literary photographic likeness of course; the symbolic uses of Russell in English literature had not yet resulted in straightforward depiction. But it is interesting to note that one of the most extended symbolic anatomisations of Russell in fiction derives fairly directly from Lawrence's sketch in *Women in Love*. Aldous Huxley's *Crome Yellow* appeared in 1921, the year after *Women in Love* was finally published.[50] Its setting is again Lady Ottoline's Garsington, alias Crome, and all the originals that make up the cast are more or less modelled on people Huxley met there – including the self-caricature, Denis Stone. The brilliant, absurd flow of ideas in the novel is interspersed with bits of poetry, readings from the history of Crome, etc. And for relief from the talk there is love-making and finally a fair. 'My Peacockian novel', Huxley aptly described *Crome Yellow* while writing it.[51] The principal source of the ideas expressed in Huxley's anatomy is one Mr. Scogan. Here is one of the descriptions of him:

> In appearance Mr. Scogan was like one of those extinct bird-lizards of the Tertiary. His nose was beaked, his dark eye had the shining quickness of a robin's. But there was nothing soft or gracious or feathery about him. The skin of his wrinkled brown face had a dry and scaly look; his hands were the hands of a crocodile. His movements were marked by the lizard's disconcertingly abrupt clockwork speed; his speech was thin, fluty, and dry.[52]

And like a lizard, Mr Scogan thrives on untempered sunlight, as this excerpt from a conversation with Denis in the garden at Crome shows:

> 'But I don't want power,' said Denis. He was sitting in limp discomfort at one end of the bench, shading his eyes from the intolerable light. Mr. Scogan, bolt upright at the other end, laughed again....
> The heat that was slowly paralysing all Denis's mental and bodily faculties seemed to bring to Mr. Scogan additional vitality. He talked with an ever-increasing energy, his hands moved in sharp, quick, precise gestures, his eyes shone. Hard, dry, and continuous, his voice went on sounding and sounding in Denis's ears with the insistence of a mechanical noise.[53]

The monologue on Mr Scogan's utopia, in which alas there is no room for Denis, ends when Denis leaves for fear of sunstroke.

This hard, laughing, relentlessly brilliant, clockwork saurian Apollo shares an unmistakable family resemblance not only with Sir Joshua Malleson but also with Mr Apollinax and Mr R*ss*ll. The resemblance to Bertie Reid is fainter because Huxley, though a devoted admirer of Lawrence and something of a blind man himself, did not deprive Mr Scogan of sexual vitality. 'Thus, while I may have a certain amount of intelligence', says Mr Scogan about himself, 'I have no aesthetic sense; while I possess the mathematical faculty, I am wholly without the religious emotions; while I am naturally addicted to venery, I have little ambition and am not at all avaricious.'[54] Yet Mr Scogan's addiction is for the most part unconvincing in *Crome Yellow*. He seems to be busy talking while others are trying to make out; he has no involvement at all with Priscilla Wimbush, the mistress of Crome. Only at the fair, when he is disguised as 'Sesostris, the Sorceress of Ecbatana', does he engage in what he hopes are self-fulfilling predictions for nubile girls who come into his tent and are told that if they go to a certain place at a certain time they will encounter 'a small man with a sharp nose, not exactly good looking nor precisely young, but fascinating.... He will ask you, "Can you tell me the way to Paradise?" and you will answer, "Yes, I'll show you," and walk with him down towards the little hazel copse. I cannot read what will happen after that.'[55] Mr Scogan in amorous disguise manifests two symbolic characteristics that recur in his various literary embodiments. But in depriving him of religious and aesthetic emotions, Huxley was going against what Russell claimed for himself. Indeed it was these emotions that Russell felt increased the pain of his awareness that the consolations of philosophy were not for him.[56] Russell would have abhorred the man-centred world that Scogan invokes in his paean to the Tube:

...I always travel by Tube, never by bus if I can possibly help it. For, travelling by bus, one can't avoid seeing, even in London, a few stray works of God....But travel by Tube and you see nothing but the works of man....All is human and the product of friendly and comprehensible minds. All philosophies and all religions – what are they but spiritual Tubes bored through the universe!...And preserve me from nature, preserve me from all that's humanly large and complicated and obscure.[57]

Russell once complained that Huxley's use of him in *Crome Yellow* involved Scogan's putting forth ideas that Russell had only jokingly argued for at Lady Ottoline Morrell's.[58] But is Mr Scogan serious in his praise of the Tube or not? Is he an advocate of the brave new world Huxley described a decade later or, like Russell, is he merely anticipating it?[59] Scogan's ironic laughter echoes throughout *Crome Yellow*. Unlike other characters in the novel such as the inspirational Mr Barbeque-Smith or the minister who eagerly awaits Armageddon, Mr Scogan is less ridiculed against than ridiculing. The logic of Russell as a literary symbol should prepare us for the difficulties of determining the bounds of irony in Mr Scogan's various disquisitions. Sometimes Huxley indicates unmistakably how boringly insensitive is Mr Scogan's dry and passionate talk. He can be alarmingly aware of what people are thinking (he knows all about the plot of poor Denis's unwritten novel), but completely insensitive to what they are feeling. The final scene is a good example of Scogan's inhuman obtuseness. As he squeezes onto a bench holding Denis and his beloved Anne to whom Denis is bidding farewell, Mr Scogan continues to propound his Russellian view that the parts of the cosmos are fundamentally discrete.

Aldous Huxley's symbolisation of Bertrand Russell in *Crome Yellow* is, with the exception of a incomplete tetralogy of forgotten novels by Gilbert Cannan,[60] perhaps the most extensive representation of him in literature. Mr Scogan is related to Mr R*ss*ll and to Mr Apollinax. He is a propounder and an embodiment of paradoxes. His laughing iconoclasm is a part of the sterile behaviour it mocks. He has godlike Apollonian affinities with light and prophecy, yet he also appears as a reptile, a satyr and a mechanical toy.

After the First World War[61] Russell relied on the experience and authority he had gained as a leading war resister to become a widely read moral and social critic, an educator and a popularizer of philosophical and scientific thought. The logic of his literary symbolism changed accordingly. In becoming a public figure Russell ceased for the most part to appear as a private symbol in literary works. Instead of an eccentric genius to be encountered at Edwardian country house weekends, he begins to be symbolised as a professional wise man, *in propria persona*, whose well-known ideas and personality readers can be counted upon to recognise.

Siegfried Sassoon's fictionalised account of his encounter with Russell during the war shows something of the change in the use of Russell as a symbol. Sassoon's *Memoirs of an Infantry Officer*, written in the late 1920s, relates how Sassoon's alter-ego hero George Sherston – a decorated infantry officer turned crusading pacifist – is referred to a mathematical philosopher named Thornton Tyrrell. Tyrrell is described by an intermediary as 'the most uncompromising character I know. An extraordinary brain, of course. But you needn't be alarmed by that; you'll find him perfectly easy to get on with.' Sherston's first impression of Thornton Tyrrell is that 'he looked exactly like a philosopher. He was small, clean-shaven, with longish grey hair brushed neatly above a fine forehead. He had a long upper lip, a powerful ironic mouth, and large earnest eyes.' Tyrrell offers Sherston some Lawrentian advice ('"Keep vital" is a more important axiom than "love your neighbour"') and gives him a copy of what turns out to be *Principles of Social Reconstruction*.[62] Tyrrell's main function, however, is to help

Sherston clarify his objections to the war in a public statement, but after making it, Sherston acquiesces in a medical board's decision that he is having a nervous breakdown and retires to a sanatorium where the psychologist Larry Rivers (not disguised because he was dead at the time of Sassoon's writing) helps Sherston to return to the war and find peace with himself. Tyrrell is not mentioned again, and the reader is left with an implicit contrast between Rivers's great sympathetic understanding and Tyrrell's rather doctrinaire view of the war to which he accommodates Sherston.[63]

Though his name is disguised, the sketch of Russell in *Memoirs of an Infantry Officer* is quite straightforward: the large eyes and ironic mouth are recognisable symbolic features of Russell, even if the reader cannot be expected to know anything about the model for Tyrrell. In all other symbolic embodiments of Russell written in the 1920s and later that I know of, the significance of the depiction depends upon the reader's knowing who Bertrand Russell is. Alfred Noyes's poems[64] ridiculing Russell's notion that there is no essential difference between a thought and a billiard ball would, for example, lose much of their point if the ideas were not identified with Russell. The best illustration of this, however, is Roy Campbell's use of Russell in his satirical fantasy *The Georgiad*. Campbell's Georgians are not to be confused with those poets customarily described as Georgian; for Campbell, Georgians are what he calls 'Nancies' – writers whose sexual proclivities he disapproves of. These poor souls come to a summer school of love at which one of the masters is that member of a 'Church-Society for sexual research', Bertrand Russell. This is part of Campbell's description of the proceedings:

Hither flock all the crowd whom love has wrecked
Of intellectuals without intellect
And sexless folk whose sexes intersect:
All who in Russell's burly frame admire
The 'lineaments of gratified desire',
And of despair have baulked the yawning precipice
By swotting up his melancholy recipes
For 'happiness' – of which he is the cook....
All who have learned this grim felicity
And swotted bliss up, like the Rule of Three,
As if life were a class-examination
And there were penance in cohabitation:

> All who of 'Happiness' have learned the ropes
> From Bertrand Russell or from Marie Stopes,
> To put their knowledge into practice, some
> With fierce determination dour and glum,
> But all with earnest faces, hither come;
> And hither, too, the poets of the land
> Even though in 'Happiness' they take no hand.[65]

Campbell is exploiting here the mathematical logician turned popularising moralist. *The Georgiad* was written in the wake of *Marriage and Morals* and *The Conquest of Happiness*, and thus had satirical opportunities not available to Eliot or Huxley. Campbell makes use of them by connecting through a culinary metaphor Russell's mathematical work and his deceptively clear and simple moral analyses. But to do this effectively Campbell has to confine himself more or less to the real Russell and leave unrealistic metamorphoses to the fantastic characters of *The Georgiad* such as the ambidextrous hero, Androgyno. Another limitation of *Campbell's* symbolisation of Russell was not so necessary. Russell is not allowed to generate any satire in *The Georgiad* and therefore he appears as a simpler symbol than in several of his previous literary incarnations. It is a pity that Campbell could not use Russell to satirise the Georgians as well as be satirised with them; as one of their teachers he is well placed to comment upon and even exploit the sexual absurdities of his pupils. The poem distinguishes in its concluding enumeration 'swotters up of philosophic blisses' from 'septuagenarian peter pans', 'Bloomsburies', 'Fabians' and 'Sissies',[66] but only Androgyno is permitted any real versatility among these groups.

As a homophobic reactionary – he was the English poet who served on the *other* side during the Spanish Civil War – Campbell was contemptuous of Russell's political as well as moral ideas, and these too are ridiculed in *The Georgiad*. Russell is presented along with George Bernard Shaw as a propounder of boring, joyless utopias where there is no conflict – 'Edens of abnegation' in Campbell's felicitous phrase, where fear of strife dominates love of life. And in making Russell a utopian, Campbell takes liberties with his physical appearance as well as his unascetic conduct. Russell has to be not only burly but also bald so that his happiness of mind

> Can be only built and lined
> Out of the tearings of his own thin hair
> On the foundations of complete despair!⁶⁷

This last line is a quotation from 'A Free Man's Worship'.

Except for his appearance in *The Georgiad* and an occasional allusion to him in a novel here and there, Russell does not appear symbolically significant in the literature of the 1930s, 1940s or even the 1950s. Joyce Cary modelled the central character of an early novel on Russell, but it was never published.⁶⁸ It is perhaps surprising that writers such as W. H. Auden made no use of Russell in their work. He is mentioned in Anthony Powell's first novel, only as an occasion to laugh at the pretentious seriousness of a young woman who reads him for mental adventure.⁶⁹ Several reasons can be found for the disappearance of Russell from poetry and fiction. First, there is the change in Russell's own life that led him away from intellectual communities in which various writers encountered and represented him; as a freelance intellectual rather than as a teacher or leader of a cause, Russell was somewhat isolated, in the 1920s and 1930s at least. Secondly, the logic of Russell as a literary symbol shows that he was repeatedly treated as a satiric or at least ironic figure by those writers who used him. Writers who were not inclined to treat him ironically do not treat him at all. An illustration of the difficulties facing a satirist who tries to treat Russell sympathetically can be found in Myra Buttle's *The Bitches' Brew, or The Plot Against Bertrand Russell*, which appeared in 1960. Roy Campbell's account of Russell's happiness recipes is far more memorable than Myra Buttle's description of the man feared by 'The National Congress for the Status Quo':

> Their enemy is Reason's great apostle,
> The sceptic, sage yet passionate Lord Russell...

The rhyme is better in the poem's concluding paean, but it is difficult not to laugh at Russell and Myra Buttle when she writes,

> ...Stand for living, banish 'hustle'
> Stand for mind against mere muscle,
> Stand, in fact, for BERTRAND RUSSELL!⁷⁰

In the 1960s Russell turns up from time to time in literary works but almost never in a revealing or significant way. All the literary praise I have seen of Russell as an angry old prophet and martyr is banal.[71] There is more genuine tribute, I think, in satiric asides on Russell such as Philip Roth's than in efforts to canonise Russell. Roth's complainer Portnoy boasts, 'Our favorite philosopher was Bertrand Russell. Our religion was Dylan Thomas' religion, Truth and Joy! Our children would be atheists...I was very honest, you see, as Bertrand Russell said I should be.'[72] Scattered literary allusions to Russell during the past five years or so, especially on the stage, may indicate another modulation is taking place in the literary symbolism of Russell. As the lines between fiction and non-fiction increasingly blur in contemporary literature, the non-fictional descriptions of Russell in published memoirs and letters become increasingly interesting both in themselves and for the way contemporary writers are beginning to use them in their fiction.[73]

During the last half century of his life Russell is symbolised in non-fiction as interestingly as he was symbolised in fiction and poetry during the first half of his life. Some of the same symbolic characteristics reappear in the non-fiction, but there are new ones as well that take into account Russell's changing career. William Butler Yeats, who was put into what he admitted was 'a state of incoherence' by Russell's epistemology and politics, described the philosopher as a 'peaky-nosed, bald-pated, pink-eyed harridan', who had, furthermore, been bald all of his or her life![74] Norbert Wiener was among the first to write of Russell's resemblance to the Mad Hatter.[75] Virginia Woolf, in her diary, thought Russell's mind like a huge shining balloon attached to the small car of his body; she recalled how marvellous Russell's mind was: it worked as if it were on springs.[76] In his autobiography, Leonard Woolf remembered Russell's arguments with Moore at Cambridge in terms of a race between the hare and the tortoise.[77] These brief examples, together with such extended autobiographical accounts of Russell as *The Early Memoirs of Lady Ottoline Morrell*, Crawshay-Williams's *Russell Remembered* or the most illuminating of them all, Russell's own autobiographies, involve different kinds of truth claims in their representations of Russell than those of poetry or fiction. The ironic mode is not as dominant, though Russell's own iconoclastic humour remains fundamental. The symbolism becomes fainter, more metaphorical, though there is still that baffling mixture of the human with the supernatural, the mechanical and the animalistic. Russell as Apollo, Dionysus, Proteus, gives way to more realistic descriptions of the genius with large eyes and short legs – a figure of unshaded light, a changeling from wonderland condemned to live in the waste land. But if there is a loss in irony and symbolic concreteness, there is also a gain. Partly because of the nature of Russell's philosophy and partly because of the non-rational preoccupations of much modern literature, autobiographical depictions of Russell make use of his ideas more comprehensively and effectively than poets and novelists have been able to do.

But this comparison cannot be pursued here. I must stop with the conclusion that for the literary symbolic logician, a history of Bertrand Russell in song and story needs to be complemented by a study of Bertrand Russell through the looking-glass.

3 Bloomsbury Letters

Let us consider letters – how they come at breakfast, and at night, with their yellow stamps and their green stamps, immortalized by the postmark – for to see one's own envelope on another's table is to realize how soon deeds sever and become alien. Then at last the power of the mind to quit the body is manifest, and perhaps we fear or hate or wish annihilated this phantom of ourselves, lying on the table. Still, there are letters that merely say how dinner's at seven; others ordering coal; making appointments. The hand in them is scarcely perceptible, let alone the voice or the scowl. Ah, but when the post knocks and the letter comes always the miracle seems repeated – speech attempted. Venerable are letters, infinitely brave, forlorn, and lost.

Life would split asunder without them.

Virginia Woolf

I

It is tempting for the literary historian to respond to the topic of this session on non-fiction prose, 'The Place of Letter-Writing in Literary History', by saying simply that it is preventive. The more one writes of them, the less one writes of it. The wording of the topic invites this kind of response because of the various meanings of the term 'letter'. In the singular it is the most elementary part of written language, and in the plural it encompasses all literary culture. It is difficult to discuss a genre so ambiguously named in twenty minutes without being completely abstract, and therefore I am going to take just one particular instance of letters in literary history. It is a modern instance because there, without complicating historical obscurities, some at least of the interesting questions concerning the uses of letters may emerge.

My instance is the place of letters in the literary history of the Bloomsbury Group, a collectivity of loving friends and relations that includes E. M. Forster, Lytton Strachey and Virginia Woolf as its principal writers. The critics Desmond MacCarthy, Leonard Woolf, Clive Bell and Roger Fry, as well as the economist John Maynard

Keynes, are also Bloomsbury writers, however; their writing does not figure importantly in the history of modern English literature, but it takes on a significance in the context of the Bloomsbury Group that it may not otherwise have. But before discussing the place – or rather the places – that Bloomsbury's letters have in the Group's literary history, it is necessary to be clear about the meaning of the term 'literary history'. I have tried elsewhere to delimit a conception of Bloomsbury's literary history that focuses on both analytic and comparative descriptions of their interconnected texts in a historical sequence. These descriptions, viewed diachronically and synchronically, involve both the similarities and the contiguities of these texts. The place of Bloomsbury's letters in this idea of literary history has to do, first, with the fictive and non-fictive, public and private genres of letters they wrote, then with the transitive nature of letters that must be taken into account in their interpretation, and finally with the textual interconnections that letters display in Bloomsbury's literary history.

II

The usefulness of the term 'text' in defining Bloomsbury's literary history is that it helps to avoid the central dichotomy in modern literary study between fiction, poetry, drama and that other kind of writing that is identified only in terms of what it is not – and to which this session of the Modern Language Association is dedicated, perhaps in propitiation of our bad literary consciences. Bloomsbury was a prose literary movement (using 'movement' in a very general way; their friendships preceded their fame and their manifestos). And although Forster and Virginia Woolf wrote high fiction, they did not, as so many of their critics have, divide their own writings or those of other authors into categories of creative and non-creative prose. Both Forster and Virginia Woolf were more interested, for example, in whether a piece of writing was anonymous in its depiction of the self than in whether a given work was to be evaluatively classified as fiction or non-fiction. Their writing combines genres in the best tradition of modernist literary practice, which does not accord with the theory that divides imaginative from discursive prose. Nowhere is this fusion clearer than in their letters.

We are not, in this session, supposed to trespass into epistolary fiction, but in considering the place of Bloomsbury's letters in their literary history these territorial restrictions cannot be completely observed because of the ways in which fiction and non-fiction intermingle in their texts. One can avoid analysing the famous deflationary 'tea-tabling' effect that Forster gets from letters in his novels and that Christopher Isherwood thought so technically important in a novel like *Howards End*. (The first sentence of the novel is, 'One may as well begin with Helen's letters to her sister.') But when letters are discussed as letters in novels, or when they take on fictive characteristics independent of any novelistic context, it becomes crampingly restrictive to keep within the boundaries of non-fiction. The epigraph to this paper, for instance, is not from one of Virginia Woolf's several essays on letters, but from a novel, *Jacob's Room*, where it nevertheless functions as a quasi-authorial essay with both fictive and truth value. The elegiac and epistemological quest of the author for her central character makes movingly significant those disembodied acts of consciousness called letters. The most fundamental distinction in Bloomsbury's letters, however, is not whether they are used in novels but whether they are private or public texts. Virginia Woolf has suggested in her essay on modern letters in *The Captain's Death Bed* that it is the privacy of modern letters which distinguishes them most sharply from those of older centuries, where they always had some public function or other. One consequence, she foolishly thought, was that modern letters such as hers and her friends' could never be published. She underestimated the social and psychological interest that would attract readers who would find aesthetically embodied in them images of lives that could not be told in biographies as well as they could be shown in letters. Our understanding of Bloomsbury's life splits asunder without these brave and forlorn acts of minds surviving their bodies' deaths.

Fiction and non-fiction mix in both the public and private letters of Bloomsbury. The personal correspondence of Virginia Woolf or Lytton Strachey indulges in hyperbolic irony where fact and fantasy are not immediately distinguishable. In the midst of the Edwardian suffragist campaign, Strachey wrote to his cousin and sometime lover Duncan Grant apropos Elizabeth Robins's play *Votes for Women* (which he thought sentimental) that he wondered how long it would take women to understand the obvious fact that 'universal buggery' was the only solution to all their difficulties. In order to take this remark unironically, it is necessary to ignore its content as well as its context – Strachey grew up in a matriarchy devoted to *The Cause* – not to mention the letter's recipient. Or one might take the letter that Virginia Woolf's editor decided was the only 'mad' one she ever wrote. In it she suggests to Strachey in 1915 that they should all subscribe to a fund to buy Clive Bell a parrot that has been taught foul language, and then persuade Bell that birds are the acme of civilisation and he should study and write about them; the parrot is to be given the name of Bell's current mistress and kept in the basement under a cloth by his wife when he is not home. The feeling here is bitter but the symbolism is not mad but fictive.

Some of Bloomsbury's private letters are fictive in their form rather than their irony or their symbolism. In 1909 several members of the Group started a game in which they wrote one another imaginary letters; each writer was provided with an archaic pseudonym: Virginia Woolf was Elinor Hadynge; Lytton Strachey was Vane Hatherley. Then under these disguises the correspondents talked about their actual lives. '...It was in fact a kind of epistolary "bal masqué"', says Quentin Bell, 'in which the disguises served only to embolden the participants.'

Bloomsbury's mixing of fiction and non-fiction in public epistolary forms is more original and interesting perhaps than their private mixtures. Members of the Group wrote the usual kind of public letters to newspapers, though their content is not ordinary. E. M. Forster's rebukes of T. S. Eliot for his remarks on the death of D. H. Lawrence, or of Bertrand Russell for his memoir of Lytton Strachey, are masterly. But his most remarkable public letter is a piece called *A Letter to Madan Blanchard*. This is a letter written from the London Library in April 1931, signed 'E. M. Forster', and sent through space and time (the mail services grow older as the distance increases) to an eighteenth-century sailor who went native in Micronesia. The letter speculates about his motives, and under the guise of giving Madan Blanchard news about the native Prince Lee Boo, who went the opposite direction, Forster is able to compare the two cultures from his twentieth-century point of view. It is a bizarre epistolary form, and part of the pleasure of reading it is in the mixing up of our expectations.

Forster's is not the only use of a fictive letter form for an essay in Bloomsbury. After his letter to Blanchard, Virginia and Leonard Woolf began to publish a series of essay-letters in their Hogarth Press, including Rosamond Lehmann's *A Letter to a Sister*, Francis Birrell's *A Letter to a Black Sheep*, Rebecca West's *A Letter to a Grandfather* and Virginia Woolf's *A Letter to a Young Poet*. All of these letters adopt fictive disguises, some quite faint, for the purposes of some kind of cultural criticism. In these kinds of public letters the preposition in the title usually identifies the basis for the letter's criticism – whether it is a letter to, from or about, whether it has to do, that is, with the sender, the receiver or a separate topic. Virginia Woolf's letter in this series blends the fictive and non-fictive with the public and private. The letter is written to a poet called John; Virginia Woolf's biography tells us it is John Lehmann, but the letter does not. *A Letter to a Young Poet* is a critique of modern poetry which breaks off in an ellipsis when the writer shifts from the public to the private; the last sentence is, 'And now for the intimate, the indiscreet, and indeed, the only really interesting parts of this letter....'

The advantage of the epistolary form for an essay in cultural criticism is shown in the longest letter Virginia Woolf or anyone else in Bloomsbury ever wrote. Virginia Woolf's feminist polemic *Three Guineas* is a book-length letter, complete with extensive notes but no salutation or signature, written by the daughter of an educated man to an educated man who asked her in the mid-1930s how war can be prevented. Before the answers get under way, the writer of the letter – who is not necessarily the author, for we are dealing here with a fictive form – introduces her remarks as follows:

> In the first place let us draw what all letter-writers instinctively draw, a sketch of the person to whom the letter is addressed. Without someone warm and breathing on the other side of the page, letters are worthless. You, then, who ask the question, are a little grey on the temples; the hair is no longer thick on the top of your head. You have reached the middle years of life not without effort, at the Bar; but on the whole your journey has been prosperous...

and so forth. What we are being given here is a justification of the public letter genre (which is also fictional) as well as an evaluation of that form that is characteristic of Bloomsbury's letters as well as those of other writers.

III

The central feature of the letter genre – public as well as private – is its inherent transitive duality. Explicitly or implicitly there is in the letter a subject and an object, a writer and a reader. Outside there may also be a correspondent and a recipient who are obviously related to the writer and reader yet not identical with them. (Some forms of public letter may have an unimportant or even non-existent recipient.) But inside the letter form there always appears to be someone addressing someone else. This is what makes the letter more closely related to the lecture and the dramatic monologue than to the reflexive diary form which lacks the convention if not, in many cases, the assumption, of an objectified reader inside the form.

The transitive character of the letter is crucial to the interpretation of the genre. In public letters the significance of the addressee needs to be clear. He, or she, or they may be the basis for the letter's criticism. *Three Guineas* is all about the world that the writer's male correspondent has made. The directness of the epistolary form (which replaces the intimacy of the private letter) makes it an effective instrument for polemics: the target is inside the letter, as it were – more so than in a lecture or even a sermon, perhaps. It is interesting in Bloomsbury's literary history that Virginia Woolf shifted in her two polemics on feminism from the milder form of the fictive lecture in *A Room of One's Own* to the angrier form of the fictive letter in *Three Guineas*. With private letters, however, the transitiveness of the communication may be more obscure because the character of the internalised object of the letter can be taken largely for granted and not displayed, as in a public letter. When published, a private letter often needs to have its intended reader and perhaps also its occasion identified for the new public reader. Bloomsbury's idea of good letters – and they wrote good letters – was, as Virginia Woolf said in *Three Guineas*, that they should include some conception of the person being written to. Forster said letters should pass two tests: they must express the personality of the writer and of the recipient. Strachey felt the first business of a letter-writer was to put his correspondent into a good humor. (He also thought that good letter-writers, such as Walpole, were androgynous, because 'the unmixed male does not express himself happily'. The theory could be interestingly applied to Virginia Woolf's letters too.) For the purposes of literary history, the most significant aspect of this agreement in Bloomsbury about the importance of a letter expressing, as it were, its object as well as its subject lies not in the writing of their letters but in the reading of them.

Remarks from a Bloomsbury letter – and not just from them, either – need to be taken in their context, which most importantly includes the person to whom the letter is being written. This, as has been noted, is easier to do in a public rather than a private letter where we have to go outside the letter and fill in the personality of the recipient or the nature of the personal relationship being assumed in the letter. The interpretation of Bloomsbury's texts depends on understanding their tone. How often the irony of them is misperceived by their critics! In letters, of course, the tone depends importantly on the person to whom the letter is being addressed. One example may suffice of the necessity in interpreting Bloomsbury's letters to grasp their transitiveness and connect what is being said to who is saying it and to whom it is being said. Virginia Woolf is sometimes accused these days of being anti-Semitic, and the evidence cited is often taken from letters in which she refers to her husband's Jewishness. What has not been noticed enough is that these references are made only to close friends who can be counted upon to understand their affectionate tone correctly. Difficult as it is to believe after Hitler, the tone is often one of a joke or an endearment. When Virginia Stephen became engaged to Leonard Woolf, she wrote to good friends such as Violet Dickinson, Janet Case or Madge Vaughan about the penniless Jew who was to be her husband. But in letters to friends who were not so close, friends such as Lady Ottoline Morrell (this is in 1912) or even Lady Robert Cecil, there is no reference at all to his being Jewish. Some will put this down to Virginia Woolf's snobbery, but it is far more likely that she would not joke about such matters with those whose responses she could not count on. The interpretation of Bloomsbury remarks should, if they are to be responsible, take into account whether the remark is a public fictive or non-fictive utterance, a piece of self-communing, or a letter to someone whose relationship with the writer helps to shape the remark.

IV

The primary justification for examining the writings of the Bloomsbury Group through its literary history is to be located in the interconnections of these writings – interconnections that bear importantly on the interpretation of the writings. Bloomsbury's texts are interconnected in various ways, through their dedications, similar subjects, analogous forms, through the backgrounds of their authors and the family resemblance of their ethical, epistemological and aesthetic assumptions, and finally through the criticism that they wrote of one another's work. A good deal of that criticism was done in the form of reviews that were by no means always exercises in mutual admiration. But a significant amount of the Bloomsbury Group's criticism of one another is contained in their letters. Some of the most revealing instances of this criticism occur in letters to the authors about their works – Strachey and Virginia Woolf on her novels and his biographies, for example, or the debate between Forster and Virginia Woolf over *Aspects of the Novel*. But some of the epistolary criticism is contained in letters written not to the author but to another member of the Group. Lytton Strachey and Leonard Woolf are revealingly critical of Forster's Edwardian novels in their correspondence. Occasionally both types of criticism are to be found about a single work, as in the interesting letter from Strachey to Leonard Woolf about his novel *The Wise Virgins* (in which a character modelled on Strachey appears) and another from Lytton to his brother commenting on the difficulties of writing to Leonard about the novel, which he did not like. Again, the inherent transitiveness of the letter is essential to the interpretation of this epistolary criticism. Biography and criticism intermingle unavoidably here, yet for all its personal impurity the criticism is among the most useful we have of Bloomsbury's writings because of the emphases it gives. The evaluation in Bloomsbury's criticism of one another's work, especially in their letters where it is not called for in the way a review exacts it, is often not as illuminating as what is singled out for attention and comment. Sometimes the illumination falls on the speaker, the auditor and the criticised text.

The place of letters in Bloomsbury's literary history might be summed up by saying that they give motives for metonymy. The letter is pre-eminently a metonymic form, and its interpretation has been neglected along with other metonymic aspects of literature, as Jakobson has pointed out, in our modern rage for analogy. If life splits asunder in Bloomsbury without letters, so does literary history. Bloomsbury's letters interconnect their texts in important ways but they are also literary texts in their own right, whether they be fictive, non-fictive, public or private. All involve contiguities of space and time, especially the private letter, for one of its organising principles is synecdoche: parts of the writer's life represented in the letter stand for the whole. But in all Bloomsbury's epistolary forms, the internalised speaker and listener must not be lost sight – or rather sound – of, whatever the letter's provenance or destination.

4 Keynes, Lawrence and Cambridge Revisited

The repulsion that D. H. Lawrence felt for Cambridge when he was the guest there of Bertrand Russell in March 1915 has become part of the mythology of modern English literary history. The primary source of the myth is John Maynard Keynes's famous memoir 'My Early Beliefs', which was first published together with an introduction by the late David Garnett in *Two Memoirs* in 1949. A review of the memoir by F. R. Leavis reinterpreted Lawrence's reaction and made it more widely known. Over the past thirty years various accounts have been published that illuminate both the character of Keynes's memoir and the actual circumstances of Lawrence's encounter with Cambridge. Now a hitherto unknown record of Lawrence's visit by no less a figure than G. E. Moore has come to light. To appreciate the interest of Moore's account it is necessary to review in some detail the commentary – by Lawrence himself as well as others – that has collected around his visit to Cambridge.

The departure point for Keynes's memoir, which was written for Bloomsbury's Memoir Club in 1938, was an earlier memoir by David Garnett about the hostility Lawrence had displayed towards Garnett's friends. When Keynes's memoir was published Garnett introduced it by briefly recounting his own, in the course of which he quoted passages from two letters of Lawrence's, one to Lady Ottoline Morrell about how the self-centred talk of Garnett's friend Francis Birrell had made him dream of beetles, and the other to Garnett himself, dated 19 April 1915:

My Dear David,
  Never bring Birrell to see me any more. There is something nasty about him like black beetles. He is horrible and unclean. I feel I should go mad when I think of your set, Duncan Grant and Keynes and Birrell. It makes me dream of beetles. In Cambridge I had a similar dream. I had felt it slightly before in the Stracheys. But it came full upon me in Keynes and in Duncan

Grant. And yesterday I knew it again in Birrell... you must leave these friends, these beetles, Birrell and Duncan Grant are done for forever. Keynes I am not sure... when I saw Keynes that morning in Cambridge it was one of the crises of my life. It sent me mad with misery and hostility and rage... [sic]

In the introduction to 'My Early Beliefs' Garnett wrote of his great admiration for Lawrence, but as a rationalist and a scientist, he opposed Lawrence's 'intuitive and dogmatic philosophy', whereas the ideas of his Cambridge friends attracted and interested him.[1]

Keynes used his meeting with Lawrence, which he thought took place before the war rather than in 1915, as a frame for the reconsideration of his early Cambridge beliefs which were derived from Moore's *Principia Ethica*. Keynes begins by admitting that he cannot recall any fragment of what was actually said during the meeting, yet he retained 'some faint remains of what was felt'. He met Lawrence at a breakfast party given by Russell, and Lawrence was morose, Keynes thought, because he had not enjoyed facing Cambridge the night before. The breakfast proceeded unsatisfactorily, with Keynes and Russell talking at rather than with Lawrence. This is all Keynes remembered, but from Garnett's memoir he inferred that Lawrence was jealous of the friends of Garnett that he had been meeting at Lady Ottoline's Garsington, in Bloomsbury, and now at Cambridge. Keynes also inferred that Lawrence was repelled by the rationalism and cynicism of pre-war Cambridge:

> Bertie gave him what must have been, I think, his first glimpse of Cambridge. It overwhelmed, attracted and repulsed him – which was the other emotional disturbance. It was obviously a civilisation, and not less obviously uncomfortable and unattainable for him – very repulsive and very attractive.

Keynes goes on to ask if there was not after all something to Lawrence's feelings about Cambridge; to answer this question he spends the rest of his memoir analysing the influence of Moore on himself and his friends. In essence Keynes finds that Moore's disciples adopted his 'religion' – meaning 'one's attitude towards oneself and the ultimate' – and ignored his morals – meaning 'one's attitude towards the outside world and the intermediate'. They became utopian immoralists, repudiating conventional morality, traditional wisdom, and believing in a pseudo-rational conception of human nature that resulted in a superficiality of judgement and feeling. The fundamental intuitions of *Principia Ethica* were beautiful in their ideality, but they were not enough. Summing up, Keynes describes himself and his friends not as beetles, but as

> water-spiders, gracefully skimming, as light and reasonable as air, the surface of the stream without any contact at all with the eddies and currents underneath. And if I imagine us as coming under the observation of Lawrence's ignorant, jealous, irritable, hostile eyes, what a combination of qualities we offered to arouse his passionate distaste; this thin rationalism skipping on the crust of the lava, ignoring both the reality and the value of the vulgar passions, joined to libertinism and comprehensive irreverence.... All this was very unfair to poor, silly, well-meaning us. But that is why I say that there may have been just a grain of truth when Lawrence said in 1914 that we were 'done for'.[2]

Keynes's memoir gave two reasons for Lawrence's 'emotional disturbance' at Cambridge: he was jealous of Garnett's friends there, and he was both repelled and attracted by the civilisation that he found at Cambridge. F. R. Leavis's influential review of *Two Memoirs*, collected under the title 'Keynes, Lawrence and Cambridge' in 1952, dismisses jealousy as an explanation and finds the significance of 'My Early Beliefs' to lie in the unwitting criticism of the Cambridge civilisation that Keynes thought Lawrence was overwhelmed by:

> That Lawrence, judging out of his experience of something incomparably more worthy to be called a 'civilization', loathed and despised what was in front of him merely because he saw just what it was, is inconceivable to Keynes.

It is ludicrous to imagine, Leavis continued later in the review,

> that Lawrence must have felt inferior and ill-educated when introduced in Russell's rooms to the dazzling civilization of Cambridge. But the thing to stress is his enormous advantage in experience. The young ex-elementary school-teacher was in a position to judge of the most distinguished intellectual among his friends...

But what for Leavis is 'most revelatory of the Cambridge-Bloomsbury ethos' in 'My Early Beliefs' is that in 1938 Keynes is still taking seriously an immature, undergraduate idea of civilisation.[3]

Leavis's review never questions the accuracy of Keynes's Cambridge recollections, not even the pre-war dating of Lawrence's visit. He also never specifies what exactly Lawrence's criticism of Cambridge civilisation was. All we are given is Leavis's criticism. The only direct evidence in Garnett's, Keynes's and Leavis's accounts of what happened to Lawrence in Cambridge is a paragraph from a letter Lawrence wrote to Garnett a month later. All the rest appears to be speculative reconstruction.

In the years since Keynes's memoir was published a number of autobiographies, letters and commentaries have appeared that reveal the incompleteness and inaccuracy of both the reasons Keynes gave for Lawrence's reaction to Cambridge. Bertrand Russell's portrait of Lawrence, first published in 1952 and reprinted in *Portraits from Memory* in 1956, agrees with Keynes's recollection of how Lawrence felt about the people he was meeting in Cambridge. 'He hated them all with a passionate hatred', Russell stated categorically, 'and said they were "dead, dead, dead".'[4] But Russell makes it unmistakably clear that his relationship with Lawrence came about during and largely because of the First World War. The Cambridge civilisation that Lawrence encountered was conditioned by the war and something of its temper became manifested the next year when Russell's college deprived him of his lectureship because of his pacifist activities. If, as it is sometimes said by literary critics, Lawrence rejected Russell's Cambridge, then so did Russell – and it was mutual. It is crucial in assessing Lawrence's response to Cambridge to realise that it was affected by the war that he agreed with Russell in opposing, though they were shortly to disagree about what to do in their opposition.

In *Sowing*, the first volume of his autobiography, published in 1960, Leonard Woolf authoritatively challenged Keynes's interpretation of G. E. Moore's influence – an influence Keynes had made central to the Cambridge civilisation that Lawrence thought was done for. Woolf flatly disagreed that he and his friends ignored Moore's morals and adopted only his religion. They were not, to be sure, as socially conscious before the war as all the younger generations became after it, but both Moore and his followers were fascinated by questions of what was right and wrong, what one *ought* to do... and argued interminably about the consequences of one's actions, both in actual and imaginary situations.

Woolf went on to point out that Keynes's memoir conflated two quite different periods of time, the Cambridge years when Woolf and his friends were undergraduates around the turn of the century and the period just before the war when they had matured and no longer argued about *Principia Ethica* as a practical guide to life.[5] The ethical point Woolf made about Moore's influence was developed later by Professor R. B. Braithwaite in an essay on Keynes as a philosopher.[6] In an effort at 'de-rhetoricising' Keynes's memoir, Braithwaite identifies three different strands of thought in *Principia Ethica*: the first has to do with the indefinable nature of good, the second with ethical pluralism, and the third with Utilitarian consequentialism. Braithwaite argues that Moore's consequentialism was familiar to Keynes in his own father's philosophy, and therefore he paid little attention to it in Moore's thought, whereas Moore's refutation of Utilitarian hedonism was new and exhilarating.

'My Early Beliefs' is a brilliantly written memoir in both its praise and criticism of *Principia Ethica*'s influence. Keynes illuminates the puritan, Platonic and neo-Platonic aspects of Bloomsbury's Cambridge as well as the power and the attractiveness of Moore's ethical methods and ideals. He is witty in his depiction of the limits of ethical disagreements over intuitive ends and in his mockery of the extremes to which his friends' rationalistic, pre-Freudian analyses of human relationships were carried. And he is deeply serious in his attack on the Benthamite tradition's 'over-valuation of the economic criterion' that has been brought to a *reductio ad absurdum* in Marxism.[7] But as an account of his early beliefs and those of his friends, 'My Early Beliefs' appears doubly mistaken in its chronology and distorted in its interpretation of Moore's influence. It is particularly interesting, therefore, to read what Moore himself had to say about a memoir connecting him with D. H. Lawrence. When David Garnett edited Keynes's memoir for its posthumous publication, he added the following footnote referring to Moore and qualifying Keynes's statement that Lawrence had probably not enjoyed the evening when he had first faced Cambridge:

Professor G. E. Moore tells me that he sat next Lawrence in Hall that night and found nothing to say to him, but that afterwards Lawrence was introduced to Professor Hardy, the mathematician, with whom he had a long and friendly discussion. From the moment of Lawrence's introduction to Hardy, the evening was a success.[8]

It would seem that *pace* Keynes (and Russell) Lawrence had enjoyed meeting at least some Cambridge dons, and this is confirmed in an unpublished letter Moore wrote to Garnett after receiving a copy of *Two Memoirs*.[9]

> 86, Chesterton Road,
> Cambridge.
>
> May 17/49
>
> Dear Mr. Garnett,
> I ought to have written before to thank you very much indeed for the copy of the two Keynes Memoirs, which was sent me by the publishers. It was very kind of you to send it to me. I have read them both through again with great pleasure; and I feel, as I felt before, that if Melchior was a 'precisian', I don't mind being called one too.
> I am afraid, from your note on p. 78, that I did not make quite clear to you what happened on that night when Lawrence stayed with Russell at Trinity. Lawrence talked that night in Russell's rooms, not specially to Hardy, but to the whole group of people who were there in a general conversation, i.e. certainly to Russell as well as Hardy, & probably to a few others as well (Hardy did not tell me whether any others were there, or who they were, but I think it is likely there were one or two more). I remember Hardy told me that what he talked about was Socialism, & I find from my Diary (which I have now looked up) that what Hardy was specially struck by was Lawrence's eloquence. My Diary also shows that you were right in thinking the meeting took place in 1915: the night in question was March 7, 1915. And it also shows (what surprises me) that when I sat next him in Hall I did not know who he was! Apparently at that time I had never heard of D. H. Lawrence. I noted that he gave me the impression of being very shy; and of course I felt shy too. But I think there is no doubt that, since afterwards, in Russell's rooms, he talked a great deal & very eloquently, he

must have enjoyed that part of the evening, and not have felt at all as he did the next morning at breakfast with Keynes & Russell. I think he must have taken a dislike to Keynes almost at first sight, and that was why he was morose, not, as Keynes supposes, because he had been facing Cambridge the night before & had not enjoyed it.

Yours sincerely
G. E. Moore

Moore's diary[10] shows that the night in question was actually 6 March. The relevant part of the entry for that day is as follows:

> <u>Hall</u> between Chapman & Russell's guest Lawrence (who is he?); L. seems very shy & only tries to speak me once [sic].

And on 7 March Moore made the following entry about hall:

> <u>Hall</u> at end next Watson: Hardy & Winstanly opp.; <u>H. talks of Lawrence's eloquence</u>; then Simpson's sermon.

(Moore's underlining may have been added later, together with a note in the margin, 'D. H. Lawrence next me at Hall.')

It may be a little surprising, given Moore's fondness for fiction, that he had not heard of Lawrence. By 1915 Lawrence had published *The White Peacock*, *The Trespasser*, *Sons and Lovers* and *The Prussian Officer* stories, not to mention a volume of poems and a play. It may also seem odd that Moore did not comment more to Garnett on Keynes's interpretation of his influence; he only notes the implicit comparison between himself and the subject of the first memoir, Dr Melchior, that Keynes made in labelling each of them a 'precisian'. (Keynes called Moore 'a puritan and precisian' and then showed how his followers became 'immoralists'; he makes a similar point about Melchior at the end of his memoir: '.... what a precisian he was, a strict and upright moralist, a worshipper of the Tablets of the Law, a Rabbi'.[11] The essay on Melchoir was written around 1931, and in it Keynes also sees himself as a kind of immoralist in his attack on the Versailles treaty.) On the other hand it is not likely that David Garnett, who never went to Cambridge, would have been the kind of person with whom Moore in his old age might have chosen to discuss the interpretation of *Principia Ethica*.

But the most significant thing about Moore's contemporary account and later recollection is their making clear that if Lawrence was repelled by Cambridge rationalism and cynicism, it was their embodiment in the personality and character of John Maynard Keynes that really upset him. It may have had something to do with views Keynes as a liberal held about the socialism Lawrence appears to have been discussing, but other accounts of Lawrence's visit and Keynes's memoir indicate that there was something much more specific at work. What it was is first intimated in letters that Bertrand Russell wrote to Lady Ottoline Morrell at the time of Lawrence's visit but were not made public until the second volume of her memoirs, *Ottoline at Garsington*, was published in 1974. On the Sunday evening of Lawrence's visit, Russell wrote to Lady Ottoline,

> I gave your letter to Lawrence who says he will come to tea with you tomorrow. I don't think he will get on with Goldie – he hates everybody here, as was to be expected. I was grateful to you for telling me Keynes was up – I am having him to dinner tonight. Lawrence had rather liked him before – but seeing him this morning at 11, in pyjamas, just awake, he felt him corrupt and unclean. Lawrence has quick sensitive impressions which I don't understand, tho' they would seem quite natural to you. They are marvellous. I love him more and more. I couldn't dream of discouraging his socialist revolution. He has real faith in it, and it absorbs his vital force – he must go through with it. He talks so well about it that he *almost* makes me believe in it. I am afraid he is not happy here, and will heave a great sigh of relief when he gets away. He can't stand the lack of vitality and force in the dons. I hope he won't visit it on me in his thoughts.[12]

One reason, of course, why Lawrence found a lack of vitality and force among the dons he met was the war in which many of the younger dons were serving. Others like Goldsworthy Lowes Dickinson were in despair about the war. Lawrence had particularly wanted to meet Dickinson before he visited Cambridge, and a widely read work of his may have helped give Lawrence the idea for the title of *Women in Love*, the novel he was shortly to begin working on again. (In *The Greek View of Life* Dickinson describes how Aristophanes accused Euripides of 'lowering the tragic by introducing – what? Women in love! The central theme of modern tragedy!'[13]) Lawrence does not seem to have met Dickinson in Cambridge, and later in 1916 he dismissed 'that old "advanced" crowd – Cambridge, Lowes Dickinson, Bertie Russell, young reformers, socialists, Fabians – they are our disease, not our hope'.[14] But in 1915 Lawrence's opposition to the war and passion for a socialist revolution made him keen to meet Dickinson. Why did Russell think he would not get on with him – because he was middle-aged and depressed about the war? Why did Russell say Lawrence hated everyone in Cambridge when the night before Lawrence had apparently enjoyed talking with Hardy and others? Russell himself, in another letter to Lady Ottoline, written perhaps the following Tuesday, also mentioned how impressed Hardy had been with Lawrence and how trivial everyone else in Cambridge had seemed by comparison. But again, Russell is writing after Lawrence had seen Keynes at Cambridge and felt him to be corrupt and unclean. That meeting, as Moore thought, changed Lawrence's mood. Why it did is suggested in the letter Russell wrote to Lady Ottoline on Monday after Lawrence had left Cambridge.

> Lawrence is gone, disgusted with Cambridge, but not with me, I think. I felt that we got on *very* well with each other, and made real progress towards intimacy. His intuitive perceptiveness is *wonderful* – it leaves me gasping in admiration.
>
> Keynes came to dinner, and we had an interesting but rather dreadful evening. Keynes was hard, intellectual, insincere – using intellect to hide the torment and discord in his soul. We pressed him hard about his purpose in life – he spoke as tho' he only wanted a succession of agreeable moments, which of course is not really true. Lawrence likes him but can't get on with him; I get on with him, but dislike him. Lawrence has the same feeling against sodomy as I have; you had nearly made me believe there is no great harm in it, but I have reverted; and all the examples I know confirm me in thinking it sterilizing.
>
> Lawrence is wonderfully lovable. The mainspring of his life is love – the universal mystical love – which inspires even his most vehement and passionate hate. It is odd that his *thinking* is coloured by Self – he imagines men more like him than they are. I think his thinking is quite honest, but there are painful things it hasn't realized.[15]

Russell's letter reveals for the first time that what sent Lawrence 'mad with misery and hostility and rage' at seeing Keynes in his pyjamas was the intimation of Keynes's homosexuality. Here again Lawrence's feelings were in agreement with Russell's but not with a number of Keynes's Cambridge friends, including Dickinson and perhaps even Hardy. Disgust with homosexuality is, it would appear from Russell's letter, the unmentioned – and when Keynes's memoir was published still unmentionable – emotional reaction that Keynes described as jealousy. Keynes's memoir, then, is an incomplete account not only of the ideas of Moore that shaped the Cambridge civilisation Lawrence was repelled and attracted by, but also of the nature and origin of Lawrence's jealousy. How inaccurate Keynes was in his chronology has been noted; he also seems to have misremembered other details about the meeting with Lawrence. There was, for example, not a breakfast together but a dinner. And the conversation, if Russell's account is to be relied upon, was not one directed by Russell and Keynes at Lawrence. In one detail, however, Russell's letter accords well with Keynes's memoir, and that is in the description of Keynes speaking as though his only purpose in life was a succession of agreeable moments. In 'My Early Beliefs' Keynes argues that the religion Moore's followers took from *Principia Ethica* held that nothing mattered but 'timeless, passionate states of contemplation and communion largely unattached to "before" and "after"'; pleasure did not play much of a role in these states around 1903, but 'as time wore on towards the nineteen-tens, I fancy we weakened a bit about pleasure'.[16] By 1915 Keynes, at any rate, had perhaps adapted Moore's philosophy to fit the early beliefs he describes in his memoir. And if they were typical of Cambridge civilisation, Lawrence may indeed have been upset by its rationalism and cynicism.

With the publication of *The Collected Letters of D. H. Lawrence* in 1962, the sexual element in Lawrence's reaction to Keynes was shown in a letter Lawrence wrote to S. S. Koteliansky about Birrell and Garnett's visit:

> I like David, but Birrell I have come to detest. These horrible little frowsty people, men lovers of men, they give me such a sense of corruption, almost putrescence, that I dream of beetles. It is abominable.[17]

But the presence of homosexuality as a motive for Lawrence's repulsion from Keynes and Cambridge was first suggested by a member of the Memoir Club who had heard Keynes read 'My Early Beliefs' in September of 1938. Professor Quentin Bell maintained in the course of his book *Bloomsbury* that appeared in 1968, six years before Russell's letters to Lady Ottoline were published, that Keynes's memoir was, in effect, a sermon on traditional values and the inadequacy of Marxism, delivered the summer before Munich to the younger generation of Bloomsbury. Certainly the date of Keynes's memoir might help to explain why Keynes wanted to remember Lawrence's visit as just before the First World War. Bell goes on to argue that Keynes's sermon had little to do with its text, in which were the excerpts from Lawrence's letters quoted by Garnett in the introduction; Keynes had hoodwinked his audience and others, such as Leavis, who assumed it was the intellectual quality of Cambridge and Bloomsbury that disgusted Lawrence, whereas Lawrence never says this. Bell declares that Lawrence's nightmare beetles 'were in fact not intellectual but erotic phenomena', and he quotes from a letter of Lawrence's, written around the time of the one to Garnett, in which Lawrence describes soldiers in terms of the sensual lust of insects. As a possible explanation of Lawrence's repulsion from Garnett's friends Birrell and Keynes and earlier Duncan Grant, Bell asked if Lawrence were not suffering from unavowed homosexual jealousy. In a footnote, however, Bell concedes that David Garnett had remained completely unconvinced by this interpretation.[18]

Why Garnett was unconvinced by Quentin Bell's arguments may have been because of Bell's insistence on Lawrence's jealousy – a motive also given by Keynes. But there can be no doubt that it was Keynes's homosexuality more than anything else that repulsed Lawrence when one reads the complete letter that Lawrence wrote to Garnett a month later and that Garnett finally published in *Great Friends* in 1979.

> Greatham, Pulborough, Sussex.
> Monday.
>
> My dear David,
>   I can't bear to think of you, David, so wretched as you are and your hand shaky – and everything wrong. It is foolish of you to say it doesn't matter either way – the men loving men. It doesn't matter in the public way. But it matters so much David, to the

man himself – at any rate to us northern nations – that it is like a blow of triumphant decay, when I meet Birrell and the others. I simply can't bear it. It is so wrong, it is unbearable. It makes a form of inward corruption which truly makes me scarce able to live. Why is there this horrible sense of frowstiness, so repulsive, as if it came from a deep inward dirt – a sort of sewer – deep in men like K and B & D G. It is something almost unbearable to me. And not from any moral disapprobation. I myself never considered Plato very wrong, or Oscar Wilde. I never knew what it meant till I saw K., till I saw him at Cambridge. We went into his rooms at midday, and it was very sunny. He was not there, so Russell was writing a note. Then suddenly a door opened and K. was there, blinking from sleep, standing in his pyjamas. And as he stood there gradually a knowledge passed into me, which has been like a little madness to me ever since. And it was carried along with the most dreadful sense of repulsiveness – something like carrion – a vulture gives me the same feeling. I begin to feel mad as I think of it – insane.

Then comes the original paragraph Garnett quoted in his introduction without any indication that it was not the beginning of the letter.

Never bring B. to see me any more. There is something nasty about him, like black-beetles. He is horrible and unclean. I feel as if I should go mad; if I think of your set, D. G. and K. and B. It makes me dream of beetles. In Cambridge I had a similar dream. Somehow I can't bear it. It is wrong beyond all bounds of wrongness. I had felt it slightly before, in the Stracheys. But it came full upon me in K., and in D. G. And yesterday I knew it again in B.

Garnett had omitted parts of that paragraph and then combined it with excerpts from the rest of the letter.

David, my dear, I love your father and I love your mother. I think your father has been shamefully treated at the hands of life. Though I don't see him, I do love him in my soul – more even than I love your mother. And I feel, because he is your father, that you must leave these 'friends', these beetles. You must wrench away and start a new life. B. and D. G. are done for, I think –

done for for ever. K. I am not sure. But you, my dear, you can be all right. You can come away, and grow whole, and love a woman, and marry her, and make life good, and be happy. Now David, in the name of everything that is called love, leave this set and stop this blasphemy against love. It isn't that I speak from a moral code. Truly I didn't know it was wrong, till I saw K. that morning in Cambridge. It was one of the crises in my life. It sent me mad with misery and hostility and rage. Go away, David, and try to love a woman. My God, I could kiss Eleanor Farjeon with my body and soul, when I think how good she is, in comparison. But the Oliviers, and such girls, are wrong.

I could sit and howl in a corner like a child, I feel so bad about it all.

D. H. Lawrence[19]

The full text of Lawrence's letter together with Moore's letter and diary and Russell's letters to Lady Ottoline give a fairly clear picture of what actually took place at Cambridge when Lawrence visited there. But by omitting the entire first paragraph and much of the third one, Garnett concealed the primary cause of the repulsion Lawrence felt for Keynes and Cambridge. Lawrence's encounter with Cambridge and his meetings with Duncan Grant and Francis Birrell cannot be understood apart from Lawrence's intense and complex reaction to homosexuality. The beetles he dreamt of were coprophagous symbols of sodomy. And his writings – especially the cancelled prologue to *Women in Love* – display his own homoerotic susceptibilities. Keynes's explanation of jealousy cannot, therefore, be dismissed in the manner Leavis does, though it may not have been the particular type of homosexual jealousy that Bell suggests. Keynes does not explain Lawrence's jealousy beyond noting that when Lawrence saw Garnett 'being seduced by Cambridge, he was yet more jealous, just as he was jealous of Ottoline's leanings that way'. Keynes's language here raises a basic question about the version of the myth in 'My Early Beliefs': did Keynes know the full import of Lawrence's letter to Garnett when he wrote his memoir? We do not have the original memoir that Garnett read to the Memoir Club (but see the postscript below). The version of it he published in his autobiography *The Flowers of the Forest* in 1955 is as reticent as his introduction to Keynes's memoir. Yet it is difficult to avoid the conclusion that Keynes must have had some idea of it, for there is a missing 'belief' in Keynes's memoir – the belief in the value of homoerotic or homosexual relationships that was held by a number of the Apostles, some of whom like Strachey and Sheppard figure in 'My Early Beliefs'. At the end of his memoir Keynes said that the ignoring by himself and his friends of 'both the reality and the value of the vulgar passions' helped arouse Lawrence's passionate distaste for Cambridge.[20] But in 'My Early Beliefs' he is still ignoring one particular kind of vulgar passion whose reality and value in Cambridge in 1915 so repelled Lawrence.

As for Keynes's other explanation of Lawrence's reaction – the attraction and repulsion he felt for an unattainable intellectual civilisation that was, however, rational and cynical – the accounts we have simply do not provide enough information for useful generalisations about Lawrence's intellectual response to Cambridge. All we really know is what he wrote to Russell before coming to Cambridge – that it was a momentous occasion for him: 'I don't want to be horribly impressed and intimidated, but am afraid I may be.'[21] He was indeed horribly impressed and intimidated, and in ways he had not anticipated. But this is not to say that Lawrence's reaction can be reduced to a defensive revulsion at the homosexual affairs of Garnett, Birrell, Grant, Strachey and Keynes. The wartime setting of Lawrence's visit importantly affected his response to Cambridge as it did his relationship with Russell. The conflict that developed between Russell and Lawrence contains a number of basic intellectual and emotional disagreements, though in the end it should not be forgotten that these two geniuses influenced each other's outlooks, as can be seen in some of the ideas of Russell's *Principles of Social Reconstruction* or in Lawrence's representation of Russell in his story 'The Blind Man'.[22] But Russell's Cambridge was not Keynes's Cambridge or even Moore's Cambridge, and all their Cambridges were different in 1903, 1914 and 1915.

There may well be more to learn about the history behind the myth of D. H. Lawrence's visit to Cambridge that was so brilliantly imagined (that is his word) by Keynes in 'My Early Beliefs' – more about the intellectual nature of his response to Cambridge's civilisation, more about the passions of its inhabitants, when we have the next volumes of letters in *The Cambridge Edition of the Works of D. H. Lawrence*, as it is called, perhaps not all that inappropriately.

POSTSCRIPT

After this article was published David Garnett's son Mr Richard Garnett very kindly sent me a copy of his father's original Memoir Club paper, which had indeed survived. This was the memoir that Keynes read – not heard, for he was not at the meeting when it was delivered, and Garnett sent it to him afterwards.[23] The first thing to be said about it is that the memoir gives the same bowdlerised version of Lawrence's letter, with the explicit references to 'men loving men' left out. Keynes may well have not known the rest of what Lawrence said in his letter. Yet Garnett does refer in the memoir to the rumour spread by Mrs Gilbert Cannan that he and Francis Birrell were having an affair.

In his Memoir Club paper and again in *The Flowers of the Forest* and *Great Friends* Garnett tells the story of his and Birrell's stay with the Lawrences. Lawrence was very disturbed by their relationship – he smelled a witch, the Memoir Club paper says – and later in the night when Birrell was afflicted with a swollen tongue, Garnett says Lawrence saw this triumphantly as a sign his dark gods had blasted his enemy where he was strongest (Birrell was a non-stop talker). In *Great Friends* Garnett went further to suggest that Lawrence 'may have put some fantastic sexual explanation upon the incident', based on finding Garnett and Birrell in pyjamas between their bedrooms.[24] None of this, however, is said in his original memoir.

When Lawrence's complete letter was included in the second volume of the Cambridge *Letters of D. H. Lawrence,* Garnett added a note rather disingenuously attributing Lawrence's 'lurid account of my friendship with Francis Birrell' to Ottoline Morrell. He went on to say that Birrell 'was attracted to me but I was unable to respond, and during our friendship which lasted from early 1914 until his death, I was quite incapable of returning his early "falling in love" with me which was rather imagined than real'.[25] Shortly after, however, Garnett was able to respond to Duncan Grant,[26] and Keynes, of course, would have known of that relationship.

David Garnett concludes his introduction to Keynes's memoir as follows:

> The reader is now in possession of the facts which led Maynard Keynes to re-examine his beliefs and those of his closest friends when they were undergraduates at Cambridge.[27]

Even with his original memoir, it is still obvious that certain facts bearing on Keynes's early beliefs and Lawrence's response to Cambridge remain implicit, if not concealed. As for Garnett's own long and full sexual history, that awaits his biographer. Here we can leave the last word to him. When as an old man Garnett was asked if he had had 'homosexual leanings' he replied simply, 'I was more leant against that leaning.'[28]

5 E. M. Forster's *Aspects of the Novel* and Literary History

Let there be those 'formidable erosions of contour' of which Nietzsche speaks (p. 171)[1]

I

Among the notes that E. M. Forster made in his *Commonplace Book* while working on *Aspects of the Novel* is a quotation from *Tristram Shandy* that asks a hard question:

> Shall we be destined to the days of eternity, on holy-days as well as working-days, to be shewing the *relicks of learning*, as monks do the relicks of their saints – without working one – one single miracle with them? (p. 122)

This is just the kind of awkward question Forster enjoyed asking, and it may help us to avoid some of the customary centenary pieties that would have irritated him. Do Forster's writings still work miracles for us, or are they really now relics of learning that we parade on academic holidays? What about *Aspects of the Novel* itself? For a quarter of a century after its publication in 1927 it was the most widely read English critical work on the most popular literary form of the time. Since the Second World War the criticism of fiction has grown enormously in complexity, seriousness, sensitivity – and bulk. After *Scrutiny*, the New Criticism, Chicago Aristotelianism, structuralism, hermeneutics, what is *Aspects of the Novel* if not a relic of learning?

In the following pages I would like to try to indicate how *Aspects of the Novel* might be looked upon as something more than just a relic, though I do not promise any miracles. I will try to show how *Aspects of the Novel* ought to be read in conjunction with a number of other texts, and not just as a theory of the novel but as a piece of writing in its own right. It is now time, in short, to look at *Aspects of the Novel* under the aspect of literary history.

It is not an aspect Forster felt very friendly towards. Time is the avowed enemy throughout *Aspects of the Novel*, and nowhere is it more disliked than in the chronicles of the pseudo-scholar:

> Everything he says may be accurate but all is useless, because he is moving round books instead of through them, he either has not read them or cannot read them properly. Books have to be read (worse luck, for it takes a long time); it is the only way of discovering what they contain. A few savage tribes eat them, but reading is the only method of assimilation revealed to the West. The reader must sit down alone and struggle with the writer, and this the pseudo-scholar will not do. He would rather relate a book to the history of its time, to events in the life of its author, to the events it describes, above all to some tendency. As soon as he can use the word 'tendency' his spirits rise, and though those of his audience may sink they often pull out their pencils at this point and make a note, under the belief that a tendency is portable. (p. 8)

Forster's mockery of pseudo-literary history is a warning to us all because we cannot escape literary history if we want to understand not just what Forster's writing means to us but what it meant to his contemporaries and to himself. Like the discussion of fiction, literary history has also developed considerably since *Aspects of the Novel*, though more recently. Old literary history with its source-hunting, tendency-labelling evasions of analysis and evaluation has been giving way to a newer literary history that attempts to move through books as well as around them. Recent literary history has been asking questions about forms as well as origins, as it tries to interrelate texts rather than just talk about influences. It has been examining manifestations of the new along with continuities of the old; it has been looking at the assumptions about the literariness of a piece of writing that are held by authors and readers, and it sees texts as combining quite different kinds of literary statements.[2]

There is another reason for looking at *Aspects of the Novel* under the aspect of literary history besides recent developments in the theory of literary history. Over the past fifteen years or so the materials of modern English literary history have become widely and extensively available in the manuscript collections of libraries and in the publication of bibliographies, biographies, autobiographies, letters, diaries and scholarly editions of Forster and his literary friends. These materials offer opportunities to pursue the answers to the new kinds of questions that literary history has been asking. The Abinger Edition of Forster's work is an excellent example of this new material, and I am considerably indebted to its late editor, Oliver Stallybrass, whose fine edition of *Aspects of the Novel* has made my discussion possible.

II

The literary history of *Aspects of the Novel* begins in Bloomsbury. In the 1920s Forster's closest Bloomsbury friends were Leonard and Virginia Woolf. They were the first people he wrote to, thanking them for their encouragement, when he finished *A Passage to India* in 1924.[3] In December 1925, Forster's most important statement on the nature of literature before *Aspects of the Novel* appeared in the Hogarth Essay series of the Woolfs' press. *Anonymity: An Enquiry* is alluded to in *Aspects of the Novel* for its theory of inspiration but it also anticipates some of the basic assumptions of Forster's theory of the novel, such as the autotelic nature of imaginative literature ('a poem points to nothing but itself'), the mixed form of the novel (part atmosphere, part information), the limits of literary study (it is only a serious form of gossip) and the unimportance of personality or biography in that anonymous state of imagination in which the reader approaches the inspiration of the writer.[4] It was also in December of 1925 that Forster declined Leonard Woolf's proposal that he write a book on psychology and fiction for a new Hogarth series (perhaps the Hogarth Lectures on Literature) that was under consideration. Leonard Woolf's suggestion may have influenced the topic that Forster chose when, several months later, he was offered the Clark Lectureship at Cambridge. If so, the influence was to be reciprocal, for the lectures that Forster gave and then published as *Aspects of the Novel* clearly left their mark on more than one of the works in the Hogarth Lectures on Literature series that began appearing shortly after Forster's book. We shall come back to the significance of the lecture form in the literary history of *Aspects of the Novel*.

Aspects of the Novel *and Literary History*

In May 1926, Forster wrote to Virginia Woolf that he was going to give some lectures at Cambridge, he thought on the novel, and he would like her advice on two points: how could one lecture on novels – what, for example, should such a course of lectures be called? And what were the best novels? (Forster did not mention in his letter that he had been offered the Clark Lectureship, whose first incumbent had been Virginia Woolf's father.[5]) They had tea together next day and argued about novel-writing, Virginia Woolf wrote to her sister, adding that she found Forster 'limp and damp and milder than the breath of a cow'.[6] There was some further correspondence between the novelists about Virginia Woolf's essay on *Robinson Crusoe*, which she had published in February. Forster wrote that he found the piece very interesting, but in his *Commonplace Book* notes he remarked on its 'dreary Bloomsbury conclusion' (p. 128). Virginia Woolf had argued in words Forster would echo in his criticism of pseudo-scholars, that biography or the history of the novel does not help increase the pleasure or the intelligence with which we read fiction because,

> however we may wind and wiggle in our approach to books, a lonely battle awaits us at the end. There is a piece of business to be transacted between writer and reader before any further dealings are possible....

That business involved seeing 'those cardinal points of perspective – God, man, nature' on which novelists gaze; but Defoe's ruthless common sense snubs these and leaves us instead with an earthenware pot which, nevertheless, pulls the universe into harmony as completely as if it had been man himself. If a writer believes in a pot with enough intensity, Forster paraphrased Virginia Woolf, it can be as satisfying as the universe (p. 128).

What Forster meant in calling this a 'dreary Bloomsbury conclusion' immerses us in aesthetics. It was just before the turn of the century, Forster later recalled, that he first heard Roger Fry lecture and detected the essential Bloomsbury undertone that it was the treatment that counted and not the subject.[7] In his 1920 retrospect to *Vision and Design* Fry put his formalism this way:

> I conceived the form of the work of art to be its most essential quality, but I believed this form to be the direct outcome of an apprehension of some emotion of actual life by the artist....[8]

Earlier Clive Bell had polemicised the formalism that he had developed with Fry out of their responses to French post-impressionist painting. Bell argued that 'Significant Form' – which he defined as lines and colours combined into forms that cause aesthetic emotion in us – was the essential quality of a work of art; 'if a representative form has value', he insisted, 'it is as form, not as representation'.[9] In her essay on *Robinson Crusoe* Virginia Woolf is using this formalism as a metaphor: Defoe's common-sense belief in the pot is intense enough to produce a form that harmonises his vision of the universe. Perhaps it was this metaphorical application of visual to literary art that Forster found dreary. At issue here is a central problem in Bloomsbury's literary aesthetics, and that is how the doctrine of significant form in the visual arts is applicable to words. The apprehension and evaluation of form in literature is very different from that in pottery. In the novel, Forster would argue, form was even less important than in drama or poetry. Clive Bell originally thought the cognitive content of literature prevented that art from having significant form; Fry, who believed in the unity of the arts, tried at various times to demonstrate how literary form could be the essential quality of words.

In 1924 I. A. Richards attacked Bloomsbury's formalism in *Principles of Literary Criticism*, denying that form is the source of value in art, dismissing aesthetic emotion as part of 'the phantom aesthetic state', disagreeing with what he took to be Bell's and Fry's separation of art from life.[10] Richards surprisingly has nothing to say in his book about the principles of criticism that apply to the novel. Perhaps his silence also helped Forster to his subject. In *Anonymity: An Enquiry*, however, which came out the year after Richards's book, Forster was closer in several respects to Bloomsbury's dreary conclusions than to Richards – particularly in the conclusion that poetry was autotelic. Richards had gone back to A. C. Bradley's well-known lecture 'Poetry for Poetry's Sake', which he delivered in 1901, as an illustration of the inadequacies of literary formalism. Fry and Bell used it as support in their respective replies to Richards.[11] It is worth noting that Bradley's lecture contains the phrase 'significant form', and that when Forster came to write the address entitled 'Art for Art's Sake' that he gave in 1941, he adopted Bradley's careful distinction between art as an end in itself and art as the supreme end of life. From *Anonymity: An Enquiry* to 'Art for Art's Sake' Forster was an ambivalent formalist, and nowhere is this more manifest than in his most influential critical work.

III

It may also have been in Bradley's 'Poetry for Poetry's Sake' that Forster found the answer to the question he had asked Virginia Woolf about what lectures on the novel could be called. At the end of his introductory lecture Forster explains that he has adopted the word 'aspects' because it is a free, scientifically vague term that allowed him to consider the different ways both reader and writer look at a novel. This enlightening explanation says something about the form of Forster's lectures and also reveals something of their value for us now. Forster as reader is but one way he approaches the novel; Forster as writer is another – and not just as a writer of novels. It was, of course, Forster's reputation as a novelist that made him an authority on novels for his audience, and his subsequent critics have been helped by *Aspects of the Novel* to understand his own novels. But Forster is also a writer in *Aspects of the Novel* itself. We will turn to this aspect of his lectures after considering them as an illustrated theory of fiction conceived of mainly from the reader's or critic's point of view.

In 'Poetry for Poetry's Sake' Bradley argued that the unity of a literary work has various 'aspects' rather than separable parts; the true critic does not separate form and content: 'the whole, the poetic experience, of which they are but aspects is always in mind...'.[12] When aspects are distinguished for purposes of evaluation, however, Bradley points out they become components and the heresies of separable substance and form arise, as indeed they do in *Aspects of the Novel*. Forster enumerates seven aspects in his lectures: story, people, plot, fantasy, prophecy, pattern and rhythm. He is not always clear about the nature of these aspects, for in one place he defines them as demands made upon the reader (pp. 74–5) but elsewhere he says that five of the aspects are critical tools, while fantasy and prophecy are something else (p. 101). There is a shift here, in other words, between aspects of fiction and kinds of novels, as Forster is aware. The discussions of novels he has classified as fantastic or prophetic are identified as 'interludes', and they call for a new invocation (pp. 102, 76).

But if Forster is inconsistent about what he means by the term 'aspects' he is unwaveringly clear that one of his aspects is more important than all of the others. It is a curious reflection of the form of *Aspects of the Novel* that few of its readers remember that it has a single unifying idea. We forget the whole in the familiarity of some of its parts – the familiarity of the Forsterian tone of voice in which we must say 'Yes – oh dear Yes – the novel tells a story', in the discrimination of flat and round characters, in the battle between plot and characters, in the possibilities of rhythm in fiction. Specific insights into particular novels and novelists also remain in the memory longer than what amounts to Forster's thesis. We recall his comments that time is the hero of *The Old Wives' Tale* and muddle the hidden god in *Tristram Shandy*; we do not quickly forget the description of the fluffy, lush home counties posing as the universe in the work of that suburban roarer Meredith, nor how the clothes of those Egyptian deformities, the characters of Henry James, 'will not take off'. But who remembers half so clearly the dualism that Forster insists characterises the novel? 'The idea running through these lectures is plain enough', he says quite accurately after the lectures on story, people, and plot, and it is

> that there are in the novel two forces: human beings and a bundle of various things not human beings, and it is the novelist's business to adjust these two forces and conciliate their claims. (p. 73)

There could hardly be a clearer instance of Bradley's heresy of separable substance and form. Again and again in his lectures Forster returns to the primacy of the aspect he calls people – the only aspect to be given two lectures. Moll Flanders, for example, is a fictive rather than a human being not because she is embodied in a self-contained work of art but because she is psychologically unreal: we can know all about her inner life in a way we can never know that of people, and this is how novels give us 'the illusion of perspicacity and of power' (p. 44). But Forster does not want to distinguish too sharply between the fictive and the human in fiction. His aim in theorising about novels is the same as it was when he was creating them: to conciliate the human and the non-human. Thus, though he calls his lectures on the aspect of character in fiction simply 'People', his famous distinction between flat and round *characters* brings us back to the realm of art. It will not do to call them flat and round people.

The inconsistencies of Forster's dualism arise from his diminishing the value of art in fiction relative to the value of the characters whom Forster isolates from their aesthetic embodiments. In her reviews and subsequent correspondence, Virginia Woolf objected to Forster's theory not because of its emphasis on the centrality of character – she agreed with him and with Arnold Bennett about that – but because of his devaluing of art. 'In most literary works there are two elements', Forster stated early in his lecture on plot, 'human individuals...and the element vaguely called art' (p. 59). This almost sounds like a doctrine of insignificant form in fiction, particularly when, as Virginia Woolf complained, the talk of art was so vague.[13]

There is another basic distinction in *Aspects of the Novel*, however, that is surprisingly formalistic in its consequences – consequences that Virginia Woolf, as we shall see, could not accept. Readers of *Aspects of the Novel* most likely remember Forster's radical separation of art from history better than they do his distinction between people and art because of his amusing image of all the novelists in the history of the novel sitting timelessly around the reading room of Bloomsbury's British Museum writing their novels synchronically. If separating people from art in novels reduces the significance of form in fiction, distinguishing history from fiction clearly enhances the work itself and therefore by implication its aesthetic form. 'History develops, Art stands still...' (p. 14). It is a crude, even vulgar motto, Forster admits, only a partial truth but one he quite cheerfully embraces and in this he is in agreement with Bell's and Fry's aesthetic theories. 'Assuredly, to understand art we need to know nothing whatever about history', Clive Bell had claimed in *Art*,[14] and Forster assumes in talking about novels that no mists from the river of time will obscure our apprehension of their significance. Thus the title of his lectures is very apt. Novels rather than novelists or traditions are what he mainly speaks about, and aspects are not developments; each stands still to be contemplated like a painting or a sculpture. Time is the enemy of value throughout *Aspects of the Novel*, not just in the literary history of pseudo-scholars.

IV

Forster's lectures on the novel are thus a mixture of formalistic and non- or even anti-formalistic ideas. He would not find much sympathy in Bloomsbury for this mixture, and yet it displayed a quintessential Bloomsbury characteristic – eclecticism. It was Clive Bell, the most uncompromising formalist of the Group, who maintained in *Civilisation* (which he finished the year Forster gave his lectures) that the civilised man would be an eclectic.[15] The clearest statement of eclecticism in Bloomsbury can be found in *Aspects of the Novel*. Forster's attitude towards it is more pessimistic than Bell's would have been. He reluctantly concluded, after expressing reservations about the double vision in his lecture on prophecy, that most of us will keep the single vision and therefore,

> be eclectics to this side or that according to our temperament. The human mind is not a dignified organ, and I do not see how we can exercise it sincerely except through eclecticism. And the only advice I would offer my fellow eclectics is: 'Do not be proud of your inconsistency. It is a pity, it is a pity that we should be equipped like this. It is a pity Man cannot be at the same time impressive and truthful'. (p. 101)

The engrained eclecticism of *Aspects of the Novel* has indeed struck some critics as pitiful, and yet it is basic for his comparative critical method. The subject of *Aspects of the Novel*, Forster stated in the middle of his lectures, was 'the books we have read' (p. 73), and he worried that they had escaped him as he theorised about the novel. He need not have worried, for the books we have read in *Aspects of the Novel* include works of criticism as well as novels. Forster's juxtaposition of novels or novelists may appear sadly eclectic to those with monolithic notions of traditions in fiction; for others, however, Forster's bringing together of novels is the most stimulating aspect of his criticism. The comparison of anonymous quotations from the fiction of Richardson and James, Wells and Dickens, Sterne and Virginia Woolf in the introductory lecture establishes the critical procedure which Forster continues in his other lectures. *The Antiquary, The Old Wives' Tale* and *War and Peace* are brought together in the lecture on story; *Moll Flanders* and *Mansfield Park* are the chief examples in the lectures on people. Plot sets the novels of Meredith alongside those of Gide, among others, and fantasy compares rather fantastically Sterne with the completely forgotten Matson, with Beerbohm and with Joyce. Prophecy pairs George Eliot and Dostoyevsky, to begin with, and then brings in Melville, Lawrence and Emily Brontë. Finally Anatole France, Percy Lubbock, James and Proust all come together in the last lecture.

Forster's eclectic use of critical works in *Aspects of the Novel* has naturally attracted less attention than the novels he compares, yet these texts provide the critical ideas, the aspects, that bring the compared novels into focus. It is a matter not merely of the extrinsic sources for *Aspects of the Novel* but of the intrinsic critical structure of the work. 'The books we have read' – the subject, that is, of *Aspects of the Novel* – include, in addition to novels, critical texts of T. S. Eliot, Aristotle, Alain, Lubbock, Wells and Henry James. They are specifically referred to but there are others present that do not get mentioned: Virginia Woolf's essay on *Robinson Crusoe*, Bradley's 'Poetry for Poetry's Sake', and the work of the critic to whom Forster dedicated *Aspects of the Novel*. Forster's lectures depend significantly on the interpretation of these texts as on the works of fiction that he discusses, and a literary history of *Aspects of the Novel* needs to examine Forster's eclectic use of them. While it is not possible to discuss all of them in detail, I want at least to note Forster's use of them and to analyse briefly his interpretations of several of them. This should still leave us time to consider *Aspects of the Novel* as a literary text in its own right and to glance at its interesting relation with what may be in the English-speaking world today the most widely read book about fiction.

V

In his introductory lecture Forster mentions three books on the novel, none of which he makes much use of. From Abel Chevalley's 'brilliant little manual', *Le roman anglais de notre temps*, he adopts the unhelpful definition of the novel as 'a fiction in prose of a certain extent' (p. 3), and then never refers to the book again. (It is hard to see what Forster found so brilliant in Chevalley's survey unless it was all the novelists he was prepared to generalise about, including Forster himself who is described as full of ideas and talent; Chevalley's attack on Henry James may have appealed to Forster too.) Walter Raleigh's *The English Novel* is referred to as a work of genuine scholarship; Raleigh is able to contemplate the river of time, though Forster does not remark that Raleigh's river stops with Scott. After a satirical digression in which Clayton Hamilton's *Materials and Methods of Fiction* is anonymously cited as a particularly egregious example of the substitution of classification for understanding – it is a work both Forster and Virginia Woolf reviewed with ridicule[16] – Forster comes back to his argument for the timelessness of fiction, and here he invokes T. S. Eliot.

Eliot was Forster's immediate predecessor in the Clark Lectureship (Raleigh was another Clark Lecturer), and he is cited to support Forster's ignoring of literary history. Though Eliot's lectures on metaphysical poetry were still unpublished, Forster quotes from *The Sacred Wood* Eliot's remarks on the business of a critic, part of which is to preserve tradition (which Forster feels he cannot do) and part of which is 'to see literature steadily and to see it whole; and this is eminently to see it as *not* consecrated by time but to see it beyond time...' (p. 15). This part Forster gladly accepts as support for his own efforts to view the novel synchronically. Eliot had also observed in *The Sacred Wood* that the critic's tools are analysis and comparison.[17] Much of modern criticism since Eliot has favoured analysis at the expense of comparison, though this cannot be said of *Aspects of the Novel* which does the opposite. Eliot's comments on tradition, quoted by Forster, disclose of course another text, one that Forster had already used in *Howards End*. Eliot's discussion of the business of the critic at the beginning of *The Sacred Wood* is in the context of making amends to Matthew Arnold, whose famous lines on Sophocles are echoed and whose essay 'The Function of Criticism at the Present Time' is approvingly quoted by Eliot. 'How astonishing it would be', Eliot went on, 'if a man like Arnold had concerned himself with the art of the novel....'[18] Forster does not, however, pursue any of the topics in the criticism of the novel that Eliot wishes Arnold had. Arnold was Forster's favourite Victorian and he may have accepted a little advice from him, such as the now rather quaint suggestion that English critics should pay some attention to foreign thought.

Forster's references, direct and indirect, to Eliot and Arnold almost invoke their critical protection at the outset of his enterprise. These critical allusions can remind us of Forster's share in Bloomsbury's early response to so different a mind and sensibility as Eliot's, and also of the continuities between Bloomsbury and the Victorians – continuities sometimes ignored in accounts of Bloomsbury's ironic attitudes towards the world of their fathers.

VI

Aristotle's *Poetics* might not count as an example of foreign thought in English criticism, so domesticated has his influence been, but the same cannot be said of the work of the French philosopher and essayist Alain, who is still an unfamiliar name to many students of English literature. Forster combines critical ideas from Aristotle and Alain in a theory of the novel that describes how timeless works of art represent time-bound human beings. Aristotle's influence is the more important, for several of the central features of Forster's theory of the novel appear to have been developed in response to Aristotelian theory of poetry and psychology.

Forster begins his lecture on plot by quoting Aristotle on character and happiness and then disagreeing with him. Forster argues that we know better than Aristotle, who said character gives us qualities but happiness or misery takes the form of action. We believe it is in our inner secret lives that we are happy or unhappy, and therefore Forster looks for a more psychological aesthetics, such as Alain's. Bloomsbury's concern with states of mind, which they derived from the philosophy of G. E. Moore, coincides with Forster's dissatisfaction with Aristotle. The *Poetics* with its analysis of tragedy into six parts may nevertheless have suggested for Forster a model for organising his lectures into seven aspects of fiction. A comparison of the two sets of analysis quickly brings out the distinctive features of Forster's theory of the novel. Aristotle's dominant idea of plot is broken into plot and story by Forster. Aristotle's character and Forster's people are where the two theories converge most closely. Aristotle's thought and diction have no corresponding aspects in Forster – and the absence of any consideration of ideas or of language in *Aspects of the Novel* is among the serious defects of Forster's analysis, a defect all the more surprising when one thinks of his own novels. Forster's aspects of fantasy and prophecy are non-Aristotelian, except perhaps as functions of the chorus, but pattern and rhythm are parts that could be included in Aristotle's conception of plot. (They also resemble faintly Aristotle's melody and spectacle, which were not parts of the epic, the genre Aristotle discusses that is closest to the novel.) It should be clear from this brief comparison that by exalting the role of character in fiction and rejecting Aristotle's primary emphasis on action in life and art, Forster divides Aristotle's idea of plot into various aspects. As a consequence, the conception of structure in the novel – the closest analogue to significant form in painting – is also fragmented in Forster's theory.

This fragmentation can be illustrated by Forster's familiar but puzzling distinction between story and plot. By defining story as a narrative of events in their temporal sequence, and plot as a narrative of events in their causal sequence, Forster obscures their relationship – though at one point, when discussing pattern and rhythm, he does say, almost in an aside, that plot is actually derived from, 'springs out of the story' (p. 102). But he never makes it clear why the arrangement of a story's incidents that is to be designated as the plot has to be limited to those incidents in a causal sequence. (And Forster does not confine his discussions of plot in Meredith, Hardy or Gide to causally arranged sequences of events.) Plot for Aristotle is σύνθεσιν τῶν πραγμάτων or τῶν πραγμάτων σύστασις. Butcher translates these phrases as 'the arrangement of incidents' and 'the structure of incidents'.[19] The incidents or happenings have to occur in a temporal sequence, of course, which can also be a causal one. But 'there is a great difference', Aristotle notes, 'between a thing happening *propter hoc* and *post hoc*' – thus possibly giving Forster the idea for his distinction between plot and story.[20] Forster, who knew Greek, indicates by his quotations from Aristotle that he was using Bywater's translation of the *Poetics*, and Bywater translates Aristotle's definition of plot as 'the combination of incidents or things done in the story', and again as 'the combination of incidents in the story'.[21] Thus he appears to make two things out of one, translating τῶν πραγμάτων not just as incidents or happenings, but as incidents or happenings *of the story*, and Forster seems to follow Bywater here.

Time outside the novel can be ignored by putting all the novelists together in the British Museum, but inside the novel Forster knows 'there is always a clock' (p. 20). In distinguishing between plot and story, Forster appears to be trying to confine the clock to one aspect of the novel, the story, which he nevertheless concedes is 'the fundamental aspect of the novel' (p. 17). In another image Forster describes the story as 'the naked worm of time' (p. 19). When *Aspects of the Novel* is juxtaposed with the *Poetics* it becomes apparent that Forster's plot is ultimately only another species of worm.

Forster's disagreements with Aristotle are not, as we have seen, merely about the meanings of plot. They extend all the way from literary criticism to happiness. The *Poetics* brings out the degree to which *Aspects of the Novel* is an anti-critical work of criticism. Forster hardly conceals the suspicion and distaste with which he regards critical methodology. They are summed up in his remark that questions about literary method of the kind Aristotle liked to ask 'have too much the atmosphere of the law courts about them' (p. 59).

VII

Alain's *Système des beaux-arts*, in spite of its title, was far less methodological in intent than Aristotle. At one point in his *Commonplace Book* Forster drew up two columns in order to compare Aristotle and Alain on character (p. 137). In one column he wrote down the passage from Aristotle he had quoted at the beginning of the lecture on plot; but the other column remained blank. Forster might have put there the beginning of his quotation from Alain that he gives in the first lecture on people: 'What is fictitious in a novel is not so much the story as the method by which thought develops into action, a method which never occurs in daily life' (p. 32). For both Forster and Alain character not plot is the soul of fiction. But Forster is uneasy about Alain's sharp division between history and fiction. In history, according to *Système des beaux-arts*, we are spectators but in fiction we are actors because there is always one character with whom we identify, who thinks for the reader, whose interior life presents in perspective other characters and objects in life. Forster agrees with Alain's discussion of character, however, because it gives him an aesthetic explanation of what makes characters real in fiction. It is a matter of knowing all about their inner, mental existences.[22] There is something of Kant's formalistic argument for the autonomy of the aesthetic in Alain's distinction between historical and fictive prose that also comes into Forster's theory.

There is, I believe, another theory of fiction that comes into *Aspects of the Novel*, one that helped Forster more than Alain did to a non-Aristotelian conception of character. It comes from Charles Mauron, another modern French aesthetician. Mauron's name appears not in Forster's text but before it. It is to him that *Aspects of the Novel* is dedicated. A month after Forster delivered his lectures, Virginia and Leonard Woolf published, as part of their second Hogarth Essay series, a pamphlet of two essays by Mauron entitled *The Nature of Beauty in Art and Literature*. They were translated with an introduction by Roger Fry. Mauron himself had been introduced into Bloomsbury by Fry who shared with him the conviction that aesthetics ought to be thought about scientifically. Forster came to know Mauron better than anyone else in Bloomsbury did, except Fry; he once wrote that after Fry Mauron was the friend who helped him most to look at pictures. There would have been ample opportunity for Forster to read Mauron's two essays in

French or English while he was preparing his lectures, which he delivered early in 1927. Fry had used Mauron's essays in *Transformations*, published in the autumn of 1926, to help answer Richards's *Principles of Literary Criticism*.[23]

The second of Mauron's essays, entitled 'Beauty in Literature', consists of an attempt to show how post-impressionist aesthetic theory can be used to discuss literary beauty. Mauron's hypothesis is that an exact analogy can be drawn between spatial volumes in painting and psychological or spiritual volumes in literature. In the spatial world,

> there remains the vast crowd of complex volumes: in the spiritual there remain the everyday realities of our soul, all the forms of our inner life.
>
> 'As the painter creates a spatial being, the writer creates a psychological being'. Such, I think, is the hypothesis that we might admit as the basis for all literary criticism.[24]

The purpose of what used to be called plastic arts is the creation of spatial being for Mauron, whereas the end of literature is the creation of psychological beings. These psychological beings are of three general types: the simplest psychological volumes are states of mind or moments of the spirit (they predominate in lyric poetry); the second are characters in drama and fiction; the third type consists of relations between psychological types, or what we call situations. 'Moments of the spirit, characters, situations and their complexes – these', it seems to Mauron, '...all literature envisages.'[25] Then carrying further the analogy to sculpture, Mauron finds that the written text is the equivalent of surface in plastic art, and thought the equivalent of volume.

Mauron did not follow up his theory, but it indicates the direction of his future criticism that was to make him a leading psychological critic of French literature. He never clarified the precise nature of his notion of psychological volumes (the relationship of words to psychological volumes does not seem at all analogous to that of lines and colours in spatial volumes) nor did he show how they could be arranged to display significant form in literature. Yet his theory suggests how post-impressionism provided aesthetic analogies for Forster in *Aspects of the Novel*. It is surely not just a coincidence that the most famous distinction in *Aspects of the Novel* – whose very title is a visual metaphor, albeit a faint one – consists of describing characters in terms of volume. The volumes of flat and round characters illustrate their psychological and moral dimensions. And earlier in his lectures Forster had remarked that the novelist, unlike other kinds of artists, uses what he calls 'word-masses' to describe himself, and these become in turn his characters (pp. 30–1).

Neither Mauron nor Forster reveals exactly how the formal relations between psychological volumes can be beautiful, though Forster implies that through round characters the novelist harmonises human beings with other aspects of his form. Mauron's 'Beauty in Literature' nevertheless offered Forster a post-impressionist literary aesthetic that suggested form in literature was a matter not just of structure or even style, but of character – the aspect of fiction Forster claimed was most significant. Thus the formalism of 'Beauty in Literature' was less dreary to Forster than other Bloomsbury theories of literary beauty. The dedication of *Aspects of the Novel* was more than a gesture of friendship.[26]

VIII

The right arrangement of flat and round characters in a novel was more important, Forster concluded, than the point of view, and this brings us to the last group of critical texts in relation to which Forster eclectically developed *Aspects of the Novel*. Inevitably they have to do with Henry James. Forster's ambivalence about the value of form in fiction is nowhere more clearly apparent than in his discussions of James's theory and practice. The theory is considered mainly in relation to Percy Lubbock's exposition of the master's method in *The Craft of Fiction*, which was published in 1921. There is no evidence that Forster was aware of Lubbock's declining the Clark lectureship, which was then offered to Forster. Forster quotes Lubbock's statement that method in fiction is governed by 'the question of the relation in which the narrator stands to the story' (p. 54) and then disagrees. For Forster 'the whole intricate question of method' – he is echoing Lubbock's words here – 'resolves itself not into formulae but into the power of the writer to bounce the reader into accepting what he says...' (p. 54). Lubbock's exposition of point of view in fiction is rather more than a matter of formulae, but the disagreement between *The Craft of Fiction* and *Aspects of the Novel* is not really about this so much as the broader issue that disturbs Forster throughout his lectures. Lubbock is concerned that readers and novelists will ignore the art of the novel and treat it as a piece of life, whereas Forster worries that in treating it as art we shall forget life. Apart from their disagreements over the achievement of Tolstoy or Dickens, it is not a very illuminating critical dispute, especially as neither critic-novelist has anything to say about language or style. Forster once called words in *Aspects of the Novel* 'the minutiae of style' (p. 86). The two most influential English books on fiction in the early modern period move without hesitation between originals and translations, as if there were no differences between them.

It is for Lubbock's master that Forster reserves his most sustained criticism. In the first lecture of *Aspects of the Novel* James is parodied by Forster himself, and in the last lecture it is Wells's parody that is quoted. *The Ambassadors* is held up as an example of a novel that sacrifices life to pattern. The grounds for Forster's dislike are rather involved, I think. They have to do with both James's content and form. Forster's unease with James's content is illustrated by the sexual imagery that he uses to criticise James in both the text of *Aspects of the Novel* and his *Commonplace* notes. James's characters' clothes 'will not take off... this castrating is not in the interests of the Kingdom of Heaven', he keeps among the vegetables 'because their reproductive organs are not prominent' (pp. 110–11, 125). The comparison of James first with Wells and then with Proust also suggests that James's fictive sexuality bothers Forster, and in more than just one way.[27]

Forster's formal objections to the art of James's fiction are more interesting for the history of criticism than his unhappiness with its sexual implications. As with the other critical works Forster uses in *Aspects of the Novel*, those connected with James help Forster to bring out his own theory. This emerges in the way Forster favours Wells in the famous controversy that began when James criticised Wells's novels for being without form and then was continued by Wells in *Boon* where he attacked James's novels for being without content. Forster quotes Wells's lethal comparison of a James novel to an empty church with a dead kitten, an eggshell and a bit of string on the altar, but not the ensuing correspondence which ended with Wells saying that James thought of literature as painting whereas he likened it to architecture. Wells's spokesman in *Boon* claimed that 'James never discovered that a novel isn't a picture... That life isn't a studio....'[28]

The aspect of the novel that is the context for Forster's criticism of James is pattern. Pattern expresses completion, Forster claims, whereas rhythm – the aspect under which Proust is discussed – conveys expansion and allows the novelist to give his characters a good run and achieve 'something else at the same time' (p. 116), that something else being artistic form. The distinction being made here between pattern and rhythm is somewhat invidious, and it suggests one of the principal objections that Forster, like Wells, had to James's theory and practice – and also more generally to Bloomsbury's aesthetics – was that their artistic analogies came from painting and sculpture. Music was a deeper art than these for Forster. One of his conclusions in *Aspects of the Novel* is that 'in music fiction is likely to find its nearest parallel' (p. 116). The distinction between aesthetic analogies carries over into the differences between fantasy, which just glances about, and prophecy, which gives the sensation of sound or song. Virginia Woolf's likening of *Robinson Crusoe* to a pot was 'a dreary Bloomsbury conclusion' at least partly because of the visual nature of the comparison. (It may also help to explain why, when her latest novel was *Mrs. Dalloway*, Forster classified Virginia Woolf as a fantasist.) But Forster's reaction to post-impressionist aesthetics should not be exaggerated. In terms of Roger Fry's binary formulation, Forster concentrated more on vision and tended to deprecate design. Yet the title of his lectures stresses the viewing of fiction. Here again Forster was eclectic.

IX

A literary history of *Aspects of the Novel* needs to do more, however, than examine the eclectic uses to which Forster put the texts of fiction and criticism with which his lectures are concerned. It should examine the form of the lectures themselves if only because Forster's eclecticism like Bloomsbury's extends beyond the ideas in his writing to the writing itself. The Nietzschean erosions of contour that Forster admired in Gide's *Les faux-monnayeurs* can also describe what is happening in *Aspects of the Novel*, and not just with the texts that Forster has used to construct his lectures. The Bloomsbury writers combined in various ways forms of fiction and non-fiction, eroding the boundaries between them. This has not always been understood or appreciated by their critics, especially when the erosions are ironic. The mixing of forms is clear enough, perhaps, in a work like *Orlando* but not always in Virginia Woolf's *Common Reader* essays. Lytton Strachey's biographies still await adequate analysis as writing that combines fictive and non-fictive genres. And with Forster critics have discussed a work like *Aspects of the Novel* in the same dichotomous spirit in which he looked at the novel. His lectures have been read as if they themselves were composed of two forces: a theory of fiction and a bunch of other things. Those other things are essential to our experience of reading *Aspects of the Novel*. The art of Forster's lectures distinguishes them from the critical texts they use and discloses to us why *Aspects of the Novel* has not become in literary history merely a relic of learning. To appreciate this we need to look more closely at *Aspects of the Novel* as a form of writing.

How can novels be lectured on? Forster had asked Virginia Woolf. The genre of the public literary lecture presented Forster with opportunities and difficulties. The public lecture form renders ineffective any prolonged or involved argument. The possibilities of exemplification are so limited that there can be little or no close textual analysis. And of course there is no place for a scholarly apparatus of notes and bibliographies. These limitations were all advantages to Forster, who contentedly classified himself and most other lecturers as pseudo-scholars. The problem of exemplification Forster handled very effectively by emphasising the comparison of passages or novels. There was another aspect of lectures that Forster exploited with great skill, and that is their colloquial opportunities. In his 'Author's Note' Forster justifies his colloquial informality by appealing to the subject of his lectures, the novel, which 'may possibly withhold some of its secrets from the graver and grander streams of criticism, and...reveal them to backwaters and shallows' (p. xvii). Here once again in *Aspects of the Novel* Forster connects the informality of lectures, the colloquialness of the novel, and the inadequacies of criticism.

Forster's defence of the talkative tone of his lectures stresses from the very outset the voice in *Aspects of the Novel*. A lecture is, of course, a script for performance. In their printed form Forster's lectures still call upon us to respond to that voice as readers, since we cannot be hearers. And in this respect Forster's lectures resemble his essays, which are unapologetically talkative. The tone of the lectures is quite close to that of the familiar essay as Forster practised it, but there is also a difference to be found in the centrality of voice in the lectures. Voice becomes more prominent in a sustained work like *Aspects of the Novel* than in the essay, which in Forster's writings is a quite short form. The recurring voice in Forster's lectures sounds in the end more familiar to us than the brief voices of the essays, however familiar their essay form is. Identifying the voice of *Aspects of the Novel* by listening to its various tones is as important to the appreciation of Forster's book as comprehending his theory of the novel is. They cannot be completely separated. We first hear Forster's voice distinctly in the invocation of the first lecture. Invocations are not exactly customary in lectures, certainly not one that calls upon the donor of the lectures as a kind of god whose integrity and *in*attention are solicited! And I think, by the way, that we must describe it as Forster's voice here and not his persona's because in a lecture the voice is the author's. In the absence of a poetics of the lecture we have to be tentative, but there does seem to be no persona in a lecture, only personality.

The prominence of voice in the form of *Aspects of the Novel* appears in the second lecture, where Forster gives us three vocal reactions to the place of story in the novel. The third of these, described as 'a sort of drooping regretful voice' that says 'Yes – oh dear yes – the novel tells a story' (p. 17) is identified as the author's. And it is his voice again that we are asked to join in a kind of chorus at the end of the lecture. We hear that voice at various times in the lectures, most notably in the passage on eclecticism when we are advised in quotation marks not to be proud eclectics. But there are other voices or tones of voice in *Aspects of the Novel* besides the deprecating one – voices that are affectionate, deflating, giggly, mocking, admiring, dismissive. Attending to them is one of the chief pleasures of reading Forster's text.

The images of *Aspects of the Novel* are another of its pleasures: the novelists in the British Museum, the flatness and roundness of characters, the fantastic and prophetic bars of light, and of course the water imagery. The novel for Forster is 'one of the moister areas of literature', and water runs through these lectures from the opening streams and shallows of criticism through the 'spongy tract' that is the novel (a rather neat pun), to the humanity with which the novel is sogged, and finally down to the open seas of prophecy. Characters also appear in *Aspects of the Novel*, and not only those from novels. The bus conductor and the golfer offer us opinions about the place of story in the novel. Curiosity is personified in the man who, when you meet him again in a year's time, will probably 'ask you how many brothers and sisters you have, his mouth sagging open, his eyes still bulging from his head' (p. 60). Finally, there are Forster's parodies of criticism as well as fiction, often done devastatingly in paraphrase.

Forster, we should remember, entitled his lectures 'aspects' because the term included the ways that both the reader and the novelist can regard the novel. The features of Forster's text that I have been reminding you of – and they are to be found in his essays as well – are not those we usually expect to find in modern criticism. They are more novelistic than critical. They tend in fact quite deliberately to undermine the seriousness of *Aspects of the Novel* as a work of critical theory. How earnest is Forster in visualising all the novelists synchronically at work on their novels round the reading room of the British Museum? He is certainly serious about time as an enemy of value in life and art but the image is surely at least partly ironical. Forster's critical vision here is double, as Virginia Woolf had said of his fictive vision.[29] His misgivings about criticism are manifest throughout *Aspects of the Novel*. We even have the standard romantic allusions to peeping and botanising on our mothers' graves and enumerating the rainbow's warp and woof. Some of Forster's doubts about the value of criticism derive from his disillusionment with the novel itself. This emerges clearly in his argument with Virginia Woolf about the importance of art in fiction. Forster was not disillusioned about criticism because he was never illusioned about it. But he wrote no more novels after he lectured on them in 1927. He continued to write criticism, however. The next set of lectures he gave after *Aspects of the Novel* was also given in Cambridge; they were lectures for the tripos in 1930, and there are autobiographical resonances in Forster's entitling them 'The Creator as Critic'. (They remain unpublished.)

Despite his scepticism about formalistic and historical criticism and his doubts about the novel, Forster succeeds through its eclectic form in making *Aspects of the Novel* a worthwhile work on the criticism of fiction. But here again Forster is characteristically ambivalent. A course of lectures, he tells his audience at the beginning of the sixth one, 'tends in its parasitic way to lead a life of its own and it and the ideas running through it are apt to move in one direction while the subject steals off in another' (p. 73). This does not happen in *Aspects of the Novel* because of the way Forster erodes the contours between subject and treatment, between criticism and creation. The erosion may limit the value of the lectures as criticism, but it augments them as writing. A novel, Forster said in *Anonymity*, is part atmosphere, part information. Criticism of the novel is similarly divided in *Aspects of the Novel*, and the atmosphere in which the theory and criticism of fiction are presented there is largely one of comic irony. The comic irony of Forster's lectures is his principal means of mixing creative and critical writing. How many of the novels he mentions are comedies.

Forster of course was not the only early modern writer to make literary criticism funny. If he had not read Ezra Pound, he certainly knew D. H. Lawrence's *Studies in Classic American Literature*, which appeared in 1923.[30] A similar relationship exists between the criticism and poetry or fiction of all these writers; Forster's own critics have shown how illuminating his ideas are when applied to his own novels. *Aspects of the Novel* is a particularly useful commentary on *A Passage to India*, for example. But unlike Pound's and Lawrence's critical humour, Forster's is not polemical in his lectures. The irony is far gentler. Yet irony it remains, and a number of reviewers complained that *Aspects of the Novel* diminished the art of its subject. Perhaps it does. But if we attend to Forster's lectures as a work in its own right, a work that will be read and enjoyed longer than the critical writings of probably all but one of his reviewers, we should be able to see how Forster's comic irony eclectically combines not only the texts of novelists and critics but also the forms of fictive and critical writing to create the art of *Aspects of the Novel*.

X

The literary history of *Aspects of the Novel* remains radically incomplete without an account of how it became, in turn, a text in subsequent discussions of the novel. And again this involves the form of Forster's book as well as its content – its significance, that is, as a work *of* literature as well as one *on* literature. There are, for example, the reviews of *Aspects of the Novel* by Arnold Bennett, E. F. Benson, L. P. Hartley, Ford Madox Ford, Edmund Wilson, I. A. Richards and of course Virginia Woolf. But also very relevant to the literary history of Forster's lectures is the Hogarth Press series entitled 'Lectures on Literature' that began appearing shortly after *Aspects of the Novel* was published by the Cambridge University Press. One of the early works in this series, Edwin Muir's *The Structure of the Novel*, is designed in part as a direct reply to Forster.

Another work, announced as forthcoming in the series but never published in it, is even more interesting. It is Virginia Woolf's long essay 'Phases of Fiction', which was serialised in the spring of 1929 but never published as a book. It can be read, I think, as another response to *Aspects of the Novel* and therefore belongs to the debate about fiction that really began when Forster wrote to Virginia Woolf for advice about lecturing on novels.

The literary history of that debate is at least a chapter in itself, but two dimensions of it need to be briefly mentioned here because they extend the significance of this Bloomsbury debate as well as confirm the usefulness of a literary history that concerns itself with intertextual relations and the development of forms.

Virginia Woolf's disagreements with Forster in her two reviews of his lectures, in their ensuing correspondence (only a part of which has been described in their biographies),[31] and in the works on fiction Virginia Woolf subsequently wrote recapitulate and extend two very well-known earlier twentieth-century disagreements over the novel. Woolf's complaint that Forster was too concerned with human emotion and not enough with aesthetic emotion in his lectures is a continuation of the dispute between James and Wells a half generation earlier. James's closing words to Wells, 'it is art that *makes* life, makes interest, makes importance...'[32] could have come from Woolf's review, and Wells's reply that he did not know what James meant by art is exactly how Forster responds. Henry James and Virginia Woolf are fond of drawing analogies between fiction and the visual arts; Wells and Forster find them misleading (though Forster uses them) and turn instead to parallels in architecture and music. In 1914 James criticised his Edwardian successors Wells, Bennett and others for their saturation approach to fiction. Just a few years later we find Virginia Woolf attacking her Edwardian predecessors for their materialistic conceptions of character. Even Forster, Woolf observes in *Mr. Bennett and Mrs. Brown*, which she wrote in the early 1920s, had somewhat spoiled his early novels by compromising with Edwardian materialism in his characterisation.

Virginia Woolf's quarrel with Bennett resembles James's argument with Wells even more closely than her quarrel with Forster. As with the James/Wells debate, it was basically about how novels should be written rather than how they should be criticised. Bloomsbury's epistemology, ethics and aesthetics had shown Woolf that Bennett's fiction was inadequate in content as well as

… Aspects of the Novel *and Literary History* … 107

in form.³³ We now know that she also attacked Bennett's notion of Mrs Brown because Bennett had revealed, in an earlier book on women, that he did not understand them or their situation.³⁴ We shall see this theme recurring in her debate with Forster. The point to be emphasised here is that the disagreement between Mr Bennett and Mrs Woolf cannot properly be reduced to a conflict between ordinary life in fiction and high-brow art.³⁵ Similarly, the disagreement between Forster and Woolf is not just a life-versus-art opposition.

These three debates disclose modern critic-novelists of different generations in recurrent disagreement about the value of their form and its nature. Half a century later the vocabulary of our debates about fiction is different but not, perhaps, the underlying concerns.

XI

The other dimension of the subsequent literary history of *Aspects of the Novel* that needs to be mentioned here is involved in the first critical disagreements of James and Wells, Woolf and Bennett, Woolf and Forster. When Forster complained to Virginia Woolf that if his notion of life in his lectures was vague, so was her notion of art – she replied that she was not writing a book on fiction, only reviewing one. We have noted that Woolf was, in fact, at work on a book about fiction at this time that was announced for years but never appeared as a book.³⁶ One of the reasons why 'Phases of Fiction' was not finally published in the Hogarth Lectures on Literature may have been because of another book on fiction that Woolf began to write at the same time she was supposed to be finishing 'Phases of Fiction'.

It was a year and a half after Forster gave his now widely acclaimed lectures on the novel, in Cambridge, that Virginia Woolf was herself in Cambridge and lecturing on the novel. These lectures were reworked into the book she called *A Room of One's Own*. It was her last and most interesting response to *Aspects of the Novel* and very different from her earlier ones. Woolf's subject in *A Room of One's Own* is women and fiction, and the fame of the book has tended to obscure the second of her two subjects. It is in her discussion of fiction, however, the Virginia Woolf implicitly, though never directly, challenges an aspect of Forster's theory of fiction that she had not mentioned before. In *A Room of One's Own* she questions not Forster's devaluing of form in fiction but his formalistic rejection of the history of the novel. Forster, after comparing passages from six novels in his opening lecture, had defended his timeless discussions of the novel in the following words:

> Does not chronology seem less important now that we have visualized six novelists at their jobs? If the novel develops, is it not likely to develop on different lines from the British Constitution, or even the Women's Movement? I say 'even the Women's Movement' because there happened to be a close association between fiction in England and that movement during the nineteenth century – a connection so close that it has misled some critics into thinking it is an organic connection. As women bettered their position the novel, they asserted, became better too. Quite wrong. A mirror does not develop because an historical pageant passes in front of it. It only develops when it gets a fresh coat of quicksilver – in other words, when it acquires new sensitiveness; and the novel's success lies in its own sensitiveness, not in the success of the subject-matter. Empires fall, votes are accorded, but to those people writing in the circular room it is the feel of the pen between their fingers that matters most. (p. 13)

Forster's obliviousness here to how the conditions of life affect the novel and determine the opportunities of its authors to become novelists in the first place displays a more extreme version of formalism than anything to be found in Virginia Woolf's various defences of the art of fiction. In *A Room of One's Own* the women novelists are not with the men under the dome of the British Museum. They are in drawing rooms and kitchens and – in the future, it is to be hoped – in their own rooms. The British Museum in *A Room of One's Own* is the place not where writers write timelessly but where the narrator goes from Cambridge to find out why women are poor.

Woolf's rejection of Forster's assumption that history develops but art stands still is all the more interesting in *A Room of One's Own* because of its form and its conclusion. The conclusion is that a woman needs five hundred pounds a year and a room of her own so that she can live in the presence of reality, think of things in themselves. To do this she must attain that unself-consciousness, that unsex-consciousness, that resembles what Forster described as the anonymous state of creation in his pamphlet on anonymity. 'All literature tends toward a condition of anonymity' for both Forster and Virginia Woolf.[37]

The resemblance in form between *A Room of One's Own* and *Aspects of the Novel* connects these two works as illuminatingly as do their critical assumptions and conclusions. The erosions of contour that *A Room of One's Own* achieves are more formidable than those in *Aspects of the Novel*. Both works combine genres in such a way that they cannot be fully understood or appreciated simply as works of criticism or non-fiction. Virginia Woolf rewrote her two lectures in a fictive form of one giant lecture that has six chapters, various personae, a narrative structure, symbolic motifs, a peroration, etc.[38] And the lecture form is insisted upon throughout. Again we have an emphasis on voice, on the role of the audience and on the identity of the lecturer not just as critic but as novelist. Both *A Room of One's Own* and *Aspects of the Novel* use comic irony throughout, mocking for example the academic setting and the very genre that they are using. Virginia Woolf's lecture is more radical in its implications than Forster's; as well, its mixture of fiction and non-fiction is more original than Forster's. There is also an important difference in their interest in the novel, for Forster is looking at present and past novels while Virginia Woolf is chiefly concerned with unwritten future ones. Nevertheless these two works complement each other when brought together through literary history.

Today *A Room of One's Own* works miracles for many readers. Forster's lectures are unlikely to do so very often, yet they are, in an important literary historical sense, a part of Virginia Woolf's lectures, just as the texts of Bradley, of Eliot and Arnold, of Aristotle and Alain, of Mauron, Lubbock, James and Wells are parts of Forster's – not to mention all the novels that Virginia Woolf and Forster allude to, including their own.

But time must have a stop even in literary history. My moral is simply that we need to re-examine where we stop it in modern literary history.

6 Towards the Literary History of *A Room of One's Own*

INTRODUCTION

In April 1990, while finishing the second volume of my literary history of the Bloomsbury Group, I came across a letter of Leonard Woolf's mentioning that Virginia Woolf might have given one of her manuscripts to the Fitzwilliam Museum in Cambridge or the Bodleian Library in Oxford. The letter was written the year after her death, and a helpful footnote by Frederic Spotts, the meticulous editor of Leonard Woolf's letters, informed me that a manuscript entitled 'Women in Fiction' and identified as 'the first draft of what became *A Room of One's Own*' was indeed owned by the Fitzwilliam.

A Room of One's Own was the only book Virginia Woolf published in her lifetime for which no substantial manuscript had yet been discovered. Only twenty or so pages of what seem at first to be notes and fragments were to be found in the Monks House Papers now at the University of Sussex. The 1928 talks at the two Cambridge women's colleges out of which the book grew have not survived; they were probably recast as an article entitled 'Women and Fiction' (not 'Women in Fiction') that Virginia Woolf published in March 1929, before bringing out *A Room of One's Own* in the autumn.

I assumed, before visiting the Fitzwilliam Museum, that their manuscript was that for the article, not the book. (An entry in the *Location Register of Twentieth-Century English Literary Manuscripts and Letters* had described it as a 'lecture' that had been incorporated into *A Room of One's Own*.) But the dark blue box that a librarian of the Fitzwilliam brought to me contained well over a hundred sheets in Virginia Woolf's not easily readable hand. This was too long for a lecture. The first page with its title and the subsequent chapter divisions made it clear that here at last was most, as it turned out, of the manuscript of *A Room of One's Own*. It had been donated by Leonard Woolf, who described it in an accompanying letter as the first draft of the book, but even he misread his wife's writing and took the ampersand in the title *Women & Fiction* as the preposition *in*.

That a man, and a professor at that, should be editing the manuscripts of *A Room of One's Own* has its ironies. But these have been eased for me through the help of two authorities on feminism and on Virginia Woolf. Naomi Black, who understands the complexities of modern feminism so well, and Susan Dick, the fine editor of the manuscripts of *To the Lighthouse* and *The Complete Shorter Fiction of Virginia Woolf*, both compared very carefully the emerging transcription with copies of the manuscript and suggested innumerable improvements.

Soon after she finished drafting *Women & Fiction* Virginia Woolf wrote a short biography of Mary Wollstonecraft in which she said of works like *A Vindication of the Rights of Woman* what readers have come to feel about *A Room of One's Own*: 'they seem now to contain nothing new in them – their originality has become our commonplace.' The drafts of *A Room of One's Own* allow us to defamiliarise the text and re-experience the originality of a work so influential that it has become our commonplace. In *Women & Fiction* the narrative structure of *A Room of One's Own* is clearly visible, yet almost every sentence of the book was revised in some way during the course of composition. Again and again Virginia Woolf rewrites her text as she strives to fuse the diverse forms of lecture and fiction, feminist argument and literary criticism, polemic and prophecy. *Women & Fiction* reflects, like *A Room of One's Own*, the fantasy of *Orlando*, which she had just published, and the mysticism of *The Waves*, which she was about to write. Yet the study of its composition differs from those of Woolf's novels because *A Room of One's Own* is a more discursive work. In its manuscript versions one can watch Woolf creatively developing her arguments through reasoning and association in images and scenes. The revisions in her drafts raise those same questions that the narrator begins to ask in *A Room of One's Own* as she goes to look at the manuscripts of Milton and Thackeray in a men's college library: 'whether the alterations were for the benefit of the style or of the meaning. But then one wd. have to decide what is style & what is meaning...'. For the narrator these questions end when she is prevented from seeing the manuscripts. Thanks to the copyright holders, Quentin Bell and Angelica Garnett, and the institutional owners, the Syndics at the Fitzwilliam Museum, and the University of Sussex, any reader can now ask such questions of *Women & Fiction*.

THE MANUSCRIPTS

'By a miracle, I've found all the pages', Virginia Woolf wrote to Ethel Smyth three years after the publication of *A Room of One's Own* (*Letters*, V, 136). She wanted to donate the manuscript to the nearly bankrupt London and National Society for Women's Service, whose secretary was Philippa Strachey, a sister of Lytton. The Society asked her to sell it for them if she could in America. Unsuccessful efforts were made first by Vita Sackville-West, who was lecturing in the States, and then by Woolf's American publisher Donald Brace. The Huntington Library in California expressed interest, a wealthy collector said he would rather have the manuscript of *Flush*, but in the end Virginia Woolf was advised to try and sell the manuscript in England. There the matter seems to have dropped.

While making some enquiries as to the whereabouts of his wife's manuscripts after her death, Leonard Woolf received a request from the Director of the Fitzwilliam Museum in Cambridge, for something of Virginia Woolf's. Leonard responded appropriately and with great generosity, giving back to Cambridge (but not to Newnham or Girton, not to King's, and certainly not to Trinity's library) the manuscript that had its beginning there. He described the gift as the first draft of *A Room of One's Own* – the manuscript Virginia had been unable to sell for Pippa Strachey's society.

The Fitzwilliam manuscript bears the title *Women & Fiction* and consists of 134 holograph leaves. It is divided into five chapters plus a conclusion, and bears various dates between March and April 1929. A closer examination reveals, however, that Virginia Woolf had not, as she thought, miraculously found all the pages. The Fitzwilliam manuscript is really two manuscripts. The rhetoric of interruption in *A Room of One's Own* together with the disconnectedness of its composition sometimes makes it difficult to recognise breaks in the manuscript's progression. But it is self-evident that the heading 'Chapter 4. Cont.' is not simply a continuation of the third chapter that it follows. The manuscript paper is also different.

The third chapter of the Fitzwilliam manuscript is continued, however, in an untitled, undated manuscript of twenty leaves to be found in the Monks House Papers now at the University of Sussex. (Also to be found in the Monks House Papers are a brief variant opening for *A Room of One's Own* and a page of notes for the conclusion of *Women & Fiction*.) The paper of the Monks House manuscript is the same as the Fitzwilliam manuscript, except for the last few pages. But discontinuities remain. The fourth chapter of the Fitzwilliam manuscript does not carry on from the Monks House manuscript. It refers, for example to the imaginary novelist Mary Carmichael, who had been called Chloe in the Monks House manuscript. Parts of the drafts for *A Room of One's Own* are therefore still missing and must be presumed lost. To make matters more complicated, some scenes in the Monks House manuscript have been redrafted again in the following Fitzwilliam leaves. These different drafts, it is clear from the dates in the Fitzwilliam manuscript, were all made within days of each other, for the entire drafting of the book that became *A Room of One's Own* was completed in a little over a month. One reason for this remarkable speed, as Virginia Woolf noted in her diary, was that 'the thinking had been done & the writing stiffly & unsatisfactorily 4 times before' (*Diary*, III, 218–19, 221–2). To understand the creative evolution of *A Room of One's Own*, we need to trace the literary history of these earlier efforts from the talks in Cambridge through the article 'Women and Fiction' to the writing of the book *Women & Fiction* and its revision into *A Room of One's Own*.

THE CAMBRIDGE LECTURES

On Saturday, 20 October 1928, Virginia and Leonard Woolf, together with Vanessa Bell and her daughter Angelica, drove from London to Cambridge where Virginia was to read a paper to the undergraduates of Newnham College. She had been invited nearly a year before and planned to come in May. The first version of her paper had been prepared in the spring, interrupting the writing of *Orlando*. But illness and the pressure to finish that book led her to postpone until the autumn both Newnham and Girton (the only other Cambridge college where women could study) which had also asked her to speak.

The Woolfs were staying with Pernel Strachey, the Principal of Newnham and sister of Philippa and Lytton. Virginia arrived nearly an hour late for the college dinner at which she was to speak. To make matters worse, according to the subsequent recollections of E. E. Phare, she brought her husband along and upset the seating arrangements. Phare thought the dinner at Newnham, though never a gourmet meal, suffered considerably from the late arrival of the guest of honour, and she recalled how uncomfortable the depiction of Fernham's poverty had made the students feel (*A Newnham Anthology*, p. 174). Phare, who went on to become an authority on the poetry of Marvell and Hopkins, was the president of the Newnham Arts Society, under whose auspices Virginia Woolf was to speak. Her report of the paper in the Newnham magazine *Thersites* is worth quoting because the paper or papers that Woolf read at Newnham and later at Girton no longer exist, and Phare's is the only contemporary account of what Virginia Woolf actually said that evening. One can glimpse through this summary the symbolism of rooms, the prevalence of male standards and style that figure so importantly in *A Room of One's Own*, and also a little of the book's ironic self-consciousness.

> Mrs Virginia Woolf visited us on Saturday, Oct. 20th, and spoke in College Hall on 'Women and Fiction'. The reasons why women novelists were for so long so few were largely a question of domestic architecture: it was not, and it is not easy to compose in a parlour. Now that women are writing (and Mrs Woolf exhorted her audience to write novels and send them to be considered by the Hogarth Press) they should not try to adapt themselves to the prevailing literary standards, which are likely to be masculine, but make others of their own; they should remake the language, so that it becomes a more fluid thing and capable of delicate usage.
>
> It was a characteristic and delightful lecture and we are most greatful to Mrs Woolf for coming to us, as well as to Miss Strachey for consenting to preside over the meeting. (No. 87, Michaelmas Term, 1928)

Half a century later, almost the only thing Phare could remember from the talk was the praise of a poem by Stella Gibbons, but she also recalled how well disposed Woolf seemed to her audience of young intellectual women, and how formidable. Another listener, U. K. N. Carter, recollected Woolf's conversation after the paper – how she surprised the young woman with a compliment on her dress. But it was the look that remained most vividly with Carter: 'the look held a hint of a smile, a hint of compassion, but it was above all an absolutely ruthless look; my pretty frock was no proof against it' (*A Newnham Anthology*, p. 175).

The next day there was a luncheon party in the rooms of George 'Dadie' Rylands that had been decorated by Carrington and overlooked the beautiful Backs and the Cam. Rylands had recently been made a fellow of King's College after having served as an assistant at the Hogarth Press. According to Leonard Woolf's diary, the other guests were Lytton Strachey and John Maynard Keynes, and Keynes wrote Lydia Lopokova that Julian Bell and Angelica had also been there. The party was thus a thoroughly Bloomsbury affair. Rylands thought later that one of the guests may have been E. M. Forster (who had given his famous *Aspects of the Novel* lectures at Cambridge the year before and was also a fellow of King's at this time). Rylands doubted, however, that the cooking of his college could have produced various partridges and a brown-flecked counterpane of sauce, as *A Room of One's Own* has it. He hoped that there had been two wines but thought it unlikely (*Recollections of Virginia Woolf*, p. 144).

The accounts of lunch and dinner in *A Room of One's Own* have entered into the mythology of Oxbridge, and it is sometimes forgotten that, while based on Woolf's experiences at Cambridge, they are fictive descriptions. (The book's reversal of the order in which Woolf had the meals is a small but interesting illustration of how she transformed autobiography into art.)

The following Friday Virginia Woolf again went to Cambridge to speak, accompanied this time by Vita Sackville-West. In the afternoon she visited her nephew Julian, a first-year undergraduate at King's, and contrasted in her diary the next day the splendour and luxury of his surroundings with Newnham's and Girton's. She stayed at a hotel with Sackville-West where they had dinner with two students from the Girton ODTAA Society. (ODTAA was an acronym, taken from the title of a recent novel by John Masefield, and stood for 'one damn thing after another'.) The guests paid for their own dinners, to the relief of the students, Woolf thought, and afterwards were shown the cold, ugly corridors and convent-cell rooms of the college. ODTAA was quite different from the Newnham Arts Society. More exclusive and informal, it discussed topics that were not limited to literature and the arts. The society was modelled to some extent on the Cambridge Heretics Society and also on the more famous male Cambridge Conversazione Society, better known as the Apostles. The Mistress of Girton, it appears, was not a member of ODTAA and did not attend Woolf's paper. In the original invitation for Woolf to speak, some reference had been made to the women's society in her 1921 sketch 'A Society'. Woolf in her unpublished reply expressed the hope that ODTAA was a considerable improvement over the society of her sketch. But the connection is illuminating because 'A Society' satirises the ignorance of women, Oxbridge, women and fiction, chastity, and war – all concerns that prefigure those in *A Room of One's Own* and later *Three Guineas*.

The only contemporary record of what Virginia Woolf said at Girton is the author's: 'I blandly told them to drink wine & have a room of their own' (*Diary*, III, 200). This does not sound quite like her Newnham paper. Woolf referred to both the Newnham and Girton talks as one lecture in her diary and again in the opening note to *Women & Fiction*, where she added that it was too long to be read in full. In the note to *A Room of One's Own*, however, Woolf says there were two lectures, or papers as she called them, both of which were too long. In her diary the day she returned from Cambridge, Woolf also recorded the 'sense of tingling & vitality' she got from such talks but indicated as well that her Girton lecture may not have been completely successful. Preparing it had been a 'long toil'. Her impression of the audience was of 'starved but valiant young women.... Intelligent eager, poor; & destined to become schoolmistresses in shoals.... I felt elderly & mature. And nobody respected me. They were very eager, egotistical, or rather not much impressed by age & repute. Very little reverence or that sort of thing about' (*Diary*, III, 200–1). In their recollections several Girton undergraduates who heard Woolf's paper suggest, like Phare at Newnham, that Woolf may have misjudged her audience. Her bleak view of their academic life and prospects did not persuade some of the readers of *A Room of One's Own* who had heard the original papers that theirs was an underprivileged gender. At Girton in particular there were three impressive, if not irreverent, young literary women in the audience who were certainly not going to become schoolmistresses.

The poet Kathleen Raine, in a review of M. C. Bradbrook's short history of Girton, remembered that they were both present at Woolf's paper forty years before. She found Woolf's criticism of her alma mater a little absurd. (Like almost all the accounts of Woolf's talks, Raine's does not distinguish between the paper she heard and the book into which it was made.) In her autobiography Raine also indicated another circumstance that made Woolf's Girton lecture different from her Newnham one. 'With

Virginia Woolf had come her friend Victoria Sackville-West: the two most beautiful women I had ever seen. I saw their beauty and their fame entirely removed from the context of what is usually called "real" life, as if they had descended like goddesses from Olympus, to reascend when at the end of the evening they vanished from our sight' (*The Land Unknown*, p. 22). Raine, herself a strikingly beautiful undergraduate, had read none of Woolf's novels, but she had probably heard something about *Orlando*, which was partly based on the circumstances of Vita Sackville-West and published the week before. *A Room of One's Own*, she felt, laid claim to unimaginable luxuries; to escape parental vigilance she had done her writing in teashops before temporarily realising the dream of a room of her own at Girton. After Cambridge Julian Bell took her to see his aunt about a job at the Hogarth Press; this time Raine felt none of the great writer's mana present. Virginia Woolf thought she had 'the mind of a lovely snowball' and offered no job (*Letters*, V, 245). Later the Press declined a volume of her poems.

M. C. Bradbook rose to be Professor of English at Cambridge as well as Mistress of Girton. Her short history of Girton briefly mentions Woolf's paper and *A Room of One's Own* immediately after a much longer and rather misleading discussion of the lesbian aspects of Rosamond Lehmann's Girton novel *Dusty Answer*. The Cambridge of the novel was Virginia Woolf's, Bradbrook says elsewhere in commenting on the book's style. *Dusty Answer* had been published the year before Woolf's talk and seems to have created something of a sensation at the College. At the time of Woolf's visit in the company of Orlando's model, literary lesbianism was in the news with the banning and forthcoming trial of Radclyffe Hall's *The Well of Loneliness* – events that would be reflected in the lesbian nuances of *A Room of One's Own*. Whatever the perceived relation of Woolf's talk to Lehmann's novel was, Bradbrook recalled in 1969 that 'we undergraduates enjoyed Mrs Woolf, but felt that her Cambridge was not ours' ('*That Infidel Place*', pp. 112–16). In 1932 (when she was twenty-three) Bradbrook had been more severe. The first issue of that famous Cambridge critical scourge *Scrutiny* contained a short dismissive essay by her that asserted Woolf's delicate perceptiveness of style was maintained 'at the cost of some cerebral etiolation'. 'Camouflage' was Bradbrook's term for the fictive art of *A Room of One's Own*: its arguments were 'clearly serious and personal and yet they are dramatized and surrounded with all sorts of disguises to avoid an appearance of argument' ('Notes on the Style of Mrs Woolf', *Scrutiny*, I, 38).

Another undergraduate who heard the Girton paper was Queenie Roth. A friend recalled that she impressed Woolf, who was going to send her a pamphlet (Gwendolen Freeman, *Alma Mater*, p. 87). Roth was not about to be a schoolmistress either. She remained in Cambridge as the wife and collaborator of F. R. Leavis, whom she married the next year. In 1935 she sent Woolf a *Scrutiny* review that praised the introductory letter to *Life as We Have Known It*, but Woolf did not recognise her name (*Letters*, V, 425). Later in the year Q. D. Leavis referred in passing to the 'crudely' manifested feminism of *A Room of One's Own* but still had praise for some of Woolf's other work (*Scrutiny*, IV, 329–30). *Three Guineas* outraged her, however, and she fiercely attacked both book and author.

THE ARTICLE 'WOMEN AND FICTION'

Virginia Woolf was still thinking about Newnham and Girton in November as she considered what to write after *Orlando*. Early in the month she appeared in court prepared to testify on *The Well of Loneliness*, but evidence of literary merit was ruled inadmissible and the book declared obscene. (Forster wrote to Leonard Woolf that Virginia, as the author of *Orlando*, ought not perhaps to have attended the trial.) The mood of *Orlando* remained with her as she recorded in her diary the desire to write something else of fun and fantasy that gave things 'their caricature value.... I want to write a history, say of Newnham or the womans movement, in the same vein.' But in the same entry she also speaks of wanting to begin the book that would become *The Waves* (*Diary*, III, 203). The next book she published was *A Room of One's Own*, in which elements of both *Orlando* and *The Waves* are to be found. But this was not the next book she completed.

For three years now Virginia Woolf had been trying to write a book on the theory of fiction for the Hogarth Press Lectures on Literature series that Leonard Woolf and George Rylands were editing. The success of Forster's Cambridge lectures provided a stimulus for the book because Virginia thought, as she said in her two reviews of *Aspects of the Novel*, that Forster had not paid enough attention to the *art* of fiction. She had begun 'Phases of Fiction', as the book was called, in 1926. But she became bored with it and wrote *Orlando* instead. Woolf took up 'Phases of Fiction' again and finished drafting it before going to Cambridge in October 1928. She rewrote it in November and December, and still had 10,000 words to write, when another book on fiction intervened instead.

The idea of making a book out of her Cambridge lectures does not seem to have occurred to Woolf until the following spring. She had written an article on the subject of the lectures at the end of the year, while working on 'Phases of Fiction', and sent it off to the *Forum* in America, where it was published in March the next year. Woolf had followed a similar procedure with two previous talks to students about reading and writing that are among her most significant critical essays. A 1926 paper read to a girls' school was published as 'How Should One Read a Book?' and then revised as the final essay and critical credo of the second *Common Reader*. In 1927, the year before she read her Cambridge papers, Woolf had gone to Oxford (accompanied by Vita Sackville-West) to speak to a mixed group of undergraduates about 'Poetry, Fiction and the Future', as she called the published article. That paper is almost a manifesto for the kind of novel she would write in *The Waves*. And later in 1931 she would give a speech on professions for women that continues the concerns of her Cambridge talks and links *A Room of One's Own* to its sequel, *Three Guineas*.

Woolf entitled her *Forum* article 'Women and Fiction'. This would also be the working title for *A Room of One's Own* as well as the heading for the paper that the speaker is trying to write in that book. If one counts the talks to Newnham and Girton as separate papers, then this was the fourth time she addressed the subject. (The first was the version prepared the preceding spring.) The article was illustrated with drawings of Sappho, Austen, Murasaki, who are among the women mentioned in the text, and George Sand, who is not. (Perhaps that was as close as the illustrator could come to George Eliot, whom Woolf does refer to.)

The *Forum* was a distinguished New York review that took its title seriously and tried to provide a non-partisan medium for intellectual debate and contemporary literature. In 1928 the editor, Henry Goddard Leach, had published Woolf's 'Slater's Pins Have No Points', which she described to Sackville-West as a Sapphist story whose point the editor had not got (*Letters*, III, 431). A serialisation of André Gide's novel *The School of Women* was begun in the same issue as 'Women and Fiction', and an essay by Valéry promised at the end of Woolf's text for the next issue. The preceding issue of the *Forum* in which Woolf's article was announced carried a piece by William Allan Neilson, the President of Smith College, arguing that the liberal arts of women's colleges should be the same as men's because educators ought 'to provide for all degrees of masculinity in female minds and all degrees of feminity [sic] in male minds, as for all other varieties of human nature' (*Forum*, LXXXI, 103). The only grave disadvantage of women's colleges, he maintained, was their lack of generous benefactors.

'Women and Fiction', while not too long to have been read as a lecture, is probably as close as we can now come to what Virginia Woolf said at Cambridge. E. E. Phare's account tallies with it (as Woolf's own comment about her Girton paper does not in the matter of wine). The article begins in the best Cambridge tradition by considering the ambiguities of meaning in its title. The past, present and future of women and fiction are all touched upon in Woolf's article as she refers to the obscurity of women's lives, the intermittent history of their literary work, the problems of style and value in women's writing, the artistic dangers of resentment, the increasing literary interest in women's relations with one another, the two kinds of modern novelist (Woolf calls them the gadfly and the butterfly in the article), and the possibilities for a more poetic fiction. Running through all of these issues is an insistence on the determining influence of the writer's environment. At the end the author calls for what has so long been denied to women: 'leisure, and money, and a room to themselves.' Not until Woolf had finished a draft of the book would she shift the final phrase to the impersonal singular 'a room of one's own'.

More revealing for the literary history of *A Room of One's Own*, however, is what the essay 'Women and Fiction' does not say. The situation of women at Oxbridge is unmentioned, and the anger of men unnoticed. There is no reference to the androgynous state of mind that, according to Woolf, a good writer needs. It may seem unlikely that her account of women's colleges was influenced by Neilson's piece in the *Forum*, which appeared before she had begun to write her book, but the coincidence of his concern with their disadvantage is arresting. 'Women and Fiction' also has little or none of the comedy, the satire of *A Room of One's Own*. There was humour in the lectures, as Phare's brief summary indicates. (William Empson, who met Woolf when he was an undergraduate at Cambridge, remembered becoming quite ill from laughing so hard at her jokes.) And there is nothing fictional in the article – no narrator or novelist named Mary, nothing about Shakespeare's sister.

Woolf says in her note to both *Women & Fiction* and *A Room of One's Own* that they are 'based' on the paper or papers read at Cambridge. A comparison of the article 'Women and Fiction' with *A Room of One's Own* makes the nature of this basis clear. It shows how the experience itself of coming to Cambridge and reading a paper to a woman's college on women and fiction became the narrative basis for the book that Virginia Woolf would begin to write some five months later. With the recovery of the manuscript versions of *A Room of One's Own*, it is now possible to follow this modernist transformation through the beginnings, endings, interruptions, repetitions, cancellations, insertions and marginalia of Virginia Woolf's creative process.

THE WRITING OF *WOMEN & FICTION*

Early in 1929, the Woolfs visited Vita Sackville-West and her husband Harold Nicolson in Berlin, where he was serving as a diplomat. After their return Virginia Woolf was ill: for three weeks she lay in bed, and for perhaps another three could not write. It was a creative illness. As she wrote later, 'I believe these illnesses are in my case – how shall I express it? – partly mystical. Something happens in my mind. It refuses to go on registering impressions. It shuts itself up. It becomes a chrysalis' (*Diary*, III, 287). Woolf had wanted to begin *The Waves*, but the subject of her Cambridge papers and article forced itself on her again in a new form now, which she described as half talk and half soliloquy. Woolf began making up *Women & Fiction* in her head as she lay in bed. Then in what she called 'one of my excited outbursts of composition', the book was drafted in about a month. 'I used to make it up at such a rate', she noted when beginning her revisions in April, 'that when I got pen & paper I was like a water bottle turned upside down. The writing was as quick as my hand could write; too quick, for I am now toiling to revise; but this way gives one freedom & lets one leap from back to back of one's thoughts' (*Diary*, III, 218–19, 221–2). It was too quick also for any easy deciphering of her manuscript. The scrawl of her handwriting illustrates the extraordinary speed with which *Women & Fiction* was written. Woolf's novels were usually written in bound quarto notebooks; the morning's work would be revised when she typed it up in the afternoon. *Women & Fiction*, however, was written on loose-leaf paper and not typed up until the holograph draft had been completed. There are no indications in the manuscript or her diary that she referred to the Cambridge lectures while composing the book that was based on them.

The first date in the manuscript of *Women & Fiction* – 'Wed. 6th March 1929' – appears at the start of 'Chapter II'. The opening chapter is undated and undesignated even as a chapter. In the note that describes its basis in a paper read at Newnham and Girton, *Women & Fiction* is not called an essay, nor is there any mention of expanding the paper, as there is in *A Room of One's Own*. Woolf may not have known yet where her essay-story was going as she began it. The opening words pick up the original title, to which the speaker-narrator keeps returning. *Women* indicates a dangerous subject, and *Fiction* lands her in the swamp and maze of literary criticism. The licence of fiction is invoked and illustrated with the image of a medieval pedlar, a device used by Woolf in one of her earliest stories. Mary Beaton, Seaton and Carmichael are all mentioned but none is developed much as a persona. There is less emphasis on the fictiveness of the narrative at the start of *Women & Fiction*; college names are undisguised, for example. But the conclusion that will be symbolised in the revised title is present from the beginning. Watching Virginia Woolf create the narrative that seeks arguments for women having 'money & a room to themselves' is among the most absorbing aspects of reading *Women & Fiction*.

The episodes of walking on the forbidden grass and being turned away from the library, of the luxurious luncheon party and the bleak fare at Newnham, were all drafted in the first chapter of *Women & Fiction* together with observations on the wealth of men's colleges, on the nature of luncheon parties and poetry before the war, and on the causes of the comparative poverty of women's colleges. The process of drafting involved more than crossings out, insertions and marginalia. It was an interruptive process. The writing starts, stops and repeats. A number of pages are unfinished, breaking off sometimes in the middle of a sentence or a series of notes. The next page often starts over again, sometimes in the middle of a sentence. The drafts of *To the Lighthouse* and *The Waves* were to some extent also written in this way, but the process seems to have more significance in the writing of what became

A Room of One's Own because its narrative is so discontinuous. The very writing of the manuscript seems to illustrate the interrupted lives that women lead. Some of the most abrupt changes in the finished book, such as the sudden appearance of soup in the midst of a reverie on some terrible reality, are present from the beginning. The seasonal dislocation in the first chapter, where the speaker prefers to describe the beauty of spring even though it was October, is originally heightened by anachronism. In *A Room of One's Own*, the reference to the great Newnham classicist Jane Ellen Harrison is an anachronistic fantasy, for she had died in April 1928, but in *Women & Fiction* the more descriptive allusion is fancifully extended back almost a generation to include the well-known dons Verrall and Sidgwick.

Some passages in the first chapter, and not always important ones, are reworked a number of times. Five versions appear in the manuscript of the joke about the professor who is said to gallop if someone whistles. Woolf heavily revised the complaint about luncheon parties in novels that describe talk instead of food. Sometimes the first version of a familiar episode or phrase is revealingly different in small details. Freud is mentioned to avoid explaining how a train of thought was started by the sight of a Manx cat. The narrator's anonymous hostess at Newnham is first described as going to Australia to farm ostriches and then identified as a science lecturer named Mary Seton (as the name is now spelled). Finally, after leaving the college at the end of the chapter, the speaker briefly becomes another of Virginia Woolf's night walkers, experiencing a sense of isolation after escaping from some thraldom. 'The day's skin is neatly rolled off; thrown into the hedge.' In *Women & Fiction* it has not yet been described as 'crumpled' with accumulated impressions and emotions.

The second chapter, now so designated and also dated, was written in six days. As in *A Room of One's Own*, it consists of a walk through Bloomsbury to the British Museum for a comical attempt to research the causes and consequences of the financial disparity between the sexes. Reflections follow, at lunch and during the walk home, on the angry power of the patriarchy and the advantages of an independent income for a woman. The general resemblance of the British Museum scenes in the manuscript to those of the book is illustrated by the similar satiric list of topics in each. Elsewhere there are various differences of detail, such as Professor X, the author of a great work on the mental, moral and physical inferiority of women, who is given a German beer-hall setting, but not the title of 'von'.

More remarkable, however, are the revisions in the second chapter that reveal Woolf thinking about anger. The word appears, is crossed out, then reinserted. The narrator's doodle of the very angry professor leads to speculation as to the causes of his anger. The narrator's anger is admitted and explained, but for ten pages Woolf tries to answer the question of why men are angry. In *Women & Fiction* these thoughts occur in a French restaurant – described twice before being dropped – whose excellent cooking continues the concern with food in Chapter 1. A pencilled note at the bottom of a page gives the conclusion that will be amplified several pages later: 'Anger:/desire to be superior./ importance to have some one inferior.' Evidence of partiarchal power in the restaurant is supplied by a newspaper (identified here as the *Evening Standard*), as in *A Room of One's Own*. And a looking-glass theory of male psychology is accompanied by a digression on men as bores, which illustrates the sex's superiority complex. Then Woolf introduces a passage on an amazing tribe of women in Central Asia who have a poet equal, perhaps, to Shakespeare. At first this tribe is read out as a fact from the newspaper, to the irritation of a young man lunching nearby. On the next page it is rewritten as a hypothetical example of male rage and deception, for if such a group were found to exist, men would either destroy the women's works or claim them as their own. These thoughts the narrator offers to her audience, again on the understanding that they are all women, for 'there are many things that no woman has yet said to a man'. The tribe, without this qualification, survived into the typescript of *A Room of One's Own* before finally being deleted.

The aunt whose legacy frees the speaker from women's jobs and allows her to think of things in themselves is, like her niece, unnamed in *Women & Fiction*. Nothing can take away the £500 a year as long as the narrator does not gamble in the stock market. This reservation was also deleted in *A Room of One's Own* (which ironically was then published just days before the great crash of October 1929). With that income she is spared the acquisitive torments of men, torments which indicate that in this respect their privileged education was more imperfect than women's. The sky and trees are no longer blocked by – Woolf originally wrote the cryptic phrase 'Milton's bogeyman', then changed this to 'the large & imposing figure of Professor X'. In *A Room of One's Own* she returned to her Miltonic allusion and substituted for Professor X the large, imposing gentleman Milton recommended for her perpetual adoration. She remembered the cancelled bogeyman, however, and brought him back in the revised conclusion to her book. At the end of the chapter a contrast, which remains only implicit in *A Room of One's Own*, is made between domestic rooms where 'there was quiet & thought & happiness' and the 'flying chaos & terror' of the street.

Drafting *Women & Fiction* as fast as her hand could write (and faster in places than can now be read), Virginia Woolf took less than ten days between 12 and 22 March 1929 to produce the long third chapter. But just when and where Chapter 3 ended and Chapter 4 began in *Women & Fiction* can now no longer be determined. The third chapter returns to the narrator's unwritten paper on women and fiction, and then moves back and forward between history and fiction. From G. M. Trevelyan's account of the situation of women and the extraordinary heroines of Shakespeare and later writers, a composite being emerges. Recorded history is a little dull for women, however, and the speaker wishes some of her audience would try using the two great searchlights of history and literature to write biographies of average Elizabethan women. Calling them 'lives of the obscure' (a title Woolf herself had already used) is still an advisable dodge in October 1928. The passage about the need for biographies of the obscure is then reworked again, and references are repeated to the Pastons and others as nearly the only sources for them.

Without such lives of the obscure, the speaker is forced into fiction, and the result is a remarkable illustration of Virginia Woolf's creativity as she drafts a version of her famous myth of Shakespeare's sister. Born in Warwickshire around 1564, the woman is given the name of Shakespeare's mother, Mary Arden, as an afterthought. The brief life of this additional Mary in *Women & Fiction* contains most of the essentials that will be reworked into Judith Shakespeare's life, except for an episode in which she is beaten by her father for gallivanting about the woods dressed as a man. There is also a cancelled passage asking how the end of her story can be told genteelly. Its evolution in her draft indicates that the fiction of Shakespeare's sister was not part of Woolf's original Cambridge talk. After going on for a page about how other women writers have been hindered from pursuing their art, Woolf breaks off and begins the third chapter again from the beginning. Here and elsewhere, the manuscript of *Women & Fiction* consists of overlapping drafts.

The revised beginning of Chapter 3 brings it closer to the published book. Some of the details from Trevelyan as well as the life of Mary Arden are skipped over and then put back in *A Room of One's Own*. The revised story of Shakespeare's sister is left unfinished; it ends not with her death but in a discussion of chastity, the difficulties of women writers and the possessiveness of men again. Then Woolf comes back to a fundamental concern of both *Women & Fiction* and *A Room of One's Own*, which is the state of mind best suited to the creation of literature. Shakespeare is the standard. The writer is compared to the carrier of a precious jar through a crowd. Examples of indifference and hostility to men writers are cited to suggest how much more discouraging is a woman's situation, and how important it is, as Emily Davies realised when founding Girton, for women to have rooms of their own. Trying to explain the result of a discouraging environment on artists, Woolf returns to Shakespeare's state of mind, and jots down the single word 'incandescent' in the margin opposite a reference to *Antony and Cleopatra*. This play and image will recur in the theory of creativity that is so important in *Women & Fiction* and *A Room of One's Own*. Shakespeare's creative mind consumed all the personal impediments, the grudges and grievances, that remain in the work of Jonson, Donne or Milton, which may explain why we have less sense of his personality than theirs. For three pages Woolf tries to describe Shakespeare's state of mind in the imagery of metallurgy.

The thought that such a molten state of mind was impossible for any woman of Shakespeare's time begins a new paragraph. In *A Room of One's Own* this is where the fourth chapter begins. But in the manuscript, Chapter 3 continues on for another half-dozen pages with discussions of pre-nineteenth-century women writers. Winchilsea, Newcastle, Osborne and Behn are all referred to, but more briefly than they will be in the revised text. The quotations to be used are identified just by first line and page number. These women are the forerunners of Jane Austen, George Eliot and the Brontës, whose masterpieces are first likened to waves of the sea and then more familiarly described as the result of thinking in common for many years. With the debts that these nineteenth-century novelists owed to their predecessors, the first part of Woolf's Fitzwilliam manuscript stops in the middle of a page – one third of the way through what will be Chapter 4 in *A Room of*

One's Own. The second part of the manuscript picks up the story in the middle of what will be Chapter 5, some thirty pages later in the book.

The gap between the two parts of the Fitzwilliam manuscript is partly filled by twenty leaves of the undated Monks House manuscript. In it Woolf continues, on the same paper as the Fitzwilliam manuscript, some time between 12 and 22 March, the survey of women writers from Aphra Behn into the nineteenth century, as in *A Room of One's Own*. There are significant differences in both organisation and detail between this version of the manuscript and *A Room of One's Own*, however. The discussion of *Jane Eyre* does not immediately analyse the awkward break in sequence that is attributed a little later to Charlotte Brontë's indignation. It is interesting to follow Woolf in the Monks House manuscript while she works tentatively towards a moral aesthetic of the novel as a structure of emotional relations depending on the author's integrity for its maintenance. One can begin to see here how her concerns with feminism, creativity and the future of the novel all come together. Sometimes Woolf's judgements are blunter in *Women & Fiction*; Rochester's description in *Jane Eyre*, for instance, is 'the portrait of a man by a woman who is afraid of men', rather than one drawn in the dark and influenced by fear. The much commented-upon statement 'for we think back through our mothers if we are women' first occurs as a parenthetical remark. Woolf does not yet work into her argument the quotations of men hostile to women's literary aspirations that will appear later in her manuscript and book. Without saying yet that the form of a woman's novel should be adapted somehow to her body, Woolf speculates through her narrator on the kind of poetic novel women may write. In *A Room of One's Own* this marks the beginning of the fifth chapter, but in the Monks House manuscript only a line-space separates it from the preceding discussion.

Virginia Woolf begins her section on contemporaries by noting the variety of books now written by women. She then digresses to describe how a visit of Emily Davies and Barbara Leigh Smith to a family of six middle-class girls moping around the table led to the founding of Girton and the writing of such books. Suddenly the speaker blushes for her topic of women and fiction, apparently because such enquiries into only one sex 'sterilise & embitter'. Then in the remaining ten leaves of the Monks House manuscript Woolf's narrator describes and reflects upon a novel written by a woman, an Oxford graduate with £300 a year, who was born at the beginning of the century. The narrator jumps into the middle of the book to get a sense of its style, which is described as plunging up and down like a boat, using too many words, putting in the wrong things and leaving out the right ones. Still, the novelist was not trying to write a realistic novel, the typical detail of which is satirised. But the test of the book will be the novel's final situation. The work does conclude successfully, but before we reach the end, Woolf drafts some of the most interesting pages of *Women & Fiction*. In these passages on the possibilities of contemporary fiction by women she continues the double fictive frame of her book by describing her narrator's reaction to the imaginary novel as she reads it. The novelist's sentence 'Chloe liked Olivia...' changes the current of the narrator's thought. Changes in current – from the first interruption on a college lawn to the last scene outside her window when a young couple come together – are one of the fundamental metaphors by which Woolf organises her book. They are also a source of the work's humour and irony.

In *A Room of One's Own* the speaker prefaces the suggestive ambiguity of the phrase 'Chloe liked Olivia...' by breaking off to be sure there are no men, no magistrates like the one who judged *The Well of Loneliness* obscene, hiding in cupboards. Originally, however, Woolf's comic interpolation follows the phrase, which is given as '"Chloe liked Olivia; they shared a ———"'. The pages of the book stick together at this point, and before she can separate them to read the next word, which is only 'laboratory', a fantasy trial, verdict and book-burning flash through her mind. After some cancellations a more serious current of thought is started, which has to do with the immense literary change that Chloe's and Olivia's relationship signifies. Until Austen wrote, all great women in literature, such as Shakespeare's jealous Cleopatra, were seen primarily in relationship with the other sex. If Chloe likes Olivia and can write – these last crucial words are inserted by Woolf – then Olivia offers readers the extraordinary opportunity of illuminating a cave where no one has been before. Woolf stops in the middle of a sentence and page here, and starts again on different paper with Chloe, who is somewhat confusingly both a character in the novel and its author. (There is no mention of Mary Carmichael.) Chloe has the great opportunity of observing the obscure lives of organisms like Olivia, whose life is 'so highly developed for other purposes, so <u>extraordinarily</u> complex, so sensitive...'. Woolf will return to these words in the second part of the Fitzwilliam manuscript, and extensively redraft the part that follows them in the Monks House pages.

The Monks House version of this section has to do with what Chloe's novel might be about. As a naturalist-novelist (the more interesting contemplative kind is not mentioned), she watches and writes about various rooms and lives of women, such as the ancient lady, seen crossing a street with her daughter, whose life of Monday and Tuesday has passed unrecorded, or the vagrants, whose faces reflect so differently the meeting of a man or a woman. Chloe might even write about shopping rather than golf or shooting, and thus win the approval of the anonymous critic who said recently that 'female novelists should only aspire to excellence by courageously acknowledging the limitations of their sex'. Woolf took the partial quotation from the August 1928 issue of the new periodical *Life and Letters* that her Bloomsbury friend Desmond MacCarthy had started editing and to which she contributed. Woolf had been disagreeing in print with MacCarthy about the capabilities of women since 1920, when she criticised a review of his on some books about women (*Diary*, II, 339–42). That criticism anticipates the arguments of *A Room of One's Own*. MacCarthy's remark in *Life and Letters* comes at the beginning of his review of a young woman's novel. Its autobiographical relevance appears in a further part of the quotation that was omitted by Woolf: 'If, like the reporter, you believe that female novelists should only aspire to excellence by courageously acknowledging the limitations of their sex (Jane Austen and, in our own time, Mrs Virginia Woolf have demonstrated how gracefully this gesture can be accomplished)....' After the publication of *A Room of One's Own*, in which Woolf used the same elliptical quotation, MacCarthy wrote in *Life and Letters* that he was horrified to find his unhappy sentence used so acidly when it was inspired by a wholehearted admiration of Woolf's work. He went on to praise her again, but still concluded obtusely that we should applaud the way she recognised her limitations. Later, however, he delighted Woolf with his favourable review of her book in the *Sunday Times*.

Twice Woolf gives the partial quotation in *Women & Fiction*, mocking the reviewer who knew the limitations of women writers but did not specify them. Were they allowed to describe shops, for example? (The reviewer is compared with the bishop who, in an anecdote referred to a number of times, was certain no woman could equal Shakespeare and no cat go to heaven.) The narrator finally comes back to the last scene of Chloe's novel. It represented something about the immensity of the soul, but had little to do with sex. Thus we come back to the start of the speaker's thoughts about women and modern fiction, and at this point, which corresponds to the end of Chapter 5 in *A Room of One's Own*, the Monks House manuscript also ends.

The discrepancies in chapter division between *Women & Fiction* and *A Room of One's Own* remain in the second part of the Fitzwilliam manuscript. Virginia Woolf began the chapter, which she headed '<u>Chapter 4. Cont.</u>' on 22 March 1929, continuing for ten leaves a chapter whose beginning is not indicated in the surviving manuscripts. Further evidence that part of the draft of *Women & Fiction* is missing appears with the reference several pages later to the novelist Mary Carmichael. Where Chloe the novelist turned into Mary is now unknown. How much material has been lost is uncertain; it may be only five to ten pages. The second part of the Fitzwilliam manuscript begins again with the words that had been used to describe the 'highly developed', the 'infinitely intricate' capacities of Olivia, though they are not the exact words used in the Monks House manuscript. The narrator is vexed that she has slipped into praising her own sex, especially when there is yet no way of measuring their ability. All she can do is note the dependence of great men upon women. The account of this is close to that in *A Room of One's Own*, but it was not part of the original draft in the Monks House manuscript. The rooms of these women are then emphasised, and here one can watch the central symbol of the book emerging. The valuable differences of the sexes are stressed, and, in a remark later cut, the speaker says that nothing would please her more than if some explorer discovered yet another sex somewhere. Next, the different rooms and lives of women that Mary Carmichael will have to represent are described, as in the Monks House manuscript. But instead of a discussion of whether she is allowed to describe shopping, a brief description of a shop is given. Returning to Carmichael's untitled novel, the speaker comments on her abilities and discusses the challenge of the last scene at greater length than in the Monks House draft. A racecourse metaphor is repeated and extended to include the men of Cambridge and the authors of books and reviews (MacCarthy's phrase echoes again) who advise and warn from the sidelines. Woolf's narrator places a bet and urges the novelist to ignore the men and think only of the jump itself, which she successfully does. The chapter ends, as in *A Room of One's Own*, with the prediction that in a hundred years Mary Carmichael will be a poet.

It took Virginia Woolf four days to write the continued fourth chapter. On 26 March, five months to the day after giving her paper at Girton, she began the fifth chapter of *Women & Fiction*. In just one week she drafted both it and the concluding chapter – a total of thirty-four manuscript pages. The structure of Chapter 5, which becomes approximately the first half of Chapter 6 of *A Room of One's Own*, is generally similar to that of the book, though much more disjointed and tentative. The chapter opens with the narrator observing a London street scene. She begins to sketch a theory of androgynous states of mind, and then considers masculine self-consciousness in the work of several unandrogynous modern writers. At the end of the chapter the narrator returns to the description of creative states of mind. The writing of the fifth chapter of *Women & Fiction* was far from being straightforward, however. Much of its interest lies in watching Woolf's attempts to create a scene that will lead her to reflections on the unity of mind required for good writing. The culminating scene of *A Room of One's Own* in which a couple get into a taxi begins in *Women & Fiction* with a girl in patent-leather shoes whom a taxi-driver chooses to pick up instead of a man. Reworking the scene, trying to describe first the sexual current that sweeps all along the street and then the relief experienced at seeing the girl greet a young man, Woolf's narrator tries to explain what she means by unity of mind. Again there are allusions to Tennyson, Rossetti and Shakespeare.

Three more or less distinct drafts of a plan for the soul can be traced in the writing of this chapter as the narrator tries to write the first sentence of her paper on women and fiction. Only the last version mentions Coleridge and androgyny. In the first version the lack of repression felt by the speaker as she sees a young woman and man together leads to the realisation that she can think back through her mothers or her fathers. She can make herself an inheritor of her civilisation or an alien in it. Instead of letting her consciousness flow undivided, she can for some special purpose accentuate the dominant sexual half of her brain, as the narrator had been doing in thinking back only through her mothers. A brief fantasy intervenes of some primeval woman who regrets her destiny of having to people the jungle instead of being free to swing through the trees. Towards the end of the first version the sexual imagery of a marriage is used to describe the creative process as one in which the author draws the curtain and sinks into oblivion. While the male and female halves of his brain mate, he may look at stars, pull the petals from a rose or watch swans. (The pronouns are Woolf's.) The imagery recurs again at the end of the fifth chapter, as it does just before the conclusion in *A Room of One's Own*.

The street scene of a young couple meeting also begins the second draft plan of the soul's male and female powers. The narrator turns to books by living authors, identified as Messrs A, B, C and D, to try out her theories on men's writing. She begins by noting with some irony that despite all their advantages, men write books that lack the power of suggestion. A self-centred male's novel is mentioned, then the work of Kipling and Galsworthy, before Woolf begins the section again, this time referring to Coleridge and the androgynous mind of Shakespeare. After the suffrage campaign is identified as the cause of modern sexual self-consciousness, the text takes up again the ego-phallic novel of an author identified as Mr A. The reworked account is essentially that of *A Room of One's Own*, including allusions once more to Victorian poetry; the characters of the novel are not named, however, and the speaker's confession of boredom is more defensive. In his review of *A Room of One's Own*, MacCarthy thought the novelist was a gifted contemporary and clearly recognisable under his initial. Woolf, writing to express her pleasure at the review, asked if he meant D. H. Lawrence, and added, 'He was not in my upper mind; but no doubt was in the lower' (*Letters*, IV, 130). Just who, if anyone, might have been in her upper mind she does not say. (Lawrence's *Lady Chatterley's Lover* had been privately printed in Italy in 1928, and at the end of the year his old friend S. S. Koteliansky told Woolf, who had probably not read the novel, that it was disgusting (*Diary*, III, 217).)

After referring to the critic Mr B, whoever he may be, the narrator of *Women & Fiction* moves on to Mr C, who turns out to be Churchill. She feels crushed by the furniture of his rhetoric – the size of the sentences, the weight of the metaphors. Victorian preachers were less vociferous. Works by Galsworthy and Kipling are criticised next, and in more detail than in *A Room of One's Own*. Their purely masculine values bore her horribly and thoughts of Mussolini's Italy follow. A list of androgynous and masculine writers, to be discussed in *A Room of One's Own*, is jotted down on the back of a manuscript page at this point. Then Woolf suggests again that the cause of all this literary cock-a-doodling lies in the work of reformers like the founder of Girton. (In *A Room of One's Own* she blames no individuals.) This leads once more to the narrator's blank page headed 'Women & Fiction', and for a dozen lines she tries to formulate what will eventually become the first sentence of the paper – that it is fatal for writers to think of their own sex. Once more she tries to imagine the violence as well as the calm, unselfconscious freedom of Shakespeare's state of mind while creating a scene in *Antony and Cleopatra* or writing a line like 'Daffodils that come before the swallow dares'. The marriage-night metaphor is used again to conclude the chapter.

The last chapter of *Women & Fiction*, entitled simply 'Conclusion', corresponds to what follows the dropping of the persona in Chapter 6 of *A Room of One's Own*. The manuscript's conclusion is briefer than that in the book, however. Woolf had jotted down notes for her conclusion in a reading notebook, used them at the start of her chapter, then cancelled them. Anticipated objections to her insistence on money and a room of one's own (the phrase first appears in the manuscript here) start with the material one rather than the comparative merit of the sexes, as in the book. The same quotation from Quiller-Couch is invoked as a reply to anticipated criticisms. Woolf began a reference to Florence Nightingale, crossed it out and then expanded it in the book. Justifying the necessity of women's books leads to the speaker's admittedly selfish complaint about the monotony of her modern reading and the need for books to influence each other.

The important discussion of what Woolf's narrator means by reality and unreality follows from the attempt to justify the existence of good books, and it differs significantly from *A Room of One's Own*. In *Women & Fiction* the narrator attempts twice to justify its indefinable intuitive basis before giving up and just illustrating what she means. As in *A Room of One's Own*, Woolf connects the experience of reality with the mystical moments that the speaker has experienced at Cambridge and in London. Masterpieces express reality too, and the list in the manuscript includes *Lycidas* and *War and Peace*, which is cancelled. Examples of the effects of unreality are more extended in *Women & Fiction*; they include muffling, swaddling, drugging, numbing and being knocked senseless or into torpor. There is no escaping unreality. Civilisation requires it but one can fight with pen, brush, piano or talk. We are close here to

Bernard's final efforts in *The Waves*. Nowhere else in Woolf's writing, except perhaps in the late 'A Sketch of the Past', does she attempt to describe so explicitly the mystical enmity of unreality that she associated with what she called her madness.

There are no perorations in *Women & Fiction*, no disagreeable quotations from men, no references to liking women and wondering again if a magistrate is in the cupboard. The women of the audience are called upon to get to work – not to write fashionable books, but to conspire, anonymously perhaps, to bring Shakespeare's sister back to life. This they can do if they are free to regard human beings in themselves, to look past Milton's bogey at reality. Such an effort, the speaker maintains, 'is worthwhile'. These are the last words of both *Women & Fiction* and *A Room of One's Own*.

THE REVISION OF *A ROOM OF ONE'S OWN*

Virginia Woolf finished *Women & Fiction* in London on 2 April 1929. The next day she went to Monks House to arrange for a new room of her own – two rooms in fact, a bedroom opening into the garden with a sitting or work room above – to be added onto Monks House. Ten days later she complained to her diary that *Women & Fiction* had been written too quickly and now she was toiling over revisions. But she thought it had conviction and predicted 'some sale' for this book of 'half talk half soliloquy' (*Diary*, III, 221). After a month of revising the manuscript as she typed it up, Woolf announced, again to her diary, that the final version was finished, but she was now uncertain whether it was a brilliant essay or a mass of opinions 'boiled down into a kind of jelly, which I have stained red as far as I can' (*Diary*, III, 223). Leonard was to read it after tea. But still the process of revising continued.

The revisions of *A Room of One's Own* were apparently made while Woolf was trying once again to finish 'Phases of Fiction'. (In the reading notebook that contains the page of notes for the conclusion of *Women & Fiction* Woolf actually started a page on 'Phases of Fiction' under the heading 'Women & Fiction' then struck it out.) She was trying to complete the rewriting of this other book on fiction even as it was being serialised in America. In her letters she was calling it her dullest and most hated book. At one point in its writing Woolf jotted down the final title for *A Room of One's*

Own and a new opening that emphasised the speaker's train of thought.

Woolf was dismayed when Harcourt Brace suggested in the middle of May that 'Phases of Fiction' be published in the autumn of 1929 and *Women & Fiction*, as it was still being called, kept over until the following spring (*Diary*, III, 227). On 16 May, however, Leonard wrote firmly to Donald Brace in an unpublished letter that his wife preferred to postpone 'Phases of Fiction' until the next year and bring out *Women & Fiction* under a different title in the autumn of 1929. This is the first mention of a change in title.

In the event, 'Phases of Fiction' was never published as a book. Woolf felt she had been wrongly pressured by her husband and Rylands into writing it for the Hogarth Press. Despite the title, 'Phases of Fiction' is far less historical than *A Room of One's Own*. Forster's aspects had been elements of the novel, but Woolf's phases were kinds of novelists classified as truth-tellers, romantics, character-mongers, comedians, psychologists, satirists, fantastics and finally poets. Some women writers are discussed – Radcliffe, Austen, Eliot, Emily Brontë – but few of the novelists considered really fit into their categories. Woolf's phases also fail to meet her objections to Forster's *Aspects of the Novel*, for there is little analysis of the art of fiction in them. Forster had argued in the introduction to his Cambridge lectures that the novel was a mirror unaffected by such things as the women's movement because subject matter had nothing to do with the mirror's acquiring a new coating of sensitiveness. He amusingly imagined all the novelists writing their novels together timelessly in the Reading Room of the British Museum. In the book that Woolf developed from her Cambridge lectures, however, women are depicted as writing their novels in parlours or bed-sitting rooms. The British Museum is where the speaker goes to find out why women are poor and why men are angry. *A Room of One's Own* is, in its way, a more direct and effective response to *Aspects of the Novel* than 'Phases of Fiction' was.

Sometime after Leonard Woolf wrote to put off the publication of 'Phases of Fiction' as a book, Virginia sent Harcourt Brace the typescript entitled *A Room of One's Own* now in the Monks House Papers at Sussex. Just how hard she had toiled to revise *Women & Fiction* into *A Room of One's Own* can be shown through a brief chapter by chapter comparison of the typescript with the manuscripts of *Women & Fiction* and also with the published book. Much of the typescript is identical with this final version, but there are also numerous, significant holograph additions and cancellations. Some of the chapter divisions of the typescript are still tentative, and a few pages present overlapping passages. Even at the typescript stage, *A Room of One's Own* was still in the process of composition.

The most obvious difference between the manuscript and the typescript is, of course, the new title's emphasis on the work's principal symbol. In Chapter 1, still undesignated as such, Woolf incorporates into her typescript the new opening and reworks the speaker's novelistic solution to the problems of lecturing on women and fiction. The frame story of the three days (revised to two in the book) that preceded the Cambridge paper is established, the image of the pedlar dropped and some of the Cambridge names are disguised, including Jane Harrison's which is reduced to her initials. Footnotes are added to document the history of women's colleges. One interesting addition is the passage on how childraising makes it impossible for women like Mary Seton's mother to acquire the kinds of fortunes men have amassed or inherited. The revised first chapter ends with a recapitulation of the day's incidents.

In revising the second chapter of *Women & Fiction*, Virginia Woolf introduced a comparison of research with the aloe that flowers once in a hundred years, and this harkens back to a similar comparison of the plant with a don's life in her sketch 'A Society'. The descriptions of the kind of men who attend to women and of the student working next to the narrator have not been muted in her revisions. Footnotes are added again for sources on men's opinions of women, and some of the literary allusions are dropped, as is the description of the cooking in the restaurant where the speaker has lunch. Also deleted is the digression on male bores. But Woolf retained the Asian tribe of women whose achievements rivalled those of Shakespeare and Einstein. She cut it only when revising the typescript for the book. In the typescript Mary Beton is given now as the aunt's name that is also the speaker's. Another addition to the manuscript involves Desmond MacCarthy again. About a month before she gave her Cambridge papers, Woolf listened to MacCarthy expressing his irritation at Rebecca West's saying that men were snobs. She retorted by criticising his condescension in *Life and Letters* about the limitations of women novelists (*Diary*, III, 195). How the later remark was worked into *Women & Fiction* has been discussed, but now in her revisions Woolf took up the earlier comment, included a description of West as 'arrant feminist', and then ascribed it all to 'Z, most humane, most modest of men' (*Room*, p. 53). The remark is introduced again at the revised opening of Chapter 4. Woolf also revised the account of male acquisitiveness, adding an observation on how large groups of people are driven by instincts beyond their control. (This, incidentally, was one of the central tenets of Leonard Woolf's political theory.) At the end of the typescript's second chapter Virginia Woolf resolves the chaos and terror of the London machine into a fiery fabric with flashing eyes; in the book it is defined further as a hot-breathed tawny monster.

Chapter 3 of the typescript is quite close to the final version of *A Room of One's Own*. The details of Mary Arden's life are worked into Judith Shakespeare's. A comparison of the artist to a jar-carrier is omitted, the portrait of Oscar Browning developed more astringently, an allusion to Lady Bessborough brought into the text from the back of a page, and a collection of opinions on male superiority called cock-a-doodle-dum is imagined. The beginning of Chapter 4, which is missing from *Women & Fiction*, starts in the middle of a page, rather than at the head of it, as the second chapter had. Woolf's continuing uncertainty about chapter divisions reappears at the end of the next chapter.

The revised discussions of women writers in Chapter 4 are more detailed, especially in the analysis of *Jane Eyre*. Additional references to other writers appear. An allusion to Mary Wollstonecraft is dropped, but the significance of Dorothy Osborne's letters is developed. There is no indication in the typescript of the gap which is to be found in the Fitzwilliam manuscript at the point where nineteenth-century women and fiction begin to be considered. The prevalence of masculine values is emphasised, and then MacCarthy on the limitations of female novelists is brought in and criticised together with another quotation, from T. S. Eliot's *New Criterion*, in which the reviewer of Dorothy Wellesley's *Matrix* (in the Hogarth Living Poets series) asserts that a metaphysical obsession is particularly dangerous in a woman. From this Woolf turns to the discussion of men's and women's sentences, giving holograph examples of both in the typescript. The woman's sentence, taken from *Pride and Prejudice*, was deleted from the final version of *A Room of One's Own*. At the end of the chapter Woolf reworked in her own hand the remarks on the future form of women's writing.

That Virginia Woolf had not yet sorted out the organisation of the book in her typescript is apparent from the brevity of Chapter 5 and the confusion over the numbering of Chapter 6. The fifth chapter is only five pages long. It begins with the various kinds of books which modern women write (she later included Vernon Lee on aesthetics), then suddenly veers into a fantasy on Florence Nightingale that exists only in the typescript. There is nothing like it in *Women & Fiction*. In her best *Orlando* manner, Woolf imagines a shell from the Crimean War crashing through the drawing room door of Nightingale's house; out steps the lady with a lamp, which marks the end of women's servitude. Quotations from Nightingale's *Cassandra* follow. Harriet Martineau is mentioned, and then Woolf brings in the anecdote from the lives of Davies and Smith that she had used in *Women & Fiction* when beginning to discuss modern women's books. There the chapter ends.

Two chapters 6 are to be found in the typescript of *A Room of One's Own*. In the first Woolf's speaker continues, as in the fifth chapter of the final version, her discussion of living writers by analysing Mary Carmichael's novel. Now called 'Life's Adventure', the novel also has named characters and a style that fears sentimentality and breaks the sequence like a switchback railway (instead of the earlier tossing boat). The satire of realistic fiction in the manuscript is removed, and the reaction to Chloe's liking Olivia changed. Woolf also adds to the discussion of women's friendship in fiction a reference to Meredith's *Diana of the Crossways*. But no indication is to be found in the typescript of the discontinuity between the end of the Monks House and the beginning of the second part of the Fitzwilliam manuscripts. There is, as well, considerable evidence of Woolf's rewriting in the typescript. The speaker now distinguishes between the naturalist and contemplative species of novelist. She criticises the multiplication of books on Napoleon, Keats and Milton, while the lives of obscure women go unrecorded. Woolf also added a passage about the spot in the back of the head that only the opposite sex can describe. References to Thackeray and Flaubert are reworked and new allusions made to Juvenal and Strindberg.

The second Chapter 6 of the typescript corresponds to the sixth chapter in the book, yet the substantial differences between them indicate the degree to which Woolf would revise her typescript again for the final printed version of *A Room of One's Own*. The crucial scene of the young couple getting into a taxi is more succinctly described in the typescript, and to it Woolf added a remark about the union of men and women making for the greatest happiness. She eliminates the passage on the primeval woman and confines the marriage-night metaphor of creation to the end of the chapter. Her theory about the mind's unity becomes the familiar one of *A Room of One's Own*, except for the retention of the botanical term 'gunandros' as a companion for 'androgynous'. The remainder of the chapter's first part, where the theory of androgyny is tested on some modern men's books, is quite different in detail from both the manuscript and the published book. Mr A, for example is referred to as a descendant of Oscar Browning, and his female characters are described not only as boneless but also as 'jelly fish adapted to his lust'. Churchill is reduced to his initial; the ridicule of his rhetoric now likens his metaphors to stuffed Wagnerian ravens and his ideas to poor little things rigged up in rouge and brocade – all of which she then drops again from the book. Another passage follows in the typescript describing a banquet at which the narrator wanted to shout the praises of unknown women in response to the Prince of Wales's extolling of fishermen. Woolf revised the more extended criticism of Galsworthy's Forsyte books in the typescript before finally cutting it from her book. She retouches the description of Fascist Italy and works into the text from the margin the list of androgynous and unandrogynous writers, to which a comment on Shelley's sexlessness is added. Also revised before being cut is a description of the violent state of mind that Shakespeare's composition of *Antony and Cleopatra* must have involved.

A line in the typescript separates these discussions from the conclusions that Virginia Woolf now brought in from the last chapter of *Women & Fiction*. Only later in revising the typescript for the book did she accomplish the transition by abandoning her narrative persona. The conclusions of the typescript nevertheless differ significantly from those of the manuscript. Woolf crossed out a beginning that defended the symbolism of money and rooms by citing Quiller-Couch on the material conditions required for the writing of poetry. In her second attempt she moved closer to the book by recapping the episodes of the previous few days. She added a scornful criticism of the comparative merits of the sexes before coming to the Quiller-Couch quotation again, and after it made an allusion to Florence Nightingale. In defending the value of good books, she altered the description of reality, which she refuses to define; she gives instead more examples of it but deletes the illustrations of unreality in *Women & Fiction*.

In the typescript Woolf introduces the peroration called for by the conventions of male eloquence, and then evades it by urging her audience simply to think of things in themselves. She does not stop with an emphasis on ends, the means to which are £500 and a room of one's own, but goes on to remark in the typescript that current writing calls for something very unpleasant when a woman addresses women. Another joking allusion is made to the magistrate of *The Well of Loneliness* trial who may be yet lurking in a cupboard. And then one more ironic quotation, which Woolf had used before in her writing, is given about how women will cease to be necessary when children cease to be wanted. The raising of these topics at the end of *A Room of One's Own* makes its criticism of the patriarchy's sexual standards stronger than that in *Women & Fiction*. Indeed there is little in the manuscripts to suggest that Woolf is softening or censoring her text to make it more acceptable to male readers, as is sometimes claimed about her revisions. At last, after urging young women on to the next stage in their sex's career, Woolf returns once more to fiction for the final invoking of Shakespeare's sister.

During the last two weeks of June 1929, Woolf worked at correcting what must have been the typescript of 'that much corrected book, Women & Fiction' (*Diary*, III, 237). It is odd that she should revert to its original title on the same day – 30 June – that she signed the contract for *A Room of One's Own* with Harcourt Brace (*Letters*, IV, 71). Two days later Woolf began the first draft of *The Waves*.

The proofs for *A Room of One's Own*, which allowed more opportunity for change, were corrected in July and August. They do not appear to have survived, but Woolf's correspondence indicates that she had to send Harcourt Brace revised proofs containing additional alterations in the first two chapters or so (*Letters*, IV, 76). On 19 August, more than four months after finishing her manuscript, she opened her diary to record 'the blessed fact that for good or bad I have just set the last correction to Women & Fiction, or a Room of One's Own. I shall never read it again I suppose. Good or bad? Has an uneasy life in it I think: you feel the creature arching its back & galloping on, though as usual much is watery & flimsy & pitched in too high a voice' (*Diary*, III, 241–2). The next day she expressed her delight with Vanessa Bell's cover which showed a view though a curtained arch or window of a room with a clock on the mantle. The clock's hands form a 'V', and Woolf thought that would cause a stir (*Letters*, IV, 81). The published dust-jacket of the Hogarth Press first edition also has a blurb describing *A Room of One's Own*. From what is known about the operations of the Hogarth Press, it is reasonable to assume that this description of the book has authorial status. Woolf would continue to comment publicly and privately on the book and its reception, but the summary on the dust-jacket can be given here as, in a sense, the last act of the book's composition. Its opening comment's generic paradox, the description of the author as an outsider, the emphasis on the relation of the sexes and hopeful forecast of a freer future for women are all completely characteristic of Woolf's writing and thought.

> This essay, which is largely fictitious, is based upon the visit of an outsider to a university and expresses the thoughts suggested by a comparison between the different standards of luxury at a man's college and at a woman's. This leads to a sketch of women's circumstances in the past, and the effect of those circumstances upon their writing. The conditions that are favourable to imaginative work are discussed, including the right relation of the sexes. Finally an attempt is made to outline the present state of affairs and to forecast what effect comparative freedom and independence will have upon women's artistic work in the future.

7 Leonard and Virginia Woolf at the Hogarth Press

I

The history of Leonard and Virginia Woolf's Hogarth Press is well documented. There is a fine checklist by Howard Woolmer of the 525 books that the Press published over a period of thirty years, and a detailed recent history of the Press has been written by J. H. Willis, Jr. John Lehmann, who was a manager and eventually a partner in the Hogarth Press, has told his story in several books; the title of the last – *Thrown to the Woolves* – sums up his view of the experience. Others have reminisced about their time working for Leonard and Virginia. But the best sources for our knowledge of the Press are Leonard Woolf's autobiographies which provide the basic information, supplemented by catalogues, accounts, correspondence and other records of the Press that have survived, together with the dozen volumes of Virginia Woolf's diaries and letters. These various documents show certain aspects of the Hogarth Press that can contribute to British Studies and the history of the book as well as to our understanding of the work of Virginia Woolf and of the Bloomsbury Group. Before considering some of the most interesting of these aspects, however, it is useful to review briefly the development of the Hogarth Press.

In March 1917, Leonard, who was thirty-seven, and Virginia, who was two years younger, bought a small hand press, some type and the other paraphernalia of printing for £19 5s 5d (Leonard kept very detailed accounts). That is about us US $750 today. They had decided several years before to learn the art of printing. According to Leonard this was to be a recreation to take Virginia's mind off her writing. According to Virginia, however, printing was to deflect the influence of the Fabian socialists Beatrice and Sidney Webb on Leonard.

The Woolfs had originally wanted to take a course in printing but discovered, as Leonard said, 'two middle-aged, middle-class persons' were ineligible because of union rules. So with the help of a friendly neighbourhood printer Virginia and Leonard Woolf brought out in July 1917, Publication No. 1 of the Hogarth Press, which consisted of two stories, Virginia's well-known 'The Mark on the Wall' and Leonard's now forgotten 'Three Jews'. Virginia set most of the type while Leonard did the machining. A congenital tremor of his hands that had kept him out of the First World War also prevented him from doing much of the typesetting, though he did do some. The pamphlet, which had four woodcuts by Carrington and a cover of Japanese paper, was sold by subscription, this method of distribution being a consequence of perhaps the most important early aim of the Hogarth Press: to print stories or poems that commercial publishers would not consider doing. The Hogarth Press thus began, we might say today, as an alternative press.

Profit on *Two Stories* was just over £7 or a little less than $150 today. Word of what the Woolfs were doing quickly got around, and Katherine Mansfield, a virtually unknown writer at this time, offered her important story *Prelude*. It turned out to be too big a job, however, and after the Woolfs set the type it had to be machined by their neighbourhood printer. Already with their second publication, then, Leonard and Virginia Woolf were forced beyond printing the Hogarth Press publications entirely by themselves. And before they had proceeded very far with Mansfield's story, they were brought the poems of Leonard Woolf's brother Cecil, who had been killed in action. These were privately printed and not even listed among the Hogarth publications. The distinction is revealing, for the Hogarth Press was never intended by the Woolfs to be a private press in this sense, and Cecil Woolf's poems was the only work the Hogarth Press printed privately.

Also while printing Mansfield the Woolfs were approached, at Roger Fry's suggestion, by James Joyce's patron Harriet Shaw Weaver, who asked them to consider publishing the unfinished *Ulysses*. The Woolfs did not much like the first four chapters she left with them, which include Bloom's defecatory musings, but it was clearly a work worth publishing if they could get a printer to do it. The laws of the time made printers as well as publishers liable for obscene works, however, and the Woolfs knew they would not find a printer for it. *Ulysses* became, therefore, the first Hogarth Press rejection.

The Woolfs then printed Virginia's famous story *Kew Gardens* along with another work outside of Bloomsbury, T. S. Eliot's *Poems*. (It may be worth noting that apart from their own work the Woolfs did not publish anything by a member of the Bloomsbury Group until E. M. Forster's *The Story of a Siren* in 1920, a work Forster had written years before but had been unable to publish.) Eliot's *Poems* together with *Kew Gardens* were the first review copies the Woolfs sent out, and, when the *Times Literary Supplement* published a favourable notice of *Kew Gardens*, the Woolfs found themselves swamped with orders and had to have a commercial printer do a second edition. Once again, Leonard recalled, the Woolfs had fortuitously to abandon the original intention of the Hogarth Press to print small books themselves. But they still considered the Press a hobby, a part-time activity to be done in the afternoons after their mornings of writing.

Two years after they started, the Woolfs bought a larger press and in 1920 engaged a paid employee. They then produced their first avowedly commercial publication, a translation of Maxim Gorky's recollections of Tolstoy which sold very well. Other Russian translations followed. The Woolfs continued to offer their books through subscription, however, until 1923 – six years after the Press had begun – when they had become so succesful that the subscriber system was given up and the Woolfs, in Leonard's words, became 'more or less ordinary publishers selling our books mainly to booksellers at the usual discount'. Yet Leonard and Virginia were hardly becoming ordinary publishers in terms of making money. After paying authors twenty-five per cent of the gross profits, Leonard calculated the net profit of the Hogarth Press during its first four years at £90 or something under $1,500 today. This was possible because nothing was spent on overhead; the Woolfs ran the Press, including storage and distribution, from their home. While becoming ordinary, if not very profitable, publishers, who had professional printers doing their books that were then sold through bookshops, the Woolfs also continued to print books themselves until 1932. They hand-printed thirty-four in all, many of them poems, but some essays by the Woolfs, E. M. Forster and others. A number of the volumes of poetry were by forgotten poets, but not all, for they included work by Robert Graves, Herbert Read, John Crowe Ransom and Edwin Muir.

A crucial event in the evolution of the Hogarth Press was the publication of a full-length book in 1922, Virginia Woolf's first modernist novel, *Jacob's Room*, which was given a post-impressionist dust-jacket by Vanessa Bell. The book was printed in Scotland by R. & R. Clark, who continued to print Virginia's novels for the

Hogarth Press. The Press's profit from *Jacob's Room* was £42 4s 6d, or about $1,750 today. This was possible, Leonard Woolf noted, by having Virginia the publisher swindle Virginia the author – that is, she took part of the profits from the Press rather than a royalty. For her later books she was paid separately by Hogarth and by Harcourt Brace and Company, which published the American editions of her books.

As the Hogarth Press demanded more of their time – manuscripts had been pouring in since the beginning of the 1920s – the Woolfs began to ask periodically if they wanted to continue with the Press. In 1922, just five years after they had started with their hand press, they were briefly tempted by an offer from William Heinemann Ltd to take over the management of the Press, leaving the Woolfs with editorial autonomy. But Leonard and Virginia declined, fearing what would happen if they lost control of their enterprise. The demands of the Press were temporarily resolved by a series of young men and women who served as managing assistants.

In 1923 the Press expanded even farther, publishing thirteen books instead of the previous year's six. The total capital invested in the Hogarth Press rose to £135 2s 3d (or more than $4,000 today). A bigger press was put in the dining room where the other had been, until the Woolfs were warned it might fall through the floor into the kitchen below, so it had to be moved to the larder. 'We printed in the larder', Leonard Woolf wrote in his autobiography, 'bound books in the dining room, interviewed printers, binders, and authors in a sitting room.' Among the books printed by the Woolfs in 1923 was that most famous of English modernist works, T. S. Eliot's *The Waste Land*, which Virginia set herself. What is the impact, one might wonder, on an author of a poem she not only reads but also sets up in type? *The Waste Land* was originally advertised in the Hogarth Press catalogue as a long poem with notes and an introduction. Eliot commented that the notes had to be expanded because the poem was inconveniently short for printing, but of the intriguing introduction promised in the Hogarth catalogue, nothing more seems to be known.

In 1924 the Woolfs moved back to Bloomsbury, setting up the Hogarth Press in the basement of their home in Tavistock Square. Instead of just literature the Press now began to publish psychiatric and political works including Leonard's own books. (They also published in 1925 *Turbott Wolfe*, the first novel of a young, unknown South African, William Plomer; the political and racial outrage it stirred up influenced the development of South African literature.) The most popular of the political offerings were pamphlets by the Woolfs' Bloomsbury friend, John Maynard Keynes. One of the chief forms of publication by the Hogarth Press was the political or literary pamphlet. Booksellers did not like them, but the Hogarth Press kept trying to advance this literary form. The Woolfs started the series of Hogarth Essay pamphlets in 1924 with Virginia Woolf's manifesto *Mr. Bennett and Mrs. Brown*. Essays by Leonard Woolf, Roger Fry, T. S. Eliot, Gertrude Stein and others followed. Nearly twenty different series were published in all, including a Hogarth Living Poets sequence that was subsidised by Yeats's friend, the poet Dorothy Wellesley. Though not nearly as remarkable as the poets Eliot was now publishing with his firm of Faber and Faber, the Living Poets did include Frances Cornford, Robinson Jeffers, Vita Sackville-West, C. Day Lewis and Edward Arlington Robinson.

More important for the success of the Press than its political and literary pamphlets or its various series was the taking over of the International Psychoanalytic Library at James Strachey's suggestion in 1924. This entailed the publication of Freud's collected papers in four volumes. Eventually, *The Standard Edition of the Complete Psychological Works of Sigmund Freud,* translated from the German under the General Editorship of James Strachey, was published in twenty-three volumes. The Freud edition and the works of Virginia Woolf were the most outstanding contributions of the Hogarth Press to modern culture. But at the time there were dangers involved. Leonard Woolf was warned against publishing Freud and other psychoanalytic works: they would be unprofitable and there was the risk of being prosecuted under the obscenity laws. Woolf took the chance, invested £200 (over $7,000 now) for books that sold steadily and were more profitable than anything else except the writings of the Press's co-owner.

The big success of *Orlando* in 1928 was another turning point in the careers of Virginia Woolf and therefore the Hogarth Press. Then the Woolfs' first best-seller, Vita Sackville-West's *The Edwardians*, was published in 1930; it sold 30,000 copies. During the decade of the 1930s, the Hogarth Press was earning the Woolfs an average yearly income more than £1000 each (around $20,000 each today). The Woolfs were now employing three typists, book-keepers or managing assistants and publishing twenty to thirty books a year that sold anywhere from 150 copies to Sackville-West's 30,000. Yet they continued to agonise over the Press's future. They still wanted to be just part-time publishers. The aim of publishing only worthwhile books appears to have been gradually modified. By 1933 the Press had lost its spring, Virginia Woolf felt, and she wanted to return to the old ideals with which they started in 1917. The assistants who had come to the Press to help the Woolfs manage it and maybe even become partners had all left. The latest was John Lehmann.

Unlike the others, Lehmann had some capital and was interested in becoming a professional publisher. But after two years as manager he left abruptly for Germany, angering the Woolfs. Yet in those years, Leonard noted, Lehmann brought to the Press some of his generation's best writers. In 1932, for example, Lehmann published the anthology *New Signatures*. Regarded as a kind of manifesto for the poets of the 1930s, it included poems by Lehmann, W. H. Auden, Julian Bell, C. Day Lewis, Richard Eberhart, William Empson and Stephen Spender. Lehmann also introduced to the Press in 1932 the work of Christopher Isherwood, the most important novelist after Virginia Woolf that Hogarth would publish in the thirties.

Lehmann reappeared and bought Virginia Woolf's half-ownership of the press in 1938 for £3000 (say $60,000 today). Lehmann was to run the Press as managing partner, while Leonard devoted about a quarter of his time to the publishing. The Press now employed seven assistants. Virginia remained, of course, as a Hogarth Press author and adviser, continuing to read manuscripts. It was also in 1938 that the Hogarth Press employed a salaried woman who was the first in the trade to sell their books to bookshops. Before then the Woolfs travelled with the books themselves or had their various assistants do so.

John Lehmann continued to bring new authors and works to the Press, including the biannual *New Writing*. Then the war changed the Press completely. It was bombed out of Mecklenburgh Square, where the Woolfs had moved the year before, and transferred to the country location of one of the Press's printers. Paper rationing seriously curtailed the Press's offerings. There had been some disagreements – occasionally resolved by Virginia – between Leonard and John over what to publish (each partner had a veto). With Virginia's death in 1941, the incompatibilities of the two partners' literary tastes increased, exacerbated by their political disagreements. John Lehmann hoped to develop the Press in various ways; Leonard Woolf was unconvinced that expansion was necessary or desirable. Finally in 1946 Lehmann offered to buy Woolf's share of the Press, but Leonard chose instead to buy him out rather than give up the Press. (In his posthumously published autobiography *The Journey Not the Arrival Matters*, Leonard Woolf wrote that Lehmann 'shares to some extent the common tendency to megalomania, and it was this which made him leave the Hogarth Press'. When Lehmann was shown the proofs of the volume, he insisted this passage be deleted and the current management of the Hogarth Press obliged.) Woolf was able to buy out his partner by selling Lehmann's half share to Chatto & Windus, which had a list similar in some respects to Hogarth's; they had published Lytton Strachey, Clive Bell and Roger Fry, for example. The Hogarth Press now became a limited company and a subsidiary of Chatto & Windus, while retaining its editorial independence under the supervision of Leonard. The Press was to remain independent until his death, which occurred in 1969, two years after the Press's fiftieth anniversary. John Lehmann began his own publishing business, which lasted only seven years, to Woolf's grim satisfaction. The Hogarth Press imprint remains today, though its distinctive wolf's head logos are no longer used. The Press itself, however, was eventually swallowed up along with Chatto & Windus, Jonathan Cape (who tried for years to buy out Hogarth) and various other publishers by the conglomerate called Random House UK.

II

I have been recounting a familiar story in order to illustrate certain principles and procedures of the Hogarth Press's history that illuminate the work of Virginia Woolf and the Bloomsbury Group as well as the history of the book in modern English literature. I shall first mention two predecessors that influenced the development of the Hogarth Press. Then I want to consider how the Press was shaped by what today we might call the management style of the Woolfs, especially Leonard, who was responsible for the daily operation of the Press. Finally I wish to say something about the implications of the Hogarth Press for Virginia Woolf's writing.

The Woolf's decision to start their own Press was influenced positively and negatively, I think, by two precursors. The first was the publishing firm that Virginia's half-brother started when she was sixteen. A great deal has been made about the effect of the Duckworth half-brothers, especially George, on Virginia Woolf's sexual development. The term 'incest' has been loosely used in some accounts, but it has been known for a long time that there was what we now recognise as sexual abuse of Vanessa and Virginia Stephen by the elder brother George. It might be argued, however, that the younger, Gerald, was the more important figure in Virginia's life. It was Gerald Duckworth, she remembered in a late memoir, who traumatically explored her genitals when she was a child. It was also Gerald to whom Virginia Woolf later offered her first two novels.

Being Leslie Stephen's stepson had obvious advantages when it came to starting up a publishing firm. Among the books published by Gerald Duckworth in his first year were works by Stephen himself (whom the Hogarth Press would also later publish), by Stephen's friend Henry James and by others such as Strindberg and Galsworthy. Books by W. H. Hudson, Charles M. Doughty, W. H. Davies and Hilaire Belloc followed, as well as translations of Ibsen, Gorky and Chekhov's stories (which were unknown in England at the time). Duckworth also started an influential series of books on art. Later writers published by him included Ford Madox Hueffer, D. H. Lawrence and Dorothy Richardson. Duckworth's distinguished list of modern books was largely owing to a publisher's reader of genius, Edward Garnett. But Gerald Duckworth and Co. Ltd also published Elinor Glyn's forgettable but immensely popular romantic novels of passion on tiger-skin rugs. (It was rumoured in the firm that she read each of her new novels to Gerald in the conservatory after lunch.) In later years the novelist Anthony Powell worked for Duckworth and encouraged the firm to publish Ronald Firbank, Evelyn Waugh and the Sitwells. Powell thought it extraordinary that Duckworth had become a publisher at all, for 'his interest in books anyway as a medium for reading, was as slender as that of any man I have ever encountered...'. Gerald Duckworth died in 1937, but his firm has continued as an independent publisher, controlled, they say, by their editors instead of their accountants.

The influence of Duckworth's firm on the development of the Hogarth Press could be viewed as both inspiring and depressing. As an inspiration, Virginia's half-brother had demonstrated what could be done by someone with some capital but little interest in books as a medium of reading. If Gerald Duckworth could start such a successful publishing business, the Woolfs could, and without the assistance of Elinor Glyns. Duckworth's Russian translations showed what kinds of modern things one might publish. As Virginia Woolf's own publisher, however, Gerald Duckworth exerted a depressing effect on her. To have to submit to Gerald again, and then wait for his approval, was there no way of avoiding this? It is clear that among the most important reasons for the Hogarth Press was the publication of Virginia Woolf's work. Wondering if the Press should be given up in 1926, the year after it had published *The Common Reader* and *Mrs. Dalloway*, Virginia Woolf wrote revealingly in her diary, 'speaking selfishly it has served my turn: given me a chance of writing off my own bat', and she doubted if publishers like Heinemann or Cape would now intimidate her. To be creatively free of intimidation, Virginia Woolf published her own books. Her third novel, *Jacob's Room*, the first that Hogarth printed, was much more experimental than the previous two published by Duckworth. The novel was in fact under option to Duckworth, but he generously released it to Hogarth and later allowed them to take over Virginia's two earlier novels as well, which lost his firm some considerable profit.

But the significance for Virginia Woof of having her own press was not only a matter of personal antipathy or critical inhibitions. It was also clearly connected with her feminism, as she indicated in her manifesto of 1938, *Three Guineas*. Explaining to a woman of some economic independence how she might put into practice her opinions on protecting culture and intellectual liberty, the narrator tells her not to dream but consider the facts of the actual world:

> the private printing press is an actual fact, and not beyond the reach of a moderate income. Typewriters and duplicators are actual facts and even cheaper. By using these cheap and so far unforbidden instruments you can at once rid yourself of the pressure of boards, policies and editors. They will speak your own mind, in your own words, at your own time, at your own length, at your own bidding. And that, we are agreed, is our definition of 'intellectual liberty'.

A more immediate and influential predecessor of the Hogarth Press was not a press but a workshop – the Omega Workshops that Roger Fry started after his revolutionary exhibitions of post-impressionist paintings in 1910 and 1912. Around the time the Woolfs were thinking of learning to print, Fry issued the first of four small books illustrated with woodcuts from the Omega Workshops. All were designed but not printed in the Workshops. The last, a book of woodcuts, was originally to be published by the Hogarth Press, but disagreements between Leonard Woolf and Vanessa Bell over who would have final control of the book led to the Omega Workshops printing the book. It is, of course, not coincidental that the Woolfs used woodcuts in the early publications of the Hogarth Press, or that they went to considerable trouble with all their hand-printed books to find unusual coloured papers for covers, which started a fashion in English publishing. Bright colours were characteristic of much post-impressionist art, and one of the two main purposes of the Omega Workshops was to bring post-impressionism into interior decoration, the other aim being to subsidise young artists by paying them to do part-time anonymous work at various crafts. A parallel with Virginia Woolf's working at the craft of printing as a relief from her art of writing has been noticed.

The inspiration of the Omega Workshops for the Hogarth Press is more than just a matter of woodcuts and decorative paper. The aesthetics of Fry and the Omega were to a considerable degree those of Bloomsbury and the Woolfs. The connection of Fry's Workshops with the English Arts and Crafts Movement of William Morris and others in the latter part of the nineteenth century has frequently been mentioned. Fry and his friends concurred with some of the aims of the Movement but not with its nostalgia for the past – which Fry characterised as lunatic medievalism. Fry objected, as Morris did, to the aesthetic hierarchy that divorced fine from decorative art; both wanted to blend the fine and decorative arts and bring them to bear on daily life. Yet Fry had no socialist intentions, and he did not share Morris's antipathy toward the use of machines in art. He laughed at the affectations of craft in the Movement. Fry wanted to introduce spontaneity into the work of the Omega as well as the sense of formal design that post-impressionism had emphasised. With the Omega Fry hoped to produce brightly designed rooms, useful furniture and serviceable pottery. But Fry disliked the English worship of the mechanically perfect finish. The Omega artists were not as a whole very interested in becoming as skilled in their crafts as those in the Arts and Crafts Movement. The instability of Omega furniture has been exaggerated, but there is a sense in which Fry would have understood what Ralph Vaughan Williams meant when he once said about making music that anything worth doing was worth doing badly.

One important parallel of the Omega Workshops and the Hogarth Press appears in the Woolfs' aim to print literary works of art by young writers that could not be published in the regular way, just as the Omega Workshops had employed young artists who had not yet established themselves. Neither the Press nor the Omega was created for profit. The Hogarth Press refused to publish something just because it would sell. The Workshop's rejection of Arts and Crafts nostalgia for past art may be also be reflected in the refusal of the Woolfs to republish classics, as they said in a fifth-anniversary statement of the Press in 1922. In its avoiding highly crafted luxurious products and emphasising utility, attractiveness and spontaneity, the Omega's intention was analogous to the Hogarth Press's plan not to 'embellish our books beyond what is necessary for ease of reading and decency of appearance'. The aim was 'cheapness and adequacy' rather than 'high prices and typographical splendour', the fifth-anniversary proclamation of the Press continued. Leonard Woolf restated in his autobiography the Woolfs' purpose not to make the Hogarth Press into the kind of private press that published finely printed books which, he said,

> are meant not to be read, but to be looked at. We were interested primarily in the immaterial inside of a book, what the author had to say and how he said it; we had drifted into the business with the idea of publishing things which the commercial publisher could not or would not publish. We wanted our books to 'look nice' and we had our own views of what nice looks in a book would be, but neither of us was interested in fine printing and fine binding. We also disliked the refinement and preciosity which are too often a kind of fungoid growth which culture breeds upon art and literature....

In particular, Leonard went on, they did not want the Hogarth Press to turn into one like Kelmscott or Nonesuch, admirable though each was in its own way. This intention is fundamental to understanding the particular nature of the Hogarth Press. The 'immaterial' content of a book was always more important than its printed form. The casualness and lack of finish in some of their printing was deliberate. In 1930 Virginia Woolf wrote a mock letter to an anonymous Hogarth customer about her pamphlet *On Being Ill*, which the Woolfs printed themselves. 'I agree that the colour is uneven, the letters are not always clear, the spacing inaccurate, and the word "campion" should read "companion".' But, she explained, as they were not allowed to learn printing, it remained 'a hobby carried on in the basement of a London house...in the intervals of lives that are otherwise engaged'. Furthermore, her unsatisfied customer could sell his or her copy for more than it cost because the edition was over subscribed.

The Hogarth Press did, however, produce some finely printed books – Vanessa Bell's decorated edition of Virginia's *Kew Gardens* is one example, Clive Bell's poem *The Legend of Monte Della Sibilla*, illustrated by Vanessa and Duncan Grant, is another. And of course there are the post-impressionist dust-jackets that Vanessa Bell designed for her sister's novels and other books published by the Hogarth Press. But the Woolfs' indifference to some aspects of the craft of printing led to a disagreement between them and the Bloomsbury artists Vanessa Bell and Duncan Grant. Two early Hogarth ghosts (books announced but not published) are volumes of original drawings by Vanessa Bell and Duncan Grant, although the Press did publish a handsome book of Fry's woodcuts.

III

In the end of the Hogarth Press was more successful than the Omega Workshops, which lasted from 1913 to 1919. Fry was not much interested in marketing his products, and the war further hurt the Workshop's chances of survival. The Omega had originally announced, incidentally, that Leonard Woolf, who had served as secretary to the second post-impressionist exhibition, would help with the business side of the Omega, but there is no evidence he ever did. It might have been better for Fry if he had, for it was Woolf's acumen and determination that kept the Hogarth Press from going the way of so many other similar enterprises. Commentators on the Hogarth Press observe from time to time that it is not really very difficult to start a new press if you have young writers willing to contribute like Virginia Woolf, Katherine Mansfield and T. S. Eliot. There is no doubt that the Hogarth Press had extraordinary good fortune in the quality of their early publications, but it was not simply a question of whom one knew. Katherine Mansfield and Middleton Murry started their own press after they saw what the Woolfs were doing; they had some of the same friends and some others like D. H. Lawrence, but their endeavour went nowhere.

When Ralph Partridge, the first assistant of the Hogarth Press, left, he intended to set up a press with the backing of Lytton Strachey and other Bloomsbury friends, but this project never even got started. The success of the Hogarth Press depended on their contributors, of course, but equally essential was Leonard Woolf's highly individual conception of how to develop a publishing business. Because not enough attention has been paid to the practical, material conditions of publishing, Leonard Woolf's contribution to modern English culture has been insufficiently appreciated.

It is quite remarkable that the Woolfs started their Press with no experience in printing or publishing – and even more surprising, with no working capital. For a contrast there is the successful career of Jonathan Cape, who served for twenty years as a manager for Gerald Duckworth before founding his own firm three years after the Hogarth Press began, with a partner and £12,000 of capital. Leonard Woolf was able to make a go of the Hogarth Press, as he said again and again, because he had no overhead expenses and no staff. It was a delusion, he insisted, to think you had to have an organisation to be a successful publisher of, say, Freud's work. How did the Hogarth Press succeed without the normal structure of a publishing business? The answer lies in the paradox that the Woolfs were successful because they were not interested in the success of their Press.

For years the Woolfs refused to publish anything they did not think worth publishing for its own sake, even though it might make money. The Press was never to be a way of livelihood for either Virginia or Leonard. In terms of Bloomsbury values, which derived from the ethics of G. E. Moore, the Hogarth Press was an intrinsic activity rather than an instrumental one, something done because it was valuable in itself rather than being a means to something else such as making money. Leonard Woolf asserted repeatedly in his autobiographies that printing and publishing were to be only part-time activities. (And in this it resembles again the Omega Workshops, which were also never a full-time occupation for Fry or the other artists involved.) As a result of their determination to remain part-time printers and publishers, however, the Woolfs eventually found it necessary to employ someone to help them run the press. Growth became inevitable, but Leonard insisted on keeping the Press as small as he could. Only in this way, he said, could he steer the business between the Scylla of being taken over by Heinemann or whoever, and the Charybdis of bankruptcy from a too rapid expansion. It was over the issue of expansion more than anything else that Leonard Woolf and John Lehmann ended their partnership.

Leonard was able to keep the Hogarth Press small and manageable, he believed, because of his seven years' experience in the Ceylon Civil Service where he was eventually put in charge of 100,000 Sinhalese. It is pleasant to think of the Hogarth Press as a by-product of imperialism. Leonard Woolf was a rigorously efficient colonial administrator, and he carried this habit over to the Hogarth Press. He himself says he was allergic to fools. Because of the efficiency Leonard demanded of himself and his employees, more than a few of them found themselves acting foolishly. There are a number of stories about conflicts between Leonard Woolf and his assistants, such as the one (there are different variants) where he quarrels with his manager over his being late to work; their watches differ and eventually in a rage they hire a taxi and drive to where they can see Big Ben to determine whose watch is right. (Another version has Virginia Woolf poking her head around the corner in the midst of the argument and asking innocently what time it was.)

In addition to appearing as a tyrant of efficiency, Leonard Woolf has also been accused of being tight about money by Bloomsbury friends, John Lehmann and others associated with the Press. There is a genteel anti-Semitism in some of these remarks, but Leonard Woolf does seem to have carried economies pretty far at times. Visitors to both Tavistock Square and Monks House in Sussex were sometimes disconcerted to find galley proofs serving as toilet paper. Yet it is clear from the history of the Hogarth Press that Leonard did not care about making money. On the other hand he was damned if he was going to lose any, and that I believe is the key to the finances of the Hogarth Press. The Woolfs would publish what they thought was worth publishing – at least in the early years – but only if they did not lose money by it. When Gertrude Stein offered her 900-page manuscript of *The Making of Americans* to the Hogarth Press, for example, Leonard offered to publish it on a commission basis; Stein declined, but the Woolfs did publish her financially feasible pamphlet *Composition as Explanation*. Though the Hogarth Press never had a year without profit, some of them were very lean. From 1924 to 1930 the Press averaged a profit of around £180 – or two to three thousand dollars a year. After that it was more prosperous, bringing the Woolfs, as I said, about £1000 or $20,000 a year. As Willis points out in his history of the Hogarth

Press, none of the publishers comparable to Hogarth such as Jonathan Cape, Chatto & Windus, Bodley Head, Faber and Faber or Gollancz could have survived on the small profits that nourished the Hogarth Press.

Still there is a sense in which, despite Leonard Woolf's desire neither to make or to lose much money, the Hogarth Press cost Virginia Woolf something. She wrote to Ethel Smyth in 1931, 'publishers told me to write what they liked. I said no. I'll publish myself and write what I like. Which I did, and for many years, owing to lack of organisation travellers etc. lost much money thereby.' It was mainly in the 1920s that Virginia Woolf's books sold less than they might have with a more conventional publisher, assuming of course a conventional publisher would have taken them the way she wrote them. But it was a price Virginia was as glad as Leonard to pay for the freedom to write and publish as she wished, for she was no more interested in making money as a publisher than he was.

IV

The way in which Leonard and Virginia Woolf ran the Hogarth Press has other interesting ramifications besides profit for the works that they published. No overhead costs, no staff meant that the Press employed no publishers' readers, no designers or publicists, not even any editors. The Woolfs read or decided not to read almost all the manuscripts that were submitted. Occasionally when they disagreed or were uncertain they would ask someone like their friend the critic Raymond Mortimer for an opinion. (Poetry was the biggest problem and Leonard Woolf said if he were publishing in other times he might well have turned down Shakespeare and accepted the Victorian versifier Martin Tupper. When a friend complained to Virginia about the poetry they were publishing, she replied they could not manufacture genius and besides she should see the manuscripts they had refused.) For the books they printed themselves, the Woolfs controlled everything. In the midst of printing Mansfield's *Prelude*, for instance, Middleton Murry pointed out to the Woolfs that the running head was given incorrectly as 'The Prelude' rather than just 'Prelude'. This was then corrected, but only for the pages not yet printed! The earlier pages are headed 'The Prelude', the later ones just 'Prelude'. This was one way of controlling costs. Again, when Laura Riding's change in marital status required that her married name of Gottschalk now be deleted from the printed title page of her poem that the Woolfs were printing, Leonard in exasperation simply printed two thick (six point) black rules across her last name and let it stand rather than print the title page again. Not surprisingly, it was the last work of hers the Hogarth Press published. For books they published but did not print themselves, the Woolfs or their printers did whatever designing or editing was required.

No editors meant that the Hogarth Press books were in effect never edited. Leonard and Virginia would read the manuscript, make what minor changes were necessary, and then send it to the printer. There was no 'house-style' other than what the printers themselves imposed, and there does not seem to have been much of that. Manuscripts were not gone over carefully; they were accepted or rejected and that was it. No detailed criticism was offered. Leonard hated asking Hogarth Press authors for changes and seems to have done so only tentatively. (The publisher of his own two novels had required significant changes about which he was very unhappy.) When Vita Sackville-West's *The Edwardians* arrived, Virginia was so enthusiastic about it that Leonard sent the manuscript straight to the Scottish printers and read it only in proof. All he suggested was that Vita consider giving the chapters titles, which she did. Occasionally, however, Leonard Woolf's rare editorial advice was firmly rejected. In 1939 he wrote to a distinguished Austrian contributor to the Press who had submitted a book with a cumbersome title that 'from a publishing point of view it is, I am sure, a great mistake to have the long title, for in England many people will be frightened by the word monotheism. Would you, therefore, agree to its appearing under the shorter title?' So confident of the persuasiveness of his judgement was he that Leonard listed in his Hogarth Press catalogue a forthcoming book by Sigmund Freud entitled simply *Moses*. Freud, however, was not persuaded, and the book, of course, appeared under its original title *Moses and Monotheism*. It does not seem to have frightened away English readers.

The way the Hogarth Press was managed, largely by Leonard, has a direct bearing on the works of both the Woolfs. Leonard had suffered from other publishers more than Virginia. His book *Co-operation and the Future of Industry* was originally written for the Home University Library series in 1915 but the publishers failed to bring it out. After two years Woolf threatened to sue, the original publishers cancelled his contract, and the book finally appeared with another publisher three years after it had been completed. For Virginia the most important aspect of publishing her own books was the freedom, the unself-consciousness it gave her, as she said, of writing off her own bat. But publishing her own books did not mean that Virginia was completely free of the pressures publishers exert on their authors. Leonard and George Rylands, an early assistant at the Press, started a series of lectures on literature in 1927 and persuaded Virginia to write one called 'Phases of Fiction', partly in response to E. M. Forster's successful *Aspects of the Novel*. Her long essay was serialised in the United States and then announced for publication by Hogarth. She struggled with rewriting what she called her dullest and most hated book while writing another book on a similar subject, namely *A Room of One's Own*. Finally she decided that Rylands and her husband were wrong to push her into publishing the book, and 'Phases of Fiction' became another Hogarth ghost.

Leonard was Virginia's only book editor, her only publisher's reader after she left Duckworth. And all that he did, he said in editing her posthumous essays, was to punctuate them where they needed it and correct verbal mistakes. It is noteworthy that the work of two of the greatest English prose modernists, James Joyce and Virginia Woolf, should have been published without the customary editorial interventions. Partly as a result of publishing her own books, Woolf at least avoided the bibliographical chaos that seems to envelop the printed work of Joyce. But this is not to say the situation of Woolf's texts is simple. The publication of her books in America by Harcourt Brace was on a take-it-or-leave-it basis. They always took them, setting their first American editions from the proofs of the Hogarth editions. Nevertheless, Virginia Woolf did not regard the Hogarth Press texts as definitive. In *Mrs. Dalloway* and *To the Lighthouse*, for example, she made substantial changes in the wording of key passages in the American proofs of her novels. The absence of any editorial assistance also contributed to errors in the Hogarth editions that went unnoticed, such as the misnumbering of sections in the third part of the first English edition of *To the Lighthouse*.

The nature of the Hogarth Press operation is revealing in other ways for the study of Virginia Woolf's writing. Vanessa Bell's dustjackets of her novels provide examples. They are, to borrow a phrase of Henry James's, 'optical echoes' of the text. Yet they were done without Vanessa having read the books; Virginia would drop in and give her sister enough of an idea about the book for a cover. A number of these jackets also had blurbs about the novel on their flaps. Given the small organisation of the Hogarth Press, it is reasonable to assume that these blurbs were written by the author. And who wrote the copy for the Hogarth Press's catalogue announcements of the Woolfs' books? Again these descriptions can be considered authorial – or quasi-authorial, perhaps, if Leonard wrote them with Virginia's approval. As for other books Hogarth published, Richard Kennedy, in his irreverent account of being a gofer in the basement of the Hogarth Press, describes Virginia Woolf writing a blurb for a novel on Spain, which the Press was publishing. How many unknown blurbs by Virginia Woolf are there in Hogarth's publication? Who knows, once the importance of the Hogarth Press for Woolf's writing has been fully recognised, we may have a thesis and perhaps a collected edition of Virginia's blurbs and catalogue announcements.

V

Virginia Woolf, of course, is the primary reason why we remain interested in the Hogarth Press today, and one of the most extraordinary aspects of the care that Leonard devoted to her – a care that ultimately made her writing possible – was his role in the creation of the Hogarth Press. But she is not the only substantial reason why the Press is part of the history of English modernism. John Lehmann has said the dazzling early promise of Hogarth as a modernist press was not sustained, except for her works. He is thinking only of literature, for surely the publication of the standard English translation of Freud is, by any standard, a great modernist achievement. It is true that the Woolfs did not find other writers of fiction like Katherine Mansfield or poets like T. S. Eliot to publish. They tried with E. M. Forster's help to publish a volume of C. P. Cavafy's translated poems; Cavafy was very grateful for the offer but did not finally commit himself to a volume of his poems in Greek, let alone English. He died in 1933, and it was not until 1951 that the Hogarth Press was finally able to bring out his poems in translation. The Press did succeed in publishing translations of modern Russian works as well as those of Rainer Maria Rilke and Italo Svevo. The Woolfs brought out the first book on

Proust in English, which was by Clive Bell. They drew attention to the new poets of the 1930s and published Isherwood's Berlin stories. And they would have published Joyce's *Ulysses* and Stein's *The Making of Americans* if they had been able to. (They even offered to publish an early version of Wyndham Lewis's anti-Bloomsbury *The Apes of God*!) Virginia Woolf's derisive private comments on Joyce's work have often been cited. It is true she did not recognise his greatness in what she said, yet *Ulysses* had a profound influence on the writing of *Mrs. Dalloway*. The important distinction here is between what the Woolfs liked and what they thought was worth publishing. They would have published *Ulysses* if the censorship laws of England had allowed them to find a printer who would do it. This no one was able to do. As for Gertrude Stein, Virginia Woolf was sceptical, again in private, about what she called her 'dodge' of repeating a word '100 times over in different connections until at last you feel the force of it'. Yet the Hogarth Press offered to publish first *The Making of Americans* and later another work on herself, Matisse and Picasso if Stein would bear the cost, which she could have done. The Woolfs did reject in the 1930s Ivy Compton-Burnett's third novel *Brothers and Sisters*, and regretted the mistake, for it does not appear that Virginia read the manuscript. Virginia Woolf always said she was not a good judge of her contemporaries' literary merit.

But was there another press in England at the time that had a better record? That this was partly a matter of luck, Leonard Woolf conceded. But it was also due to the Woolfs' realisation that the publishing conditions of their time created the need for an alternative press. The historical moment of the Hogarth Press has passed; even if one could find another Virginia Woolf, it would not be possible for many reasons to do anything similar now to what they did nearly eighty years ago. But the example of their Press illuminates the history of the book in English modernism. Virginia and Leonard Woolf's Hogarth Press was a remarkable enterprise of book publishing – and not just for the works that they published, but for the ways in which they published them. The values by which they resisted becoming professional printers or commercial publishers still seem worth thinking about today.

8 Wittgenstein in Bloomsbury

I

In 1931 as he was beginning his metamorphosis from the *Tractatus Logico-Philosophicus* to the *Philosophical Investigations*, Ludwig Wittgenstein wrote down some remarks on the famous work of a don at Trinity College, James Frazer. *The Golden Bough*, along with Spengler whom Wittgenstein had also been reading, led him to reflect on historical explanation. 'We can equally well see the data in their relations to one another and make a summary of them in a general picture without putting it in the form of an hypothesis regarding the temporal development', he wrote. An *'übersichtliche Darstellung'* or clearly detailed overview, he continued, makes possible 'that understanding which consists just in the fact that we "see the connections". Hence the importance of finding *intermediate links*. But in our case a hypothetical link is not meant to do anything except draw attention to the similarity, the connection between the facts' (*Remarks on Frazer*, pp. 8e–9e).

Wittgenstein was writing about Frazer's anthropological data that he felt had been given a narrow spiritual interpretation. On the occasion of the 17th International Wittgenstein Symposium, which this year includes discussion of the Bloomsbury Group, I would like to try relating Wittgenstein's view of historical connection to the links between his earlier philosophy and the Bloomsbury Group, not to argue a thesis about development or influence but just to draw attention to the similarities – and also in this case the dissimilarities – between Wittgenstein's ideas and attitudes, and those of the Bloomsbury Group. Bloomsbury is revealing for this purpose because over a period of some two decades there were encounters of various kinds between him and that collectivity of loving friends and relatives that included the economist John Maynard Keynes, the novelists and essayists Virginia Woolf and E. M. Forster, the biographer Lytton Strachey, the painters Vanessa Bell and Duncan Grant, and the critics of art, literature and politics Roger Fry, Clive Bell, Desmond MacCarthy and Leonard Woolf.

Bloomsbury was not, as is sometimes suggested, a school, a conspiracy or some form of corporate entity. But the Group's members themselves recognised their distinctness in backgrounds, ideas, beliefs and feelings that they shared for two generations or more.

Wittgenstein's and Bloomsbury's various encounters have naturally been mentioned by biographers, editors and critics but it is usually the insignificance, if not the antipathy, of these relations that are represented. Wittgenstein said with justice, according to Keynes himself, that Bloomsbury lacked reverence (*Collected Writings*, X, 448). The irreverent Lytton Strachey found Wittgenstein fearfully boring in 1912 and mocked him in letters to his brother James as 'Herr Sinckel-Winkel' and 'the Witter-Gitter man' (Monk, pp. 48, 68). Nor did Wittgenstein like Strachey's first book, an introduction to French literature, which he thought a gasping effort (McGuinness, *Wittgenstein*, p. 119). Virginia and Leonard Woolf met Wittgenstein at a lunch of the Keynes's in 1925; they thought him cruel to Lydia Keynes, whom he reduced to tears after she remarked on the beauty of a tree (Skidelsky, p. 208). Wittgenstein also had at this time a conversation with that most obscure member of the Bloomsbury Group, Saxon Sydney-Turner, in which, according to Virginia Woolf's derisive fantasy, the dim Turner 'talked without ceasing, some say in an obscure Austrian dialect, of the soul, and matter' until Wittgenstein was so impressed he offered himself as a bootblack just to hear more (V. Woolf, *Letters*, III, 212). Wittgenstein for his part came to think that Virginia Woolf's upbringing made her believe people's worth was measured by their successful careers (Rhees, p. 207). Leonard Woolf found the *Tractatus* too difficult, though he read Moore all his life (Interview). So it seems, did Clive Bell, who thought Keynes understood Wittgenstein as well as anyone except A. J. Ayer (*Old Friends*, p. 59). E. M. Forster, whom Keynes includes among those lacking reverence in Bloomsbury, had needed to have Moore mediated to him through his Apostolic friends. Duncan Grant remembered just two of Wittgenstein's opinions about music and art – that everything Beethoven said was true, and that a still-life by André Derain which Keynes had bought was without merit (Interview). Clive and Vanessa Bell's son Julian, who was at Cambridge in the early 1930s, satirised the author of the *Tractatus* in a verse epistle for failing to be silent on ethics and aesthetics while insisting others had to be. Another younger member of Bloomsbury, Frances Partridge, who had read moral philosophy at Cambridge, found Wittgenstein's conversation in the presence of women facetious and trivial in the extreme (*Memories*, p. 160).

In the face of this testimony the subject of Wittgenstein's relation to Bloomsbury does not seem promising. But there are other connections to be made between Wittgenstein and the Group besides biographical ones. Outside of philosophy, the discussion of Wittgenstein's historical milieu has been dominated by biography in various forms – reminiscent, scandalous, authorised, popular, photographic, fictive, filmic. (A generation ago one of Wittgenstein's executors expressed in print the wish that all concern with his private life might be obliterated with the push of a button – an appalling idea, but sometimes one can understand the exasperation.) Comparatively little attention has been paid, however, to Wittgenstein's cultural relation to his times, and most of that has been confined to his European background. The English context of Wittgenstein is still left mainly to the memoirs of his friends and disciples, where, as Professor von Wright has noted, he sometimes appears as culturally illiterate (*Wittgenstein*, p. 3). England's importance for Wittgenstein has been often overlooked, while his criticisms of English culture have perhaps been overemphasised. Fania Pascal has pointed out that 'Wittgenstein was not a refugee who came to England asking for asylum and who would feel in some special way indebted to the country. He came of his own free choice.' He came twice in fact; the second time when he might have had a philosophical career in Austria or Germany. England, and particularly Cambridge and Trinity College gave him the freedom, the tolerance that allowed him to associate as much or as little as he wished with colleagues and students (Rhees, pp. 55–6). As Wittgenstein himself said to Keynes in 1938 when he decided to become a British citizen, England was 'a country in which I have spent on and off the greatest part of my adult life, have made my greatest friends and have done my best work' (*Cambridge Letters*, p. 294).

As a way of drawing attention to Wittgenstein's English connections, I want to focus on the Bloomsbury Group, the members of whom were as serious in their criticisms of England as Wittgenstein but who also understood the profound importance of English freedom and tolerance. And though I shall rely on various illuminating biographies and autobiographies, the context I am trying to describe is more than biographical.

We can begin with the biographical fact, however, that Wittgenstein's relation to Bloomsbury came principally through his long, important and at times close relationship with a person whose role in Bloomsbury was crucial for the Group and for himself. John Maynard Keynes was largely responsible for bringing Wittgenstein into that most famous of secret undergraduate societies, the Cambridge Apostles, from which the Bloomsbury Group had developed a decade earlier. Though Wittgenstein did not remain an Apostle very long, it was through the Apostles that he came into contact with Bloomsbury. Most of the Bloomsbury Apostles were disciples of G. E. Moore, who dominated the Apostles during Bloomsbury's Cambridge education. Moore's significance for Wittgenstein has too often been dismissed with Wittgenstein's crack that Moore 'shows you how far a man can go who has absolutely no intelligence whatever'. That remark was not made to a philosopher; it was reported by F. R. Leavis, who was antagonistic to Cambridge philosophy and the Bloomsbury Group (Rhees, p. 51). Rather different is the attitude towards Moore described in Norman Malcolm's memoir of Wittgenstein (pp. 66–8). Whatever Wittgenstein's attitude to Moore's philosophy was around 1930 when he knew Leavis, Wittgenstein's last philosophical writings, published as *On Certainty*, were devoted to philosophical problems that Moore had raised.

Bertrand Russell was obviously another connection between Wittgenstein and Bloomsbury. The Group's relationship with Russell was not as close as that with Moore. Wittgenstein's admiration for Russell's work was very different from Bloomsbury's because only Keynes could appreciate the value of the work in symbolic logic that preoccupied Wittgenstein. Other members of Bloomsbury were interested in Russell's more popular works of philosophy, including the social and ethical writings that Wittgenstein detested. Strachey and Keynes among others were influenced by Russell's *The Problems of Philosophy* as well as the essays Russell published in *Mysticism and Logic*. The parallels of the title essay with Wittgenstein's *Tractatus* have been pointed out by Brian McGuinness. Russell's ideas appear to have prepared Bloomsbury for Wittgenstein's own mixture of mysticism and logic. Russell had also been an admirer of *Principia Ethica* and for a time he modelled his own ethics on it. When he urged Wittgenstein in 1912 to read the book, however, his pupil found he did not like it at all (Wittgenstein, *Cambridge Letters*, p. 13). But by then Moore, if not Bloomsbury, was having second thoughts about his book.

A comparison of *Principia Ethica* with the *Tractatus* suggests some profound differences between Bloomsbury and Wittgenstein. Bloomsbury liked to refer to *Principia Ethica* as their bible, but their interpretation of Moore has been misrepresented by Keynes. His famous account of Moore's influence in the memoir 'My Early Beliefs' should not be accepted uncritically in tracing the effect of Cambridge on Wittgenstein's early beliefs.[1] Keynes argued in his memoir, written some thirty years after the fact, that Bloomsbury took what he calls Moore's religion, which involved attitudes towards themselves and the ultimate, and ignored Moore's morals, which involved attitudes towards the outside world and the intermediate. Moore's followers became Utopian immoralists, says Keynes: they repudiated conventional morality, traditional wisdom – including the reverence Wittgenstein missed – and adopted instead a pseudo-rational conception of human nature that resulted in superficial judgements and feelings. The fundamental intuitions of *Principia Ethica* about love, beauty and knowledge were insufficient; nevertheless Keynes found that at least they liberated him and his friends from the overvaluations of economic concerns by Bentham and Marx. They also freed him from nineteenth-century notions of moral obligation (Keynes, *Collected Writings*, X, 436–46). This was a liberation that Wittgenstein also needed.

Keynes's view of Moore's early influence was authoritatively challenged from Bloomsbury by Leonard Woolf in his autobiography. Woolf pointed out the chronological confusions of the memoir – three different periods were conflated by Keynes – and he flatly denied that he and his Bloomsbury friends had adopted Moore's so-called religion while ignoring his morals. Later the Apostle and philosopher R. B. Braithwaite developed Woolf's criticisms and 'de-rhetoricised' Keynes's memoir by showing that Moore's consequentialist ethics were already familiar to Keynes in his father's utilitarianism, whereas his critique of utilitarian hedonism was exhilaratingly new to the young Keynes.[2]

Furthermore, the relevance of Moore's ethics to Bloomsbury's philosophical ideas cannot be separated from his epistemological realism or his analytic methods. To reduce the importance of *Principia Ethica* to the ideals of aesthetic experience and love in the final chapter is simplistic. But it is worth noting that Moore and Bloomsbury did not include religious experience in the Ideal because they did not believe in God's existence, and here is a profound difference between Bloomsbury and Wittgenstein. For

Bloomsbury values, however, the most fundamental principle of *Principia Ethica* was its distinction between instrumental and intrinsic good. Questions about good as a means and good as an end are continually being explored in Bloomsbury writings and reveal the basis of the Group's values. Almost as important were Moore's concept of the indefinable nature of good and his principle of organic unities which holds that organic wholes are what they are – wholes, not sums of their parts. To this principle Moore applies the epigraph of *Principia Ethica*, Butler's 'Everything is what it is and not another thing.' Wittgenstein thought the quotation marvellous and considered using it as the epigraph for the *Philosophical Investigations*. Moore's personal impact was also crucial, of course, as Keynes testifies, and here parallels are to be seen between the intensity, purity and moral force of Moore and Wittgenstein, which is not to say their personalities were alike. Yet for the disciples of both Moore and Wittgenstein, the philosophical was inseparable from the personal.

A comparison of Moore's and Wittgenstein's philosophy is beyond the scope of this paper. All I want to emphasise here is that Moore's significance for Bloomsbury cannot be left to Keynes's brilliant and misleading text. It should be remembered that the thought of Russell and Moore as well as Wittgenstein was shaped by Cambridge philosophical traditions very familiar to Bloomsbury. Virginia Woolf's father and Maynard Keynes's, for instance, were both Cambridge utilitarian philosophers. To see connections between Moore's Bloomsbury disciples and Wittgenstein, we need to look first at the evidence of Wittgenstein's involvement with the Apostles in pre-war Cambridge.

II

In October 1911, Wittgenstein appeared, unannounced and unknown, in Bertrand Russell's Trinity College rooms. Just a year later he briefly became an Apostle, joining that secret undergraduate brotherhood that included among others Russell, Whitehead and Moore as well as MacCarthy, Fry, Forster, Woolf, Strachey and Keynes. The mixture of undergraduates with older, now inactive members in the Society was one of the most important features of the Apostles. It brought young men such as Strachey, Woolf or Keynes into frank, intimate intellectual discussion with the likes of

Moore and Russell. The Apostolic spirit, as described by Henry Sidgwick, was

> the pursuit of truth with absolute devotion and unreserve by a group of intimate friends, who were perfectly frank with each other, and indulged in any amount of humorous sarcasm and playful banter.... Absolute candour was the only duty that the tradition of the society enforced.... (*Memoir*, pp. 34–5)

One can see here what might have attracted Wittgenstein to the Apostles, and also what repelled him.

Wittgenstein's links with the Apostles came naturally through Russell and Moore, whose lectures he was attending and attacking. As Russell's protégé, Wittgenstein was introduced to Strachey and then Keynes, who was teaching at King's. (Another active Apostle, the mathematician Harry Norton, had also been attending Russell's lectures on logic with Wittgenstein.) Russell thought rightly that Wittgenstein would not make a very good Apostle, but Strachey was convinced that Russell wanted to keep Wittgenstein to himself. It is clear from the letters of the time that Russell had misgivings about the Bloomsbury Apostles, their friends and even their guru. To Ottoline Morrell he wrote in 1912 of the contrast Wittgenstein was 'to the Stephens and Stracheys and such would-be geniuses' (McGuinness, *Wittgenstein*, p. 135). Russell it appears was somewhat envious of Moore's influence at this time, and Wittgenstein reassured him that *Principia Ethica* could not compare with Russell's or Frege's work on logic (*Cambridge Letters*, p. 13).

After becoming a member, Wittgenstein's reaction to the Cambridge Conversazione Society, as they publicly called themselves, involved him more directly in Bloomsbury. Among the active Apostles at Cambridge when Wittgenstein was elected were several members associated in various ways with Bloomsbury, including the poet Rupert Brooke (who was not attending meetings of the Society) and Lytton Strachey's brother James, who lived in London. There was also the Hungarian aristocrat Ferenc Békássy as well as Francis Bliss, who was elected with Wittgenstein. Békássy seems to have been in love with Bliss, whom Wittgenstein so detested that he threatened to leave the Apostles. The Austrian does not seem to have been fond of the Hungarian either. An account survives of Wittgenstein's behaviour at the Apostles in an unpublished letter of Saxon Sydney-Turner to James Strachey in December 1912. After

Békássy had read a paper, 'Wittgenstein complained that there was nothing to discuss and that the proceedings were futile; reminded that he had said the same a week before he replied that he could not have if he could have then imagined this.' Turner went on to say, however, that Wittgenstein admired the economist Gerald Shove and even liked Lytton Strachey when he spoke at the Apostles (Sydney-Turner, Strachey Papers).

Keynes wrote Strachey that Wittgenstein's objections to the Apostles were that they were not Apostolic enough – did not, presumably, pursue truth with enough devotion and candour. Wittgenstein may also have been unimpressed by Apostolic humour. The result was a crisis in the Society because undergraduates once chosen could not quit the Apostles without being ritually cursed, as had once happened in the nineteenth century. Moore asked Lytton Strachey, who was influential in the Society at this time, to come to Cambridge and talk with Wittgenstein about the purpose of the Apostles. Strachey seems to have persuaded Wittgenstein not to resign for a while. But Wittgenstein took no more role in the Society, though he did plan for a while to give a series of lectures at the Working Men's College in London where E. M. Forster and other Apostles were teaching. In 1913 Wittgenstein did leave the Society and was accordingly damned. Yet a letter to Moore written next year suggests that Wittgenstein had not lost all interest in the Society (*Cambridge Letters*, p. 77). Wittgenstein's letters to Keynes at this time also reveal how much Wittgenstein cared for their friendship despite what happened in the Apostles.[3] The friendly association with Moore continued as well for more than a year, until Wittgenstein became enraged with Moore over university regulations and told him to go to hell.

The influence of Strachey and the relationship with Keynes do not indicate that Wittgenstein was repelled by or indifferent to Bloomsbury at this time. But there were still deep differences in their outlooks, especially in religion and politics. One of Wittgenstein's favourite texts, for example, was the biblical 'For what shall it profit a man, if he shall gain the whole world and lose his own soul?' Strachey, on the other hand, had exclaimed in an early review of William Blake 'What shall it profit a man...if he gain his own soul, and lose the whole world?' Both E. M. Forster and Virginia Woolf picked up Strachey's irreverent inversion in their writings. (Wittgenstein's wealth – he was richer than anyone in Bloomsbury – may have made him particularly sensitive to the original text.) Again, at the first Apostles meeting Wittgenstein attended, Moore had read an old paper on conversion; he cited Tolstoy's novels among other works, and asked if a lasting moral conversion to a new life in which one sees life steadily and whole were possible. Wittgenstein's response, according to Russell, was that such a conversion consisted in getting rid of anxiety and feeling secure. (Wittgenstein's notion of conversion here anticipates the illustrations of mystical experience he later gave in his lecture on ethics – McGuinness, *Wittgenstein*, p. 114.) As for the political divergencies between Wittgenstein and Bloomsbury at this time, they can perhaps be seen in their attitudes towards the issue of women's suffrage. The Stracheys and the Stephens as well as Russell were actively involved in the campaign, whereas Wittgenstein was opposed to women's suffrage because, as he told his friend David Pinsent, all the women he knew were idiots (Pinsent, p. 44). One wonders about his sisters, and whether his attitude would have been different had he then met some of the women of Bloomsbury.

There is, finally, one significant aspect of Wittgenstein and Bloomsbury in pre-war Cambridge that is seldom if ever mentioned in the various accounts we have of his involvement with the Apostles. Again this may be due to the influence of Keynes's memoir. The departure point for Keynes's memoir was the visit to Cambridge of D. H. Lawrence, another young genius with whom Bertrand Russell had became involved. Keynes's linking of Ludwig's name (in Bloomsbury only Keynes called Wittgenstein by his first name) with Lawrence's as critics of Cambridge irreverence is rather curious, for the real basis of Lawrence's disgust with Cambridge does not seem to have been shared by Wittgenstein. Keynes concluded in 'My Early Beliefs' that Lawrence's passionate distaste for Cambridge was aroused by the way Keynes and his friends ignored 'both the reality and the value of the vulgar passions...'. Keynes fails to reveal that there was one particular vulgar passion not ignored in Moore's Cambridge, a passion Lawrence described as 'men loving men'. The beetles that Lawrence dreamt of after seeing Keynes in Cambridge could be symbolic of sodomy. Lawrence's own homoerotic susceptibilities figured in his repulsion. (See above, pp. 68–83.) This was not Wittgenstein's case. Like Strachey and Keynes as well as Moore at this time, but not Russell, Wittgenstein's most intense and intimate relationships were with men. Russell told Ottoline Morrell that he did not think Wittgenstein would like the Society because of 'their practice of being in love with each other, which didn't exist in my day – I think it is mainly due to Lytton' (McGuinness, *Wittgenstein*, p. 118). Strachey may indeed have been influential here, though Russell is not correct about Apostolic homosexuality in his time. It is not at all clear that Wittgenstein's objections to the Apostles were the consequence of men loving men in the Society. The importance in Wittgenstein's life of David Pinsent is displayed in the dedication of the *Tractatus*. (It is interesting to note that Pinsent had himself been looked over by Keynes as a candidate for the Apostles – Pinsent, p. xiv). More than two years after Pinsent's death Wittgenstein wrote to Russell, 'Every day I think of Pinsent. He took half my life away with him' (*Cambridge Letters*, pp. 161–2). For Wittgenstein as well as the Bloomsbury Apostles the very great value of love was not limited by the gender of the lovers.

III

With the First World War, the political divergencies of Wittgenstein and Bloomsbury can be seen more sharply. Wittgenstein (who was convinced England would win the war) fought for Austria. Most of Bloomsbury refused to fight for England, although the members of the Group were not all pacifists. Nor were all the Apostles; Bliss, Brooke and Békássy all died in the war, as did Pinsent. Keynes went to work for the Treasury where, according to his critical Bloomsbury friends, he was figuring out how to kill Germans as economically as possible. It was Keynes who tried to keep track of Wittgenstein during the war, intervening on his behalf when he was finally captured. For the other Bloomsbury Apostles Wittgenstein became remote. When he re-emerged, it was as the author of the *Tractatus Logico-Philosophicus*. Wittgenstein's relation to the Bloomsbury Group after the war can best be understood through that work.

Wittgenstein refers in the *Tractatus* to writing a book on 'the world as I found it' (5.631).[4] The world he found in the *Tractatus* is in many ways very different from the worlds as members of Bloomsbury were finding them during and after the war. First of all, the world of the *Tractatus* is very difficult to understand. Its detailed discussion of the nature of propositions which occupies so much of the book remains deep in the province of logicians. In his preface, however, Wittgenstein said the meaning of the *Tractatus* could be summarised as 'what can be said at all can be said clearly; and whereof one cannot speak thereof one must be silent' (p. 27). And he told Russell that the logic of propositions was just a corollary to a theory of language which distinguishes what can be said from what can be shown (*Cambridge Letters*, p. 124). This still leaves the reader untrained in symbolic logic (which included everyone in Bloomsbury but Keynes) to cope with the implications of Wittgenstein's picture theory of meaning and to try to distinguish what can be said clearly from what cannot be said at all. Nevertheless, Wittgenstein's conception of philosophy in the *Tractatus* as an activity of logical clarification of what can be said in propositions was something the followers of Moore might have accepted. Moore's and Russell's pursuit of clarity influenced Bloomsbury, yet the Group would hardly have agreed with Wittgenstein's insisting 'everything that can be thought at all can be thought clearly' (4.116).

Moore's discussions of the nature of perception and the meaning of good were aspects of his philosophy that Bloomsbury found most illuminating for their fiction, biographies and essays. The *Tractatus* relegated epistemology to psychology and ethics to philosophical silence. Wittgenstein's austere conclusion to the logic of propositions that 'the sense of the world must lie outside the world' (6.41) was something Bloomsbury may not have understood. There appears to be an unbridgeable abyss between the religious sensibility of Wittgenstein here and the secular world as Bloomsbury found it. If the early beliefs of Bloomsbury did accept what Keynes called Moore's religion, that religion had little in common with Wittgenstein's beliefs in the *Tractatus*. More accessible to Bloomsbury than its logic was the mysticism of the world Wittgenstein presented in the *Tractatus*. If Wittgenstein's work can be described as mystical, so can that of Virginia Woolf, E. M. Forster, Clive Bell and even perhaps Lytton Strachey. The luminous remark of the *Tractatus* 'not *how* the world is, is the mystical, but *that* it is' (6.44) could describe certain of the mystical moments in novels like *Mrs. Dalloway*, *To the Lighthouse* and *The Waves* as well as those in works of Forster such as 'The Road to Colonus', *The Longest Journey* and *Howards End*. (Wittgenstein's formulation in his notebooks for the *Tractatus* is even more relevant: he said that for art, 'the miracle is that the world exists' – *Notebooks*, p. 86e). Mysticism in Wittgenstein and in Bloomsbury seems also to be directed towards external nature and beyond rather than occurring in a withdrawal from the world into the self. Again, mystical experience in Bloomsbury's writings is not always desirable, nor does it seem to have been for Wittgenstein. There are desolating mystical moments, in *The Waves*, *A Passage to India* and the autobiographies of Virginia and Leonard Woolf. In Wittgenstein's lecture on ethics one of the mystical experiences mentioned involved feelings of guilt and of God's disapproval. But Bloomsbury's mysticism was not theistic.

Although meaning and value were not outside the world for Bloomsbury, there is also an important aesthetic sense in which the group could have agreed with the idea in the *Tractatus* that 'the contemplation of the world *sub specie aeterni* is its contemplation as a limited whole', and that 'the feeling of the world as a limited whole is the mystical feeling' (6.45). This brings in the complicated question of aesthetics in the *Tractatus* and Bloomsbury. At first glimpse again, the worlds of Wittgenstein and Bloomsbury appear opposed. Aesthetics in the *Tractatus* lies outside the world in the silent realm of value. Aesthetics in Bloomsbury was a recurrent topic of discussion among the Group's artists and critics. The advocacy of post-impressionism in the writings of Roger Fry and Clive Bell did much to transform English taste. While Wittgenstein does not seem to have been much interested in post-impressionism art, visual imagery is apparent in his picture theory of language. The fundamental distinction between what propositions can say and what they can show has analogies to literary theory from Aristotle to Henry James in the distinction between narrative and drama, telling and showing. The art that Wittgenstein responded to most deeply, of course, was music, a preference shared in Bloomsbury by E. M. Forster. Next perhaps was architecture. The severely functional form of the house Wittgenstein designed for his sister and the eclectic modern house that Roger Fry created for himself earlier reflect again the differences between Fry's English and Wittgenstein's Austrian taste. (Wittgenstein sent some photographs of his house to Keynes, hoping he would not be too disgusted by its simplicity – *Cambridge Letters*, p. 224). What would Wittgenstein have thought of the rejection of traditional English finish and prettiness in the products of the Bloomsbury Omega Workshops, which lasted through the period he was writing the *Tractatus*? He may well have respected the attempt to abolish the hierarchical distinction between the fine and decorative arts.

To return to aesthetics and the *Tractatus*, Wittgenstein's parenthetical comment that 'ethics and aesthetics are one' (6.421) was not something Bloomsbury critics would have accepted. Lytton

Strachey in his early Apostle papers used Moore's notion of organic unity to discriminate between the good and the beautiful in literature.[5] Following the celebrated post-impressionist exhibitions of 1910 and 1912 Bell in *Art* and Fry in various articles argued for the irrelevance of ethics to aesthetic appreciation. Behind the fusion of art and ethics in the *Tractatus* there is a more interesting connection made in Wittgenstein's notebooks that suggests, for all the differences in aesthetics, some illuminating connections can be seen between his ideas about art and Bloomsbury's. Wittgenstein said in his notes that the link between art and ethics was that 'the work of art is the object seen *sub specie aeternitatis*' while 'the good life is the world seen *sub specie aeternitatis*' (*Notebooks*, p. 83e). The essential disinterestedness of art was also a fundamental conviction of Bloomsbury's aesthetics, which suggests that both Bloomsbury's and Wittgenstein's aesthetic attitudes descend mainly from Kant, though Spinoza may also be relevant. Something of Wittgenstein's notebook idea remains in the *Tractatus* statement about the mystical contemplation of the world as a limited whole (6.45). In Bloomsbury's aesthetics the emphasis was on organic rather than limited wholes. Aesthetic contemplation for them was ultimately mystical too, but this did not mean one had to be silent about it. Clive Bell's famous concept of significant form has a mystical aspect. (The theory may owe as much to Plato as Kant; behind the appearance of the picture's content lies the reality of its form.) The pictorial analogies in the *Tractatus* are all representational, however. Wittgenstein's notions of aesthetics around the time of the *Tractatus* could not really be described as formalist yet they may well have involved another influential source of aesthetic theory that interested both Wittgenstein and Bloomsbury besides Kant, and that is Tolstoy.

Bloomsbury aesthetics has sometimes been misinterpreted as an extension of the *fin-de-siècle* aestheticism of Walter Pater and Oscar Wilde. But as Forster and others argued, art for art's sake did not mean only art really mattered; art was certainly not more important than love in Bloomsbury. The historical misunderstanding of Bloomsbury's aesthetics has obscured the importance of Tolstoy's ideas for the aesthetics of Roger Fry and therefore Bloomsbury, including not just the painters and critics but Forster, the Woolfs and Strachey. Fry in his important 1909 'Essay in Aesthetics' described Tolstoy's *What is Art?* as the beginning of useful speculation in aesthetics. For Fry this came from Tolstoy's suggestion that art had no essential connection with natural beauty and his recognition that art is the communication of feeling. Fry and Bell developed from these ideas the concept of disinterested aesthetic emotion that significant form evokes. Bell's theory in *Art* also tentatively suggests that artists transmit through significant form the emotion they feel for reality. Fry and Bell dismissed, however, the peculiar aesthetic judgements that Tolstoy's theory led him into. And Tolstoy's concern for the moral and social functions of art does not enter much into Bloomsbury's aesthetics. Nevertheless, it was Tolstoy's stimulus more than any other recent aesthetics at the end of the century that led to Bloomsbury's emphasis on the emotional responses of – in Virginia Woolf's words – the common reader or common seer (*Roger Fry*, pp. 105–6). The importance of Tolstoy's religious writings for Wittgenstein's development during the war is well known; he was also interested in *What is Art?* but how must he have felt about an aesthetics that dismissed Beethoven? Later, Wittgenstein criticised Tolstoy's idea that the significance of art was to be found in its being understood by everyone, and he also wrote of what could be learned from Tolstoy's bad theories of how art conveys emotion. Wittgenstein maintained that the artist's feelings in creating a work were of no concern because 'the work of art does not aim to convey *something else,* just itself' (*Culture and Value*, pp. 17e, 58–9e). This could have been said by Fry or Bell around the time of the *Tractatus*.

IV

I have been trying to describe the similarities and differences between the Bloomsbury Group and Wittgenstein's world of the *Tractatus Logico-Philosophicus* – its conception of philosophy; its theory of what language can say, show and not say; and its ethical, mystical and aesthetic attitudes. Two further less philosophical aspects of the *Tractatus* are relevant to Bloomsbury. The first is that the *Tractatus* is a literary as well as a logical work. Wittgenstein described the *Tractatus* to a prospective publisher as 'strictly philosophical and at the same time literary; but there's no gassing in it' (McGuinness, *Wittgenstein*, p. 288). In his preface Wittgenstein hoped at least one person would read his book not just with understanding but with pleasure. The value of his work, he believed, consisted in the way his thoughts were expressed, about which he had some misgivings, and in their truth, about which he had none (pp. 27–9). The literary form of the *Tractatus* has endured better than its truth, which has been effectively criticised by many philosophers including its author. Wittgenstein's analysis of the logic of propositions is carried out in a figurative and aphoristic style of extraordinary compression; the work's obscure motto about how anything that one knows can be said in three words suggests how self-consciously this idiom was cultivated. The elliptical prose in the *Tractatus* was well described as syncopated by C. D. Broad (Passmore, p. 352). It could also be called symbolistic in its absence of transitions. The literary nature of the *Tractatus* is not just a matter of prose style. It is a deeply paradoxical, even ironical work. The irony of the *Tractatus* is inherent in the very numbering of its propositions, which almost comically subvert the mathematical precision of logical importance claimed for them (p. 31). Paradox, of course, has been a familiar aspect of logic since at least Zeno. The paradoxical nature of the *Tractatus* is proclaimed from its first sentence to its last. How obscurely the work argues that everything which can be thought or said can be done so clearly. Russell in his introduction was the first but not the last commentator to observe how 'Mr Wittgenstein manages to say a good deal about what cannot be said...' (p. 22). The *Tractatus* quite self-consciously dismantles itself, though this is not necessarily self-defeating. The process is one of discovery as Max Black has said: the ladder at the end is thrown away only after it has served its purpose (*Companion*, p. 386). As a literary work, the *Tractatus* shows what cannot be said. Approaching the poetic composition that Wittgenstein later said philosophy ought to be (*Culture and Value*, p. 24), the work embodies meanings that prose summary cannot convey. Wittgenstein's theory, if not his practice, would have been appreciated in some quarters of Bloomsbury but not all. How different the intention of the prose in the *Tractatus* is from Keynes's in his *A Treatise on Probability*, which appeared two years before the *Tractatus*. In the preface Keynes described his work as belonging to the tradition of empirical philosophers who 'conceived their subject as a branch rather of science than of the creative imagination, prose writers hoping to be understood' (*Collected Writings*, III, xxv). Aside from the innuendo that imaginative writers do not hope to be understood, Keynes's dichotomy of science and creative imagination is one of the things the *Tractatus* tries to transcend.

Some of the meanings of the *Tractatus* as a poetical composition belong to another non-philosophical aspect of the *Tractatus* – its character as a war book. Though Wittgenstein's pre-war notes dictated to Moore insisted that the propositions of logic could show something but not say it, the emphasis on the limits of expression – on the unspeakable, the inexpressible – takes on further meaning in the book he wrote at the front and as a prisoner of war. The *Tractatus* can be seen as a response to Karl Kraus's bitter appeal in Vienna at the start of the war: 'He who encourages deeds with words descrates words and deeds and is doubly despicable.... Let him who has something to say come forward and be silent!' (*Reader*, p. 71). Wittgenstein said he meant to include a sentence explaining that his work consisted of two parts: 'the one presented here plus all that I have *not* written. And it is precisely this second part that is the most important' (Engelmann, p. 143). Value exists silently in this unwritten part, beyond the world as he found it during the war – a world whose logic he described in a book dedicated to the friend killed in the war who, Wittgenstein said, took half his life away. And what the *Tractatus* does manage to say is said enigmatically, disjointedly. It may be understood only by those who have already had the same thoughts, says the first sentence of the preface, whose last sentence admits how little has been done when the problems of logic are solved (pp. 28–9). Logic itself turns out to consist only of tautologies. Whatever Wittgenstein manages to say about the unsayable, the *Tractatus* is a bleak book, and very much of its time.

The year the *Tractatus* was published as a book, 1922, has been described as an *annus mirabilis* of modern English literature. That year saw the publication of Eliot's *The Waste Land* and Joyce's *Ulysses*, as well as important novels by D. H. Lawrence and Sinclair Lewis plus volumes of later poetry by Thomas Hardy, W. B. Yeats and A. E. Housman. In Bloomsbury there was Woolf's first modernist novel *Jacob's Room*, Strachey's collected essays and Forster's account of Alexandria where he served with the Red Cross during the war. A further literary paradox of the *Tractatus* is that, though written in German, it became an English modernist work. C. K. Ogden and F. P. Ramsey's translation in a bilingual edition gave the book much wider currency than it had had the previous year when published in the last issue of an obscure German periodical. A few years after its appearance Herbert Read included the mystical conclusion in his influential book *English Prose Style* – but as an example of a scientific rather than an artistic style. Later critics recognised that the numbered propositions of the *Tractatus* had their own rhetoric. The obscurity, fragmentariness, paradoxes and ironies of the *Tractatus*, its reflexive critique of language and exploration of the boundaries of expression, its distinguishing philosophy from science, its stoicism, its background of war are all in a way modernist. Wittgenstein's concern with silence and the limits of expression are recurrent preoccupations of modernism variously reflected in Bloomsbury works. It does not seem very farfetched to compare the *Tractatus* with *The Waste Land*, which the Woolfs published at their Hogarth Press, or with Virginia's *Jacob's Room*, that elegiac novel without a hero that narrates fragmentedly a story of emptiness and loss having to do with the unknowableness of a young man like Rupert Brooke, dead in the war. *Jacob's Room* is closer to the *Tractatus* in tone than those other Bloomsbury war books Lytton Strachey's *Eminent Victorians* and Maynard Keynes's *The Economic Consequences of the Peace*. There is none of their satirical irony in Wittgenstein's writing. The difference here is a manifestation of that lack of reverence Wittgenstein felt in Bloomsbury. Laughter sounds throughout Bloomsbury's writings, including Virginia Woolf's. Among the works of the philosophers the Group knew and read, it is heard most in Russell. The play of irony in Bloomsbury's writings distinguishes it sharply from the moral intensity of Wittgenstein's philosophy. Nevertheless it is a superficial reading of Bloomsbury's work that would conclude the Woolfs, Forster, Keynes, Strachey, Fry, Bell or MacCarthy were less serious than Wittgenstein in their criticisms of modern culture.

V

When the *Tractatus* was finally published as a book Wittgenstein presented one of his author's copies to Keynes, and throughout the 1920s Keynes was Wittgenstein's link with Bloomsbury. Keynes replied with a concluding article on reconstruction in Europe he had written for a series of *Manchester Guardian* supplements at the end of 1922. It was another year before he felt able to respond personally, not because he did not wish to renew the friendship with Wittgenstein but because he did not know what to say about the *Tractatus* other than it was 'a work of extraordinary importance and genius' which, rightly or wrongly, was dominating 'all fundamental discussions in Cambridge since it was written' (*Cambridge Letters* p. 201). (Later when he tried to explain Wittgenstein's philosophy to the Apostles he could only half remember it – Skidelsky, II, 208.) Keynes did comment on the *Tractatus*, however, in the article he sent Wittgenstein. Calling him 'our newest Spinoza' – a reference not only to the Spinozistic allusions in the *Tractatus* but also to its Latin/English title which Moore had suggested, Keynes told his newspaper audience that Wittgenstein's book offered only 'frozen comfort' for those who looked to philosophy for some kind of creed. He then quoted in his own translation proposition 6.52: 'We feel that even if all *possible* questions of knowledge be answered, our problems of life are still not touched at all. But in that event there is obviously no question left; and just this is the answer.' Philosophy had, in short, 'run dry' (*Collected Writings*, XVII, 449). Wittgenstein responded that he would have preferred a letter. He did thank Keynes for sending him his books, including *A Treatise on Probability* which Wittgenstein in turn did not feel up to reading, though he was much interested by parts of *The Economic Consequences of the Peace* and later by Keynes's Hogarth Press pamphlet *A Short View of Russia* (*Cambridge Letters* pp. 205–7, 222). Keynes had found what he felt might be a new religion in his visit to Russia with Lydia Lopokova after their marriage in 1925. He thought the West overestimated the economic inefficiency of Russian communism and underestimated its religious power. In characteristically paradoxical fashion Keynes contrasted irreligious Protestant capitalism with its 'congeries of possessors and pursuers' to religious atheistic communism, whose 'emotional and ethical essence centres around the individual's and the community's attitude toward the love of money'. Perhaps the Russians with their new faith were going to solve that moral problem of the age, the love of money (*Collected Writings*, IX, 259, 267–8). Wittgenstein – who had already, in the words of his notary, committed financial suicide (Monk, p. 171) – said he was glad to see Keynes knew there were more things between heaven and earth than had been dreamt about in philosophy (*Cambridge Letters*, p. 222). Wittgenstein did not refer to the oppressive absence of freedom Keynes, like Russell, also found in Russia, and which distinguishes Bloomsbury's attitude towards Russian communism from those of George Bernard Shaw and the Webbs. Keynes's pamphlet may, indeed, have had some influence on Wittgenstein's wish to live in Russia.

How characteristic of Bloomsbury was Keynes's initial response to the cold philosophical consolations of the *Tractatus*? The book was certainly talked about in Bloomsbury. Leonard Woolf could not get through it, but Lytton Strachey owned a copy and discussed it in a way to suggest he was familiar with the course of its argument (Partridge letter). For some indication of what such discussion may have been like in Bloomsbury during the 1920s we can turn again to the Cambridge Conversazione Society, where Wittgenstein's relations with Bloomsbury had begun. Particularly good Apostle papers were reread at meetings sometimes attended by older members; in 1925 the Society heard a remarkable paper that illustrates the impact of the *Tractatus* on discussion that was not of the fundamental philosophical kind mentioned by Keynes. The paper's author was that extraordinary young mathematical philosopher and economist, Frank Ramsey, who was Wittgenstein's main philosophical contact with Cambridge in the 1920s. Ramsey could not be called a member of Bloomsbury but he became associated with various members, especially as a Fellow of King's College with Keynes and later Julian Bell. (Did Virginia Woolf borrow his name, if not its spelling, for the philosopher in *To the Lighthouse* who struggles to get beyond 'if p then q' to the frontier of knowledge at r?) Ramsey's brief paper addresses the question of what general intellectual conversation could be about after the *Tractatus*'s insistence on what it could not be about. Ramsey's answer is that there is really nothing to talk about seriously any longer. Scientific, historical and political topics are suitable only for discussion by experts because others lack the necessary information. As for philosophy, writes Ramsey, 'the conclusion of the greatest modern philosopher is that there is no such subject as philosophy; that it is an activity not a doctrine; and that, instead of answering questions, it aims merely at curing headaches'. Moore's absolute has gone the way of God; ethics and aesthetics are really branches of psychology, which is either a science or just a way of comparing personal experiences. About literature and other arts, 'we do not and cannot discuss whether one work of art is better than another; we merely compare the feelings it gives us'. Thus, Ramsey concludes, 'there never seems to be anything to talk about except shop and people's personal lives, neither of which is suited for general conversation'. The paper ends with a cheerful 'What I Feel' rejoinder to Russell's recent lecture 'What I Believe'; again Wittgenstein's view is accepted that philosophy provides not belief but relief from feelings of mental discomfort.

Ramsey's paper, which was published with other writings after his tragically early death in 1931 and read by Strachey and probably others in Bloomsbury, is a brilliantly delightful and absorbing discussion of the idea that there is nothing to discuss.[6] The paradox is a Tractarian one, but where Keynes found cold comfort Ramsey finds humour: in the silence where one cannot speak, laughter echoes. Some in Bloomsbury would not have found the prospects of Ramsey's paper all that dismaying. Among the Group personal lives were quite suitable to general conversation, of course. In addition to gossip they also talked a lot of shop about writing and painting, and they liked to listen to their own authorities on history, politics and economics. As for Ramsey's diminishment of aesthetics to feeling, Bloomsbury's was an aesthetics not just of form but of impersonal and personal feeling. The reader's responses are where Virginia Woolf and to some extent Forster locate critical attention. Philosophy for Bloomsbury as well as Ramsey was more than therapy, and good either on the whole or as a whole was still discussed in the Group. The mysticism of the *Tractatus* does not figure in Ramsey's paper, which may be an illustration of Wittgenstein's later comment that Ramsey was 'a bourgeois thinker. I.e. he thought with the aim of clearing up the affairs of some particular community' (*Culture and Value*, p. 17e). The remark has relevance in the context of Ramsey's Apostle paper, and displays another fundamental difference between Wittgenstein and Bloomsbury too. For all their individuality, Bloomsbury was a group, a community of old friends. Wittgenstein by comparison was an isolated figure. He did write once of the few people that formed his cultural circle but others, he said, remained foreign to him (*Culture and Value*, p. 10c). Bloomsbury attracted followers too but in the original Old Bloomsbury, there were no disciples.

VI

The return of Ludwig Wittgenstein to Cambridge was announced ironically by Maynard Keynes to his wife in January 1929 as a second coming: 'Well', he wrote, 'God has arrived. I met him on the 5:15 train. He has a plan to stay in Cambridge permanently' (Monk, p. 255). Wittgenstein had revisited England in 1925 with Keynes's financial assistance and reassurances that he wanted to resume their intimate friendship. While staying with Keynes and his wife in Sussex, Wittgenstein met other members of Bloomsbury who lived nearby. When Wittgenstein returned to Trinity College in

1929 as a research student, Ramsey became his supervisor. Keynes had encouraged Wittgenstein to come back to Cambridge, and through him Wittgenstein came into relation with Bloomsbury again in a number of ways. Friendship with Moore was revived; it endured to the end of their lives. But Wittgenstein's friendship with Keynes altered in the course of the remarkable decade that began with Wittgenstein as a graduate student and ended with his succeeding Moore as professor of philosophy.

Keynes also brought Wittgenstein back into the Apostles in 1929 and arranged for him now to resign formally (without being damned) and become an inactive member. Among the younger Apostles that Keynes introduced Wittgenstein to were Richard Braithwaite, Anthony Blunt, George Rylands, who was closely associated with Bloomsbury, and the young Julian Bell, who was reading history and English at King's, and writing poetry. A year after meeting Wittgenstein, Bell published in a Cambridge magazine edited by Blunt, Robin Fedden and Michael Redgrave an imitation eighteenth-century verse epistle that satirised 'the ethical and aesthetic beliefs of Herr Ludwig Wittgenstein (Doctor of Philosophy)'.[7] The epistle was addressed to Braithwaite; originally it had been addressed to Ramsey but he died just before it was published. Braithwaite recalled years later how Julian Bell detested Wittgenstein and fought with him every time they met (Interview). He had even tried to argue with Keynes about Wittgenstein, Virginia Woolf wrote to her other nephew Quentin, but got nowhere (V. Woolf, *Letters*, IV, 51).

Julian Bell's satire is most memorable not for its poetry, ideas or wit, but for its subject. It has been quoted in histories of philosophy and reprinted in collections of Wittgenstein studies. The epistle contrasts the poet's own good sense with his subject's 'sainted insanity'. Bell takes his stand in heroic couplets with Epicurus, Rabelais, Voltaire especially, and others including those in the Cambridge school of rational common sense. His one certain truth is fundamental to Moorean Bloomsbury, and that is 'Value is known and found in States of Mind'. (Bell had originally written 'Value resides alone in States of Mind' – a not uncommon misinterpretation of Moore's ethics that he changed when his poem was reprinted.) With this simple creed the poet takes on the logician because Wittgenstein does not stick to his trade but 'pontificates on art' among other things. (Examples of Wittgenstein's finding tricks in Milton, mastery in Dickens and political power in the

English king were deleted when Bell revised his poem; he also removed a complaint that Wittgenstein bored and damned those Bell admired or loved.) To defend the muse against 'Omniscient Wittgenstein' Bell's satire first criticises his claim 'All statements about Value nothing mean'. But Wittgenstein is not consistent here, as Bell goes on to write in lines that have often been quoted:

> For he talks nonsense, numerous statements makes,
> Forever his own vow of silence breaks;
> Ethics, aesthetics, talks of day and night
> And calls things good or bad, and wrong or right.
> The universe sails down its charted course,
> He smuggles knowledge from a secret source:
> A mystic in the end, confessed and plain,
> The ancient enemy returned again;
> Who knows by his direct experience
> What is beyond all knowledge and all sense.

The couplets here and elsewhere are rather disjointed but the points they make echo criticisms that were being made of the *Tractatus*. (It was Ramsey who said in 1929 that we should take the claim that philosophy is nonsense seriously 'and not pretend, as Wittgenstein does, that it is important nonsense!' – *Foundations*, p. 263.)

Continuing with Herr Wittgenstein's ethical and aesthetic beliefs, the poet claims less convincingly that the philosopher's mystery is 'but a State of Mind' which one day science will understand as it has the sick visions of saints. Bell's faith in science here is not characteristic of Bloomsbury, which like Wittgenstein and others was critical of the way it was combining with technology. More interesting for Wittgenstein's relation to Bloomsbury is Bell's urging of tolerance in contrast to Wittgenstein's pontifications. Religion is 'the ancient enemy returned' that the poem refers to earlier and associates with mysticism. (An allusion to the Fifth of November and 'the good old English feelings' with which religious fanatics like Guy Fawkes had once been intolerantly dealt with was also omitted in Bell's revision together with the reassurance that maniacs could now find heaven in a padded cell.) The remainder of the poem is occupied with the religious aspects of Wittgenstein's beliefs. Here Bell is very much with Bloomsbury. Voltaire is invoked again and then Marx on the opium of the people. Life's brevity and the silent spaces that frightened Pascal are calmly faced and Ludwig pitied for his painful asceticism. Some of the criticism here is quite off the mark. Bell seems not to know of Wittgenstein's work as an engineer and then architect when he writes

> For had he ever used his hands or eyes
> He might have turned from learning to be wise.

The poem continues with a description of natural beauty in landscape and the season that Bell celebrates in his lyric poetry; the conclusion is that beauty teaches better than religion how to accept the world. The tone reverts back to satire with the evoking of the classical shepherdess 'fair Chloe' who might persuade Wittgenstein that 'all Good, all Beauty lies' not in transcendent worlds but in 'Chloe's eyes'. There may well be an ironical allusion here to Wittgenstein's attitude towards women.

Although Julian Bell's poem suggests a reaction to Wittgenstein among some members of the Group, the satire cannot be taken as a typical work of theirs. Bloomsbury did not write public poetry, for one thing; for another, their literary work (like Wittgenstein's philosophy) was modernist, while Bell's poem is a neoclassic pastiche. Bloomsbury was much interested in the eighteenth century too, but they were also concerned with the limits of expression and with mysticism, neither of which had to be equated with theistic religion. These concerns leave no trace in Bell's satire. It is perhaps significant that when his writings were edited by his brother and published in 1937 by the Hogarth Press after Julian's death in the Spanish Civil War, the satire on Wittgenstein was not included.

There is an interesting disclaimer at the end of Bell's *Epistle* which appeared only when the poem was reprinted in a collection of satirical verse in 1932. The poem, says its author, is 'not intended as a personal attack, nor as a criticism of purely logical and philosophical achievements of Dr. Wittgenstein, but solely as a criticism of certain views on art and morals advocated by him three years ago'. The note was added because of Wittgenstein's notorious hostility to anyone referring to his ideas in print, according to Braithwaite who had experienced some of that hostility himself (Interview). When the poem was first published in 1930, Fania Pascal remembered how 'it released accumulated tension, resentment, perhaps fear. For no one could ever turn the tables on Wittgenstein and pay him back in kind' (Rhees, p. 31). And many years later I. A. Richards wrote of how shrewdly Julian Bell had taken Wittgenstein's measure, and he found 'the best couplets have a fine shocking impact' (*Letters*, p. 197). Wittgenstein's only reported response, according to Frances Partridge, was to lump Cambridge aesthetes together as 'these Julian Bells!' (Partridge, p. 160).[8] Bell's note is a little disingenuous, however, because his poem is, in part, a personal attack on the manner in which omniscient Ludwig laid down the law; the satire also reflects on the ideas of 'the great logician' because they are involved with his ethics and aesthetics.

As for the views referred to that Wittgenstein was advocating three years before, there is a record in the only public lecture Wittgenstein ever gave, at C. K. Ogden's invitation, for the Cambridge Heretics' Society in 1929 or 1930. (The Society's name was apparently derived from the requirement that in religious discussions arguments from authority were disallowed; both Virginia Woolf and Lytton Strachey had lectured to the Heretics in the 1920s.) The lecture was on ethics. It begins with Wittgenstein now accepting Moore's definition in *Principia Ethica* that ethics was 'the general inquiry into what is good', which for Wittgenstein includes aesthetics and, it soon appears, religion. Such an inquiry is no longer a subject for silence. But what can be said about it involves the misuse of language because words express only relative or natural matters of fact, while ethics and aesthetics were about absolute or supernatural judgements of value. Three examples of absolute experience are given by Wittgenstein: first there is wonder at the world's existence, as in the *Tractatus*; next and closer to more traditional religious experience is a state of mind in which one feels absolutely safe; last is the feeling of guilt, as if God disapproves of our behaviour. Though the descriptions of these experiences remain nonsensical for Wittgenstein, he still respects deeply the tendency, his own tendency, as he says in one of his brilliant metaphors, 'to run against the boundaries of language' which are 'the walls of our cage' ('Lecture', p. 12).

Wittgenstein's lecture displays his affinities with Bloomsbury and his differences from them around the time he began to change his philosophy. Preoccupation with the confines of language is naturally a literary preoccupation. The would-be writer (modelled partly on Desmond MacCarthy) in Virginia Woolf's 1931 novel *The Waves*, says at the end of the book that he now needs only 'a little language....a howl; a cry' (p. 191). But Bell's poem is a reminder of how distant from Bloomsbury were Wittgenstein's concerns with guilt and God. Bloomsbury also remained irremediably interested in the aspect of ethics that Wittgenstein dismissed as 'chatter' just before his return to Cambridge ('Lecture', p. 13).

VII.

With Wittgenstein's second coming, the relationship to Bloomsbury through Keynes began to be noticed in Cambridge. When Wittgenstein told F. R. Leavis during their brief relationship around 1930 to give up literary criticism, Leavis believed 'the easy aggressiveness of the injunction was the consequence of frequenting the Bloomsbury *milieu* in which he was "Ludwig" to Keynes and company' (Rhees, p. 79). (Leavis thought of retorting 'Give up philosophy, Wittgenstein', not knowing that Wittgenstein had done so once and would try to do so again.) That Wittgenstein was influenced by Bloomsbury in his attitude towards literary criticism and that the Group had little use for this form of writing which they practised a good deal (though not in Leavis's judgemental way) are both very doubtful assumptions. But those in Bloomsbury who were interested in the early work of Moore and Russell were also more receptive to Wittgenstein's ideas than Leavis, who deplored the irrelevance of analytic philosophy to literary studies.

Leavis's perception that Wittgenstein associated with Bloomsbury was becoming out of date. His relationship with Moore would continue and develop, but the intensity of Wittgenstein's friendship with Keynes was something that Keynes, now married and with many interests beyond Cambridge, continued to find fatiguing. 'The truth is', he wrote Wittgenstein in 1929, 'that I alternate between loving and enjoying you and your conversation and having my nerves worn to death by it. It's no new thing! I always have these twenty years' (*Cambridge Letters*, p. 234). Keynes became more a benefactor of Wittgenstein's than a close friend or philosophical colleague. When Keynes reviewed the posthumous volume of Ramsey's work in 1931 for the *New Statesman and Nation*, he referred to Wittgenstein 'wondering if his next book will be finished before time's chariots are too near', and then described Wittgenstein's current attitude towards philosophy 'as a sort of inspired nonsense having great value indeed for the individual but incapable of being exactly discussed' (*Collected Writings*, X, 337–8). It sounds as if Keynes had heard Wittgenstein's lecture to the Heretics, but his remark also refers to Ramsey's criticism of Wittgenstein's view that philosophy was important nonsense. Keynes's comments in his review are his and Bloomsbury's last on Wittgenstein's work. During the 1930s Keynes must have heard of Wittgenstein's developing ideas through his friend and economics colleague Piero Sraffa, whose important influence Wittgenstein acknowledged. Keynes eventually saw something of what Wittgenstein's next book was to be when he helped elect him to Moore's professorship at the end of the 1930s; but he appears to have written nothing about it.

Lytton Strachey died in 1932, Roger Fry two years later, Virginia Woolf in 1941 and Maynard Keynes in 1946. After twenty years, Bloomsbury's direct links with Wittgenstein were mostly ending as he began his later investigations around 1931. But there are still connections to be found between Bloomsbury and the Wittgenstein of the *Philosophical Investigations*. I want to conclude this survey by mentioning a few further aspects of their association. They concern Bloomsbury's principal writers Virginia Woolf, Lytton Strachey and E. M. Forster, as well as a late friendship in Wittgenstein's life.

Wittgenstein read Virginia Woolf's *To the Lighthouse*, which he liked with some reservations, and also possibly *Mrs. Dalloway*.[9] One thing both Woolf and Wittgenstein understood, particularly in their earlier lives, was the pull of suicide. After Woolf drowned herself, Wittgenstein told Rush Rhees that she could not rid herself of her father's belief that personal worth was measured by achievement in art, science or politics; this had led to her idea that the lack of rooms of their own kept women from being great composers, etc. 'Wittgenstein said this was obviously *not* the reason', Rhees reported, without saying what the real reason might be (p. 207). Why Wittgenstein thought Leslie Stephen measured people's worth by their successful careers is unclear. Rhees himself confuses Virginia Woolf's and Frank Ramsey's fathers, which limits the usefulness of his memoir.[10] It is possible, however, to see the contrast of Woolf's feminism and Wittgenstein's misogyny in their attitudes towards the work of Otto Weininger. A large claim has been made by Wittgenstein's latest biographer for Weininger's influence. Wittgenstein did put him in a 1931 list of people he had been influenced by, but his position there is not among the early influences but the later ones.[11] The significance of Weininger's anti-Semitic, misogynist and homophobic book *Sex and Character* appears in various remarks Wittgenstein wrote in 1931.

Weininger's book may be alluded to with 'the monumental work entitled *The Mental, Moral, and Physical Inferiority of Women*' that the speaker in Virginia Woolf's *A Room of One's Own* (1929) imagines a Teutonic professor writing. Wittgenstein did admit that Weininger had been very wrong on women and on the female element in men, however (Rhees, p. 106), and Weininger's ideas on androgyny may have contributed to Woolf's in her book.[12]

Wittgenstein's appreciation of Freud's interpretations and his scepticism about Freud's explanations provides another later connection with Bloomsbury. The Woolfs' Hogarth Press was publishing the authorised edition of Freud's work in English, translated by James Strachey. The influence of Freud on his brother Lytton's biographical art is clear in *Elizabeth and Essex*, which appeared in 1928. Wittgenstein continued to read or remember Lytton Strachey's biographies. In his lectures in the 1940s he cited the famous conclusion to Strachey's *Queen Victoria*, which was published the year the *Tractatus* appeared in a German periodical in 1921. Strachey imagines Victoria's dying state of mind that carries her back through her life to her earliest memories. According to Peter Geach, Wittgenstein used the famous passage to repudiate the notion that such an imaginative but unverifiable description of mental experience is meaningless. It has meaning, Wittgenstein said, 'through its connection with a wider public "language game" of describing people's thoughts...' (Geach, p. 3). It would be intriguing to explore the relations between Wittgenstein's discussions of mental acts and Woolf's fictive techniques of free indirect style by which she renders her characters' states of mind. Then there are the literary implications of Wittgenstein's discussions in the *Investigations* of seeing aspects. 'Seeing as, ...' for example is the subject of Virginia Woolf's first published story, 'The Mark on the Wall'. It would also be interesting to note links between Wittgenstein's later emphasis on conceptual multiplicity and the pluralism, eclecticism and avoidance of system that Bloomsbury derived largely from Moore. (Montaigne's 'the journey not the arrival matters', which Leonard Woolf took as the title for his last volume of autobiography, could have served Wittgenstein as another motto for his later philosophy.)

There is finally an interesting connection between the idea of connection itself in Wittgenstein and Bloomsbury. Wittgenstein's remarks on the interpretation of connections in Frazer and Spengler have provided the departure point for my description of relations between Wittgenstein and Bloomsbury. Indeed, the very conception of the Bloomsbury Group that I have been assuming is illuminated by Wittgenstein's fundamental notion of overlapping and criss-crossing similarities that constitute family resemblance. But in England in the 1930s connection was often described in a famous phrase of two words that, according to Goronwy Rhees, 'had more influence in shaping the emotional attitudes of the English governing class between the two world wars than any other single phrase in the English language' (Rosenbaum, *Edwardian Bloomsbury*, pp. 476–7). The words were 'Only connect...', the ambiguous, elliptical epigraph to E. M. Forster's 1910 novel *Howards End*. The things to be connected in that novel range from class through love, but in the 1930s they also became gay code and communist catchwords. Though Forster frequented King's College and the Apostles, he had little or nothing to do with Wittgenstein, but his was an influential English voice of the time. Wittgenstein in Cambridge may well have been familiar with the various interpretations of the words that could describe his own interest in cultural comparisons. Yet very different from Wittgenstein's convictions were many of Forster's liberal Bloomsbury beliefs, such as his refusal to believe in belief, as he says in his widely quoted essay 'What I Believe'. Wittgenstein did believe in belief, but he also made many of the criticisms of contemporary scientific, industrial civilisation that Forster and Bloomsbury did. Yet how would Wittgenstein have responded to Forster's famous hypothetical choosing to betray, if he had the guts, his country rather than his friend? Would Wittgenstein have given Forster's two cheers for the variety and for the criticism that democracy allowed? Perhaps he would at least have agreed with Forster that 'only Love the Beloved Republic' deserved three cheers ('What I Believe', pp. 65–73).

Indeed Wittgenstein may never have been completely separated from what is sometimes derogatorily referred to as the Bloomsbury milieu. His late love for Benedict Richards involved Wittgenstein in another Bloomsbury association. Richards, an undergraduate studying medicine at King's, was born in 1924, the son of two doctors. Before the First World War his mother Noel Olivier belonged to a group of friends and relatives Virginia Woolf called the Neo-Pagans. Included were the Olivier sisters and Rupert Brooke who was deeply in love with Noel, and whose death was tragic for her. The Neo-Pagans were also friends with various members of Bloomsbury including Keynes, Virginia herself, Vanessa

Bell, David Garnett and James Strachey. James was in love at the time with both Noel and Rupert. Years later, Noel Richards and James Strachey fell in love. The Richards had what today is called an open marriage, and during the 1930s when Ben Richards was growing up, Noel and James were often together in London and on holidays. (Later Noel's niece Anne Olivier Popham married Julian Bell's brother Quentin.) Wittgenstein was not ignorant of Ben Richards's background and the presence in it of James Strachey, a brother Apostle he had first met in 1912. Whatever effect, if any, this may have had on their relationship, it seems worth noting that friendship and love brought about the last connection of Ludwig Wittgenstein and the Bloomsbury Group.

Notes

NOTES TO CHAPTER 1: THE PHILOSOPHICAL REALISM OF VIRGINIA WOOLF

This essay was published in *English Literature and British Philosophy: A Collection of Essays* that I edited with an introduction in 1971. It is reprinted by permission of The University of Chicago Press, © 1971, all rights reserved. Citations of Virginia Woolf's then unpublished letters and manuscripts have been changed to published sources when possible and some quotations slightly corrected. Although more authoritative and complete editions of Woolf's diary, essays, stories and novels have now been edited by Anne Olivier Bell, Andrew McNeillie, Susan Dick, as well as the various editors of Blackwell's Shakespeare Head Edition of Virginia Woolf's works, I have retained my original references to Woolf's published work partly as a reminder that this essay is now a quarter of a century old. I have also shortened the ending of the essay.

1. *The Letters of Virginia Woolf*, ed. Nigel Nicolson and Joanne Trautmann (London, 1971–80), III, 85–6.
2. Volume and page numbers following references to Virginia Woolf's essays refer to *Collected Essays* (London, 1966), 4 vols.
3. Maxime Chastaing's misleadingly entitled *La philosophie de Virginia Woolf* (Paris, 1951) is the most extended attempt to relate philosophy to Virginia Woolf's work, but the results are paradoxical. Ignoring the evidence of Virginia Woolf's non-fiction, Chastaing extracts from contextless quotations taken from Virginia Woolf's novels a philosophy of redemption and grace that condemns empiricism by espousing it and showing the unendurable results.
4. John Maynard Keynes, 'My Early Beliefs', *Two Memoirs, Essays and Sketches in Biography* (New York, 1956), pp. 239–56.
5. The fullest treatments to date (1971) of the importance of *Principia Ethica* for Virginia Woolf's work are to be found in Irma Rantavaara's *Virginia Woolf and Bloomsbury* (Helsinki, 1953) and J. K. Johnstone's *The Bloomsbury Group* (London, 1954).
6. Leonard Woolf, *Sowing* (London, 1960), pp. 146–9.
7. Quoted in Floris Delattre, *Feux d'automne* (Paris, 1950), p. 239.
8. Leonard Woolf, *Beginning Again* (London, 1964), pp. 24–5.
9. *Letters*, I, 357, 364.
10. *The Philosophy of G. E. Moore*, ed. P. A. Schilpp (New York, 1952), p. 535.
11. G. E. Moore, 'The Refutation of Idealism', *Philosophical Studies* (London, 1922), p. 20.
12. Bertrand Russell, *Autobiography* (London, 1967), I:73.
13. G. E. Moore, 'Autobiography', *The Philosophy of G. E. Moore*, p. 22.
14. Bertrand Russell, *My Philosophical Development* (New York, 1959), p. 12.

15. 'The Refutation of Idealism', p. 25.
16. Arnold Kettle, *An Introduction to the English Novel* (New York, 1960), II, 106n.
17. John O. Nelson, 'Moore, George Edward', *The Encyclopedia of Philosophy*, ed. Paul Edwards (New York, 1967), V, 378–9.
18. Page numbers following references to Virginia Woolf's diary refer to *A Writer's Diary*, ed. Leonard Woolf (London, 1953).
19. G. E. Moore, *Principia Ethica* (Cambridge, 1965), p. 27.
20. Jean Guiguet, *Virginia Woolf and Her Works* (London, 1965), p. 385.
21. *Principia Ethica* is even quoted, though not named, in *The Voyage Out*, p. 82. (All references to Virginia Woolf's fiction as well as to *A Room of One's Own* refer to the uniform edition of her works published by the Hogarth Press, 1929–53. In the cases of *Jacob's Room*, *Mrs. Dalloway* and *The Waves*, the second uniform editions are used, the first now being out of print.)
22. R. F. Harrod, *The Life of John Maynard Keynes* (London, 1951), pp. 112–13.
23. G. E. Moore, 'The Nature and Reality of Objects of Perception', *Philosophical Studies*, pp. 53, 60 and 70ff.
24. See for example Ralph Freedman, *The Lyrical Novel* (Princeton, 1963), pp. 229–30.
25. Virginia Woolf's criticism of Joyce's method in *Ulysses* is also put in terms of 'our sense of being in a bright yet narrow room, confined and shut in, rather than enlarged and set free' outside and beyond the consciousness he represents (II, 107–8).
26. Quoted in John D. Gordan, *New in the Berg Collection, 1959–1961* (New York, 1964), p. 31.
27. See G. E. Moore, 'Mr. McTaggart's "Studies in Hegelian Cosmology"', *Proceedings of the Aristotelian Society*, II (1901–2), 177–214, and 'A Defense of Commonsense', *Philosophical Papers* (New York, 1962), pp. 32–59.
28. There are echoes of both the techniques and images of T. S. Eliot's poetry in *Jacob's Room* and other novels of Virginia Woolf, especially those with settings in London. 'Whispers of Immortality' was among the poems published by the Woolfs in 1919; it provides an interesting contrast to *Jacob's Room* in its use of philosophy.
29. Quoted in Charles G. Hoffmann, '"From Lunch to Dinner": Virginia Woolf's Apprenticeship', *Texas Studies in Literature and Language*, X (Winter 1969), 626.
30. E. M. Forster, 'The Early Novels of Virginia Woolf', *Abinger Harvest* (London, 1936), p. 109.
31. See the discussion of the distinction between introvertive and extrovertive mysticism in Ronald W. Hepburn, 'Mysticism, Nature and Assessment of', *Encyclopedia of Philosophy*, V, 429.
32. Virginia Woolf, *'The Hours': The British Museum Manuscript of 'Mrs Dalloway'*, ed. Helen M. Wussow (New York, 1996), p. 153.
33. *A Writer's Diary*, p. 57.
34. Clarissa Dalloway's idea of acts of consciousness detached from the perceiver is not unlike G. F. Moore's description of a belief (in

the common-sense view of the world) 'that there *may* have been a time when acts of consciousness were attached to *no* material bodies anywhere in the Universe, and *may* again be such a time...' in *Some Main Problems of Philosophy* (London, 1953), p. 11.

35. Bertrand Russell, *History of Western Philosophy* (London, 1961), p. 764. Russell's critique of Bergson originally appeared in *The Monist* in 1912.
36. See *A Writer's Diary*, pp. 76–7; Noel Annan's *Leslie Stephen* (Cambridge, Mass., 1952), pp. 98ff; and Quentin Bell's 'The Mausoleum Book', *A Review of English Literature*, VI (Jan 1965), 9–18.
37. M. C. Bradbrook, 'Notes on the Style of Mrs. Woolf', *Scrutiny*, I (May 1932), 37.
38. *Abinger Harvest*, p. 110.
39. Erich Auerbach, *Mimesis: The Representation of Reality in Western Literature* (Princeton, 1953), p. 536. Two recent studies of *To the Lighthouse* both use Auerbach's insight and emphasise the perspectives or viewpoints in the novel, but neither discusses the necessary objective reality on which these focus. Avrom Fleishman's 'Woolf and McTaggart', *ELH*, argues that McTaggart influenced Virginia Woolf through his ideas about selfhood, love, time and psychic communication. McTaggart's ethical ideas may have influenced Virginia Woolf to some extent through their importance for the Apostles (including Moore), but McTaggart's idealism, which entailed a denial of the reality of time, space and matter, is remote from her fictional world. Fleishman's principal illustration is *To the Lighthouse* but his interpretation does not take into account Mr Ramsay's role in the novel. Mitchell A. Leaska's *Virginia Woolf's Lighthouse: A Study in Critical Method* (London, 1970) is one of the few studies of the novel to give Mr Ramsay his due and reduce Mrs Ramsay to human proportions. Leaska's method of analysing points of view in the novel (and analysing samples from them stylistically) does not consider the realistic philosophical implications of the multipersonal novel and thus does not recognize how Lily Briscoe's final synthesis depends upon them.
40. In an illuminating criticism of *The Waves* based on a study of the two earlier complete versions of the novel that differ basically from the published third version, J. W. Graham argues in 'Point of View in *The Waves*: Some Services of the Style', *University of Toronto Quarterly*, XXXIX (April 1970), 193–211, that beginning with *Orlando* and essays written around the same time Virginia Woolf became increasingly dissatisfied with the use of psychology and personality in her fiction and sought to represent more the impersonality that appears in *The Waves*. In support of this interpretation of her development, Graham discusses how *The Waves* grew out of the framework of a mind thinking the novel – an ur-narrator whose vestiges can be found in the lyrical interludes and in the uniform style of the different soliloquies. But underneath the change from personality to impersonality lies a continuing preoccupation with consciousness that develops steadily from Virginia Woolf's early work and that is another reason why Virginia Woolf is more accurately to be described as an epistemological novelist rather than a psychological one. The concern with

perception underlies the growth of *The Waves* as well, for there Virginia Woolf moves from an ur-consciousness to the six that finally are dramatised in the novel.
41. 'The Refutation of Idealism', p. 28.
42. *Explorations* (New York, 1962), p. 373.
43. *Essays and Introductions* (New York, 1961), pp. 404–6.

NOTES TO CHAPTER 2: BERTRAND RUSSELL: THE LOGIC OF A LITERARY SYMBOL

Originally presented at the Bertrand Russell Centenary Celebrations, McMaster University, October 1972, this lecture was reprinted in *The University of Toronto Quarterly*, XLII (Summer 1973), 301–27 and then in *Russell in Review*, ed. J. E. Thomas and Kenneth Blackwell (Toronto, 1976), pp. 57–87. I am grateful for permission to republish from the editors and the University of Toronto Press. In reprinting the essay here I have added a footnote from the supplement I wrote entitled 'Gilbert Cannan and Bertrand Russell' in *Russell: The Journal of the Bertrand Russell Archives*, XXI–XXII (Spring–Summer 1976), 16–25. Some of the quotations in the original piece have been removed or reduced, and the discussion of Lawrence's story 'The Blind Man' has been somewhat revised.

1. Quoted in Hugh Kenner, *The Pound Era* (Berkeley, 1971), p. 12.
2. *English Literature and British Philosophy*, ed. S. P. Rosenbaum (Chicago, 1971).
3. See for example 'Books that Influenced Me in Youth', *Fact and Fiction* (London, 1961), and *The Autobiography of Bertrand Russell, 1872–1914* (London, 1967).
4. Constance Malleson, 'Fifty Years, 1916–1966', *Bertrand Russell, Philosopher of the Century*, ed. Ralph Schoenman (London, 1967), p. 20.
5. 'On Denoting', *Logic and Knowledge*, ed. R. C. Marsh (London, 1956), pp. 47ff.
6. *The Principles of Mathematics*, 2nd ed. (London, 1937), pp. 358–60.
7. *Nobel Lectures, 1901–1967: Literature*, ed. Horst Frenz (Amsterdam, 1969), p. 449. Russell says in his *Autobiography, 1944–1967* (London, 1969, p. 30) that the prize was for *Marriage and Morals*, but the only works mentioned in the presentation to him were *A History of Western Philosophy*, *Human Knowledge: Its Scope and Limits*, *Sceptical Essays* and 'My Mental Development'.
8. Russell, for example, wrote letters of philosophical advice to the poet Robert Nichols, but the ideas expressed there are so familiar that it would practically be impossible to establish their influence on Nichols's poetry. For Russell's letters see Christopher Hassall, *A Biography of Edward Marsh* (New York, 1959), pp. 509–11, and the Bertrand Russell Archives at McMaster University, Hamilton, Ontario.
9. There is extreme variation in the reactions of writers and critics to 'A Free Man's Worship'. Joseph Conrad wrote to Russell, 'For the

marvellous pages on the Worship of a free man the only return one can make is that of a deep admiring affection, which, if you never see me again and forgot my existence tomorrow, will be unalterably yours *usque ad finem*' (*Autobiography, 1872–1914*, p. 225). But T. E. Hulme wrote that 'what Mr Russell has to say on the subject in "A Free Man's Worship" is so extremely commonplace, and is expressed in such a painful piece of false and sickly rhetoric, that I have no patience to deal with it here' (*Speculations*, London, 1924, pp. 29–30). Later on in his career Russell himself came not to think well of the essay. (See 'How I Write', *Portraits from Memory*, London, 1956, p. 196.) Casual satirical allusion to Russell's famous essay can be found in Campbell's *The Georgiad*, for example, and in Edgell Rickword's 'The Encounter', where the speaker is afraid that his companion Twittingpan will expound the essay:

> 'Lord Russell says...' I feared he would begin
> an exposition of the free man's worship,
> that neo-anabaptist, compelled to dip
> not now from mystic but hygienic motives.

(*Collected Poems*, London, 1947, p. 58). Fortunately Twittingpan is distracted at this moment and his allusion to Russell is left unfinished.

10. *Anatomy of Criticism* (Princeton, 1957), pp. 308–12, 365.
11. *Autobiography, 1944–1967*, p. 34. 'The Perplexities' is included as the first work in *The Collected Stories of Bertrand Russell*, ed. Barry Feinberg (London, 1972).
12. *Autobiography, 1872–1914*, p. 217 n.2, and Lester E. Denonn, 'Bibliography of the Writings of Bertrand Russell', *The Philosophy of Bertrand Russell*, ed. Paul Arthur Schilpp, 4th ed. (New York, 1963), II, 815.
13. 'Bibliography', II, 761.
14. *The Philosophy of Mr. B*rtr*nd R*ss*ll*, ed. Philip E. B. Jourdain (London, 1918), p. 3.
15. Ibid., pp. 81–2.
16. Ibid., pp. 3–4.
17. Ibid., pp. 56, 92.
18. Katherine Anne Porter, Bertrand Russell and Mark Van Doren, 'Lewis Carroll: *Alice in Wonderland*', in *The New Invitation to Learning*, ed. Mark Van Doren (New York, 1942), p. 209.
19. 'The Prelate and the Commissar', *The Humanist*, XIII (Sept–Oct 1953), 206–7.
20. Jourdain, p. 29.
21. *Autobiography, 1914–1944*, p. 19 n.
22. T. S. Eliot, *The Sacred Wood* (London, 1920), p. 66.
23. 'Style and Thought', *The Nation*, XXII (23 Mar 1918), 770. This review is unsigned, but Alan Wood identifies it as Eliot's in his biography of Russell (*Bertrand Russell, The Passionate Sceptic*, London, 1957, pp. 94–5).
24. *Ottoline: The Early Memoirs of Lady Ottoline Morrell*, ed. Robert Gathorne-Hardy (London, 1963), p. 257.

Notes 195

25. *Autobiography, 1914–1944*, pp. 58–9.
26. Ibid., pp. 173–4.
27. Eliot reviewed *Why I Am Not a Christian* in the *Criterion*, VI (Aug 1927), 177–9. Eliot had criticised Russell the year before in the *Criterion* for his pamphlet *What I Believe*; Eliot grouped Russell with H. G. Wells and George Bernard Shaw, adding parenthetically, 'I am sorry to include the name of Mr. Russell, whose intellect would have reached the first rank even in the thirteenth century, but when he trespasses outside of mathematical philosophy his excursions are often descents' (*Criterion*, IV, Jan 1926, 6.) There are also two interesting unpublished letters from Eliot to Russell about *Why I Am Not a Christian* in the Russell Archives at McMaster. In the first, Eliot noted that he was raised an atheist, but Russell was apparently brought up and obviously remained an Evangelical; the letter concludes advising Russell to stick to mathematics. Russell apparently replied that his piece was a work of propaganda, not theological speculation, and Eliot rejoined that he still did not see a justification for bad reasons, though what he most disliked was the smell of rotting Protestantism in Russell's writing.
28. Donald Gallup, 'The "Lost" Manuscripts of T. S. Eliot', *Bulletin of the New York Public Library*, LXXII (Dec 1968), 650. The poem appears in *The Complete Poems of T. S. Eliot* (London, 1969), p. 31. Earlier versions are given in T. S. Eliot, *Inventions of the March Hare: Poems, 1909–1917*, ed. Christopher Ricks (London, 1996), pp. 344–5.
29. If it were necessary to confirm the identity of Mr Apollinax, there exists in the Russell Archives a letter from Vivien Eliot, written at the time of her husband's breakdown, offering Russell congratulations on the birth of his son and assuring him that even if the baby's ears are not pointed at birth they will become sharper as time goes on. Russell has added a pencilled note to the letter explaining that this is 'an allusion to his poem about me, "Mr. Apollinax"'. Vivien Eliot's letter also suggests the friendliness with which both Eliot and Russell took the poem.
30. In a minor and devious way Russell also turns up in *The Waste Land*, suitably enough in a disguise again. F. H. Bradley is there in the notes to the poem, of course, and Russell claimed to have suggested to Eliot the vision of the disintegrating yet unreal London that Eliot put into Part V of the poem. (See *Autobiography, 1914–1944*, p. 18 n.) But it is at Madam Sosostris's, the famous clairvoyante, that we shall find a trace of Russell. Eliot acknowledged that he may have taken her name, slightly changed, from Aldous Huxley's *Crome Yellow*, which appeared shortly before Eliot composed the main part of *The Waste Land*. (See Grover Smith, 'The Fortuneteller in Eliot's *Waste Land*', *American Literature*, XXV, Jan 1954, 490–2.) And Huxley's Madame Sesostris was, as we shall see, Bertrand Russell in double disguise. Eliot could hardly have been unaware that the character disguised as Madame Sesostris in *Crome Yellow* was rather closely modelled on a man he not only knew well but also had depicted earlier in one of his own poems. Eliot's Madame Sosostris bears no

real resemblance to Russell, though she does have a number of characteristics that have been associated with Russell as a symbol: she is disguised, she has extraordinary mental powers, and through her wicked pack of cards she is a dealer in metamorphoses, some of which have sexual implications.

31. Lawrence's novel was completed in 1916 but had to wait four years for publication; it was privately printed in the United States and England in 1920, and issued in a trade edition in June 1921 (Warren Roberts, *A Bibliography of D. H. Lawrence*, London, 1963, pp. 44–5). In the private editions, Sir Joshua's name was Malleson but in the first trade edition it was changed to Mattheson (and misprinted Matheson once). Professor John Slater has pointed out to me that Lady Constance Malleson herself wrote a *roman à clef* about her relationship with Russell and others. *The Coming Back*, published in 1933, has Russell disguised as a Castilian-cum-Cambridge astronomer. T. S. Eliot and Lady Ottoline Morrell, among others, figure in the novel, but the thinness of the fiction and its disguises make *The Coming Back* of little literary interest.

32. Sir Joshua appears in 'Breadalby', Chapter VIII of *Women in Love*.

33. D. H. Lawrence, 'A Propos of *Lady Chatterley's Lover*', *Phoenix II*, ed. Warren Roberts and Harry T. Moore (New York, 1968), p. 512.

34. 'The Mythology of Friendship: D. H. Lawrence, Bertrand Russell and "The Blind Man"', *English Literature and British Philosophy*, pp. 285–315. Paul Delany has suggested that James Barrie was also used as a model by Lawrence in his story (*D. H. Lawrence's Nightmare* (New York, 1978, pp. 372–3).

35. 'The Crown', *Phoenix II*, p. 412.

36. *Autobiography, 1914–1944*, p. 53.

37. The typescript is printed as an appendix to *D. H. Lawrence's Letters to Bertrand Russell*, ed. Harry T. Moore (New York, 1948), but it is possible to have an accurate idea of what Lawrence was commenting on only in the one facsimile page of the typescript that is reproduced facing page 88. The original typescript is at the Humanities Research Center, University of Texas.

38. The nature of the disagreement between Lawrence and Russell can be illustrated from Lawrence's comments on Russell's conception of morality. Russell wrote in his typescript, 'What is essence of *morality*? A man's acts affect others therefore others are interested in what he does. A *moral* act is one conformable to the desires of the others affected by the act. Why should a man be moral? Because action against the desires of others makes him disliked, which is disagreeable to him.' Through these statements Lawrence has scrawled 'NO! NO!' and in the margin he insisted that the essence of morality is 'the sense of Truth' and asked Russell, 'Why do you use "moral" when you only mean, "well-behaved"?' (*Lawrence's Letters to Russell*, p. 88).

39. In his book, Russell, for example, adopts Lawrence's idea expressed in his comments on the typescript, that a genuine community requires an organic common purpose.

40.	*Lawrence's Letters to Russell*, pp. 59–60. 'The Danger to Civilization' is in Russell's *Justice in War-Time* (Chicago and London, 1916).
41.	*Autobiography, 1914–1944*, pp. 22–3. In the original draft of his autobiography, completed in 1931 and now in the Russell Archives, there is no mention of Lawrence; Russell's account of Lawrence was not written until the 1950s.
42.	*Lawrence's Letters to Russell*, p. 61. In his next letter to Russell, Lawrence wrote: 'We are not really enemies: it is only a question of attitude' (p. 62).
43.	Ibid., p. 63.
44.	*Autobiography, 1914–1944*, p. 22. Russell misquotes Lawrence's letter in his autobiography by silently omitting parts of it.
45.	'The Blind Man', *The Complete Short Stories of D. H. Lawrence* (London, 1955), II, 357, 349, 355.
46.	Ibid., pp. 359–60.
47.	*The Collected Letters of D. H. Lawrence*, ed. Harry T. Moore (New York, 1962), I, 566.
48.	'The Blind Man', pp. 363–5.
49.	Ibid., p. 361.
50.	Huxley wrote *Crome Yellow* in the summer of 1921 (*Letters of Aldous Huxley*, ed. Grover Smith, London, 1969, p. 13).
51.	*Letters of Huxley*, p. 198.
52.	*Crome Yellow* (London, 1921), pp. 21–2.
53.	Ibid., pp. 240–2.
54.	Ibid., p. 273.
55.	Ibid., pp. 286–7.
56.	See for example 'My Mental Development', *The Philosophy of Bertrand Russell*, I, 19–20.
57.	*Crome Yellow*, pp. 252–3.
58.	Ronald W. Clark, *The Huxleys* (New York, 1968), p. 224.
59.	Russell's *The Scientific Outlook*, which appeared just before *Brave New World*, anticipated a number of Huxley's ideas in that novel.
60.	Cannan's *Pugs and Peacocks* appeared several months before Huxley's novel. The character of the aristocratic mathematician Melian Stokes is a member of that family of symbolic representations created by Eliot, Lawrence and Huxley. In the sequel *Sembal* (1922) Stokes plays a smaller role, but in *The House of Prophecy* (1924) he is again a major figure. These last two novels are crudely anti-Semitic even by the standards of the 1920s with their use of a megalomaniacal Jew as the central character. They are not the kinds of novels one would expect from the author of *Mendel* (1916), Cannan's most successful novel, which portrayed a Jewish painter resembling Mark Gertler. Cannan became insane, suffering himself from megalomania according to one account, and a fourth volume of these 'Novels of a New Time' was never completed. Melian's prehistorical appearance, mechanical movements, brilliant intelligence, pointed wit, and political as well as philosophical concerns can all be recognised in other literary treatments of Russell. But again, as in 'The Blind Man', Stokes is a sexual innocent, and Cannan's treatment is not basically satiric.

61. Though written in the 1920s, *Crome Yellow* harks back to Huxley's experiences at Garsington during the war; the temporal setting of the novel is left quite vague in relation to the war, however.
62. *Memoirs of an Infantry Officer: The Complete Memoirs of George Sherston* (London, 1937), pp. 477–9. Sherston underlines in the book of lectures Tyrrell has given him such Lawrentian sentiments as 'What integrates an individual life is a consistent creative purpose or unconscious direction' (pp. 489–90). This quotation is to be found on page 229 of *Principles of Social Reconstruction* (London, 1916).
63. Sassoon never regretted his pacifist activities, and letters in the Russell Archives show that Sassoon remained a supporter of Russell throughout his life. During the war, however, Sassoon's friend Robert Graves – the David Cromlech of *Memoirs of an Infantry Officer* – wrote to Russell accusing him of exploiting Sassoon for pacifist purposes when Sassoon was mentally ill. (Graves's letter to Russell is in the Russell Archives.) Another poet of the war, David Jones, alludes to Russell's activities more favourably; a soldier in his poem *In Parenthesis* – first published in 1937 – suggests ironically that one of his bloodthirsty patriotic mates might want, among other things, to 'garrotte Mr. Bertrand-bloody-Russell with the Union Flag...' (*In Parenthesis*, New York, 1961, p. 143). (Russell does not figure significantly in Pat Barker's *Regeneration*.)
64. W. B. Yeats refers to Noyes's poem on Russell written in the 1920s, though I have been unable to locate it (*W. B. Yeats and T. Sturge Moore: Their Correspondence, 1901–1937*, ed. Ursula Bridge, New York, 1953, p. 114). Noyes wrote another poem on the same theme, entitled 'Thoughts and Billiard Balls', and published it in *Punch*, CCXXXII (30 Jan 1957), 195.
65. Roy Campbell, *The Georgiad* (London, 1931), pp. 17–18.
66. Ibid., p. 62.
67. Ibid., pp. 38–9.
68. The novel was called *Arabella* and written in the middle 1930s. According to Andrew Wright, 'The principal figure in *Arabella* is Professor Willie Hoopey, the victim and the disciple of both Nazism and Communism. He is credulous, intelligent, learned; Cary told me that Hoopey was suggested to him by the character of Bertrand Russell. Hoopey's journey to Paris and a series of taxi accidents, to Germany and the Nazis, to Soviet Russia and a Sovietized Washington, is a progress from one inadequate philosophical position to another. Although from the beginning, as a Blake-quoting believer in man as an artist, he is anti-violent, and remains so in the face of violence, his journey is necessary before he can discover that behind systems, above man, beyond philosophy, is God.' Wright concludes that *Arabella* is not a great novel (*Joyce Cary: A Preface to his Novels*, London, 1958, pp. 51–2). There are also some distinct echoes of Russell in the character of Sir Robert Tinney in Cary's last, unfinished novel, *The Captive and the Free* (1959). Sir Robert is a physicist who went to jail for conscientious objection in the First World War, who likes upsetting people's apple-carts, and who uses a Rational Truth Society to help

discredit Preedy, a faith-healer whom Cary contrasts favourably with Tinney.
69. Antony Powell, *Afternoon Men* (Boston and Toronto, 1963), pp. 21, 30, 51–2.
70. Myra Buttle [Victor Purcell], *The Bitches' Brew, or The Plot Against Bertrand Russell* (London, 1960), pp. 5, 87.
71. One exception may be Czeslaw Milosz's novel *The Seizure of Power* (New York, 1955). As described by I. F. Stone, this story of the Polish underground in the Second World War includes a resistance fighter who 'had taken the name Bertrand as his "*nom de guerre*, in honour of Bertrand Russell. After the war he wanted to devote himself exclusively," so Milosz describes him, "to mathematical logic." But it was more than admiration for the *Principia Mathematica* which explained why a man in the Polish underground took the name of the British philosopher. "Bertrand," as Milosz pictures him, was somehow different. "It was difficult," he writes, "to find fault with him because he was an exceptionally good shot." Yet in the eyes of the underground group leader, "Bertrand" had many failings. He "made no secret of his contempt for the army and for war." His "companions in the battalion scornfully called him a pacifist." It is when we come to the final touch of his portrait that we fully understand his identification with Bertrand Russell. "One day," Milosz relates, "he had brought a wounded German to safety under fire." [P. 59. See also p. 65.] It was this survival of an objective of humanity, and this willingness to take risks on its behalf, which marked "Bertrand" as one of Russell's brood' (I. F. Stone, 'To Oppose the Stream', *Bertrand Russell, Philosopher of the Century*, p. 56). There is also a novel by Harvey Swados, called *Celebration* (1974), which according to Sheila Turcon of the Russell Archives at McMaster is about the elderly Russell and his notorious secretary Ralph Schoenman but put into an American setting.
72. *Portnoy's Complaint* (New York, 1969), p. 231.
73. This is especially true in the theatre, where parodies of Russell appear to have begun with the revue *Beyond the Fringe* (1961). One of the original members of the cast was Alan Bennett, who mocked Russell's and Lady Ottoline's memoirs in his play *Forty Years On*. At one point in the play within the play Russell mentions to 'Lady Sybilline Quarrell' that 'I had no contact with my own body until the spring of 1887, when I suddenly found my feet. I deduced the rest logically' (*Forty Years On*, London, 1969, p. 42). In Tom Stoppard's *Jumpers*, Russell is invoked as a logician, lecher and peace-maker by the central character, a philosopher named George Moore, and his wife Dorothy, as the following excerpt shows:

> GEORGE: Do I say 'My friend the late Bertrand Russell' or 'My late friend Bertrand Russell'? They both sound funny. (*Pause.*)
> DOTTY: Probably because he wasn't your friend.
> GEORGE: Well, I don't know about that.
> DOTTY (*angrily*): He was *my* friend. If he hadn't asked me who was that bloke always hanging about, you'd never have met him.

> GEORGE: Nevertheless, I did meet him, and we talked animatedly for some time.
> DOTTY: As I recall, *you* talked animatedly for some time about language being the aniseed trail that draws the hounds of heaven when the metaphysical fox has gone to earth; he must have thought you were barmy.
> GEORGE (*hurt*): I resent that. My metaphor of the fox and the hounds was an allusion, as Russell well understood, to his Theory of Descriptions.
> DOTTY: The Theory of Descriptions was not what was on his mind that night. For one thing it was sixty years since he'd thought it up, and for another he was trying to telephone Mao Tse Tung.
> GEORGE: I was simply trying to bring his mind back to matters of universal import, and away from the day-to-day parochialism of international politics.
> DOTTY: *Universal import!* You're living in dreamland!
> GEORGE: Oh really? Well, I wouldn't have thought that trying to get the local exchange to put you through to Chairman Mao with the wine-waiter from the Pagoda Garden hanging on to the bedroom extension to interpret, showed a grasp of the real world...
> (*Jumpers*, London, 1972, p. 31).

74. *W. B. Yeats and T. Sturge Moore*, p. 114 passim.
75. *Ex-Prodigy* (New York, 1953), pp. 194–5. Wiener recalls how the three most important philosophers at Trinity College were known as the Mad Tea Party of Trinity: Russell was the Mad Hatter, McTaggart the Dormouse and G. E. Moore the March Hare.
76. Virginia Woolf, *Diary*, ed. Anne Olivier Bell (London, 1978), II, 295, 147.
77. *Sowing* (London, 1960), p. 134.

NOTES TO CHAPTER 3: BLOOMSBURY LETTERS

This paper was read at a session of the Modern Language Association on Nonfictional Prose: The Place of Letter Writing in Literary History, December 1980, and printed in *Centrum*, New Series, I (Fall 1981), 113–19. It is reprinted by permission of the editor. My conception of literary history is given in the introduction to *Victorian Bloomsbury: The Early Literary History of the Bloomsbury Group* (London and New York, 1987), 1–18. Also referred to is Roman Jakobson's 'Two Aspects of Language and Two Types of Aphasic Disturbances', *Fundamentals of Language*, ed. Jakobson and Morris Halle (The Hague, 1955), pp. 69–82.

NOTES TO CHAPTER 4: KEYNES, LAWRENCE AND CAMBRIDGE REVISITED

This article was originally published in *The Cambridge Quarterly*, XI (1982), 252–64. I have added a postscript and expanded the notes.

1. John Maynard Keynes, *The Collected Writings*, ed. Donald Moggeridge and Elizabeth Johnson (London, 1972), X, 430–2.
2. Keynes, X, 433–50.
3. F. R. Leavis, 'Keynes, Lawrence and Cambridge', *The Common Pursuit* (London, 1953), pp. 255–60.
4. Bertrand Russell, 'D. H. Lawrence', *Portraits from Memory* (New York, 1956), pp. 111–16.
5. Leonard Woolf, *Sowing: An Autobiography of the Years 1880–1904* (London, 1960), pp. 144–9.
6. R. B. Braithwaite, 'Keynes as a Philosopher', *Essays on John Maynard Keynes*, ed. Milo Keynes (Cambridge, 1975), pp. 237–46.
7. Keynes, X, 446.
8. Keynes, X, 433.
9. David Garnett papers, Harry Ransom Humanities Research Center, University of Texas at Austin; quoted by permission of the Center and Mr Timothy Moore.
10. G. E. Moore papers, Cambridge University Library; quoted by permission of Mr Timothy Moore.
11. Keynes, X, 428, 435.
12. Ottoline Morrell, *Ottoline at Garsington: Memoirs of Lady Ottoline Morrell, 1915–1918*, ed. Robert Gathorne-Hardy (London, 1974), pp. 56–7.
13. Goldsworthy Lowes Dickinson, *The Greek View of Life*, preface by E. M. Forster (London, 1957), p. 158.
14. D. H. Lawrence, *Letters*, III, ed. James T. Boulton and Andrew Robertson (Cambridge, 1984), p. 49.
15. Morrell, p. 56.
16. Keynes, X, 441.
17. Lawrence, *Letters*, II, ed. George J. Zytaruk and James T. Boulton (Cambridge, 1981), p. 323.
18. Quentin Bell, *Bloomsbury* (London, 1968), pp. 73–7, 119–20.
19. David Garnett, 'D. H. Lawrence and Frieda', *Great Friends: Portraits of Seventeen Writers* (London, 1979), pp. 88–9.
20. Keynes, X, 450.
21. Lawrence, *Letters*, II, 300.
22. See 'Bertrand Russell: The Logic of a Literary Symbol', above, pp. 37–59.
23. Keynes, X, 430.
24. Garnett, *Great Friends*, p. 88.
25. Lawrence, *Letters*, II, 320.
26. For Garnett's and Grant's relationship, see Frances Spalding, *Duncan Grant: a Biography* (London, 1977).

27. Keynes, X, 432.
28. Quoted in Richard Garnett, *Constance Garnett: A Heroic Life* (London, 1991), p. 296.

NOTES TO CHAPTER 5: E. M. FORSTER'S *ASPECTS OF THE NOVEL* AND LITERARY HISTORY

Delivered at the Forster centenary conference held at Concordia University in Montreal, May 1979, this lecture was then published in *E. M. Forster: Centenary Revaluations*, ed. Judith Scherer Herz and Robert K. Martin (Toronto, 1982) and is reprinted by permission of the editors. The notes have been slightly revised and expanded.

1. Page references in the text are to E. M. Forster, *Aspects of the Novel*, ed. Oliver Stallybrass (London, 1974). Among the various materials included in this edition are the preparatory notes Forster made in his *Commonplace Book*.
2. See for example Ralph Cohen, 'Genre Theory, Literary History and Historical Change', *Theoretical Issues in Literary History*, ed. David Perkins (Cambridge, Mass., 1991), pp. 85–113.
3. Forster's letters to the Woolfs are in the Sussex University Library and the Berg Collection of the New York Public Library. See also *Selected Letters*, ed. Mary Lago and P. N. Furbank, 2 vols. (London, 1983–5).
4. *Anonymity: An Enquiry* (London, 1925; rpt. *Two Cheers for Democracy*, ed. Oliver Stallybrass, London, 1972), pp. 77–93.
5. The Trinity College Cambridge Clark Lectures for 1927 had originally been offered to Percy Lubbock, but he declined. The College appears to have wanted some lectures on fiction. Walter de la Mare had given the Clark Lectures on the art of fiction in 1922 but they were never published. (See Ronald Schuchard, Introduction to T. S. Eliot's Clark Lectures, *The Varieties of Metaphysical Poetry* (London, 1993), pp. 19, 320.)
6. *The Letters of Virgina Woolf, 1923–1928*, ed. Nigel Nicolson and Joanne Trautmann (London, 1977), III, 266.
7. See *The Bloomsbury Group: A Collection of Memoirs, Commentary and Criticism*, ed. S. P. Rosenbaum (Toronto, 1975), p. 25.
8. Roger Fry, *Vision and Design* (London, 1920), p. 194.
9. Clive Bell, *Art* (London, 1914), pp. 8, 25.
10. I. A. Richards, *Principles of Literary Criticism* (London, 1924; rpt. London, 1961), Chapters I, II and III.
11. See Roger Fry, *Transformations* (London, 1926), Chapter I, and Clive Bell, *Landmarks in Nineteenth-Century Painting* (London, 1927), pp. vii–x.
12. A. C. Bradley, 'Poetry for Poetry's Sake', *Oxford Lectures on Poetry* (London, 1909), pp. 16–17.
13. For Virginia Woolf's reviews of *Aspects of the Novel* see B. J. Kirkpatrick, *A Bibliography of Virginia Woolf*, Revised Edition (London, 1967).

For the correspondence between Forster and Virginia Woolf see *The Letters of Virginia Woolf*, III, 437–9; Quentin Bell, *Virginia Woolf: A Biography* (London, 1972), II, 134–5; and P. N. Furbank, *E. M. Forster: A Life* (London, 1978), II, 146–7.
14. Bell, *Art*, p. 98.
15. Clive Bell, *Civilisation* (London, 1928), p. 170.
16. Forster's review is included as an appendix to Stallybrass's edition; Woolf's is in *The Essays of Virginia Woolf*, ed. Andrew McNeillie (London, 1988), III, 43–7.
17. T. S. Eliot, *The Sacred Wood* (London, 1920; rpt. London, 1960), p. 37.
18. Eliot, p. xiii.
19. Aristotle, *The Poetics*, trans. S. H. Butcher, ed. John Gassner, 4th ed. (n. p., 1951), VI, 6 and VI, 9. 1450a.
20. Aristotle, X. 3. 1452a.
21. Aristotle, *De Poetica*, trans. Ingram Bywater in *The Basic Works of Aristotle*, ed. Richard McKeon (New York, 1941), pp. 1460–1.
22. Alain's discussions of history and fiction are in Chapters 5 to 8 in Part 10 of *Système des beaux-arts* (Paris, 1920; rpt. Paris, 1926), pp. 316–28.
23. In April 1925, Forster met Mauron in France to work on a translation of *A Passage to India* (Furbank, *Forster*, II, 138). Fry heard Mauron read 'Beauty in Literature' in Pontigny in September 1925, and wrote to Virginia Woolf that he had arranged to translate it. (Fry's unpublished letters to Virginia Woolf are at the University of Sussex.)
24. *The Nature of Beauty in Art and Literature*, trans. Roger Fry (London, 1927), pp. 66–7.
25. Mauron, p. 78.
26. Mauron in turn translated *Aspects of the Novel* in *Mesures* in 1928. (The translation is not listed in B. J. Kirkpatrick's bibliography of Forster.)
27. Forster thought that in *The Turn of the Screw* James was 'merely declining to think about homosex, and the knowledge that he is declining throws him into the necessary fluster' (*Aspects*, p. 134).
28. *Henry James and H. G. Wells: A Record of Their Friendship, Their Debate on the Art of Fiction, and Their Quarrel*, ed. Leon Edel and Gordon N. Ray (Urbana Ill. 1958), p. 244. (The ellipses are Wells's.) According to Edel and Ray, James's review of contemporary fiction, 'The Younger Generation' started the debate. Forster was, surprisingly, not mentioned at all by James in this 1914 survey written for the *Times Literary Supplement*, though he had published four novels by then. James's ignoring of Forster may have contributed to Forster's dislike of him.
29. See 'The Novels of E. M. Forster', *Collected Essays* (London, 1966), I, 342–51.
30. Forster refers to Lawrence's articles on Melville in *Aspects*, p. 99.
31. Bell and Furbank mention only a single exchange of letters. There are two more letters from Forster and one from Virginia Woolf about *Aspects of the Novel*.
32. *James and Wells*, p. 267.
33. See 'The Philosophical Realism of Virginia Woolf' above, pp. 1–36.

34. See *The Diary of Virginia Woolf*, ed. Anne Olivier Bell (London, 1978), II, 339–42.
35. See for example Samuel Hynes, 'The Whole Contention between Mr. Bennett and Mrs. Woolf', *Edwardian Occasions* (New York, 1972), pp. 24–38. Hynes is right to stress that the debate between Virginia Woolf and Arnold Bennett has a broad context but it is even broader than he suggests, as Virginia Woolf's reactions to Bennett's *Our Women* (see previous note) and Forster's *Aspects of the Novel* indicate. Bennett was clearly a more self-conscious artist in writing novels than Wells was and perhaps even than Forster; he also realised the potential importance of post-impressionism for literature, and that is more than can be said of Henry James.
36. See J. Howard Woolmer, *A Checklist of the Hogarth Press, 1917–1938* (London, 1976), p. 165.
37. *Anonymity*, p. 81.
38. See 'Towards the Literary History of *A Room of One's Own*' below, pp. 110–41.

NOTES TO CHAPTER 6: TOWARDS THE LITERARY HISTORY OF *A ROOM OF ONE'S OWN*

This is a slightly revised version of the preface and introduction to the transcription of Virginia Woolf's *Women & Fiction: The Manuscript Versions of 'A Room of One's Own'* (Oxford, 1992).

The edition of *A Room of One's Own* used here is the first English one published by the Hogarth Press on 21 October 1929. B. J. Kirkpatrick's *A Bibliography of Virginia Woolf*, 3rd ed. (Oxford, 1980) is the indispensable source for the history of Virginia Woolf's writings. References to the equally indispensable editions of Woolf's letters and diaries are to *The Letters of Virginia Woolf*, ed. Nigel Nicolson and Joanne Trautmann, 6 vols. (London, 1975–80) and *The Diary of Virginia Woolf*, ed. Anne Olivier Bell, 5 vols. (London, 1977–84). Also essential are the *Letters of Leonard Woolf*, ed. Frederic Spotts (New York, 1989) and Brenda R. Silver's *Virginia Woolf's Reading Notebooks* (Princeton, N.J., 1983).

A Newnham Anthology (Cambridge, 1979) was edited by Ann Phillips. George Rylands's recollections have been included in *Recollections of Virginia Woolf*, ed. Joan Russell Noble (London, 1972). ODTAA is defined in Eric Patridge's *Dictionary of Slang and Unconventional English*, 8th ed. (New York, 1984). Woolf's story 'A Society' was first published in *Monday or Tuesday* (London, 1921) and is collected in *The Complete Shorter Fiction of Virginia Woolf*, ed. Susan Dick, 2nd ed. (London, 1989). Kathleen Raine's review of Bradbrook's history appeared in the *Daily Telegraph*, 30 Jan 1969; her autobiography, entitled *The Land Unknown*, was published (London, 1975). M. C. Bradbrook's history is *'That Infidel Place': A Short History of Girton College, 1869–1969* (London, 1969). Q. D. Leavis's attack on *Three Guineas* appeared in *Scrutiny*, VII (Sept 1938), 203–14. Gwendolen Freeman's *Alma Mater: Memories of Girton College, 1926–29* was published by Girton College in

1990. Leonard Woolf's diaries are in the Monks House Papers at the University of Sussex, and J. M. Keynes's correspondence with Lydia Lopokova is at King's College, Cambridge. Desmond MacCarthy's remarks on Woolf occur in the August 1928 and December 1929 issues of *Life and Letters*; his *Sunday Times* review, which Woolf clipped for her *Three Guineas* scrapbooks, appeared on 26 January 1930.

NOTES TO CHAPTER 7: LEONARD AND VIRGINIA WOOLF AT THE HOGARTH PRESS

This essay was originally given as a talk for the University of Toronto Centre for the Book and the Friends of the Victoria College Library, which has one of the most complete collections of Hogarth Press books. It was also given at the Harry Ransom Humanities Research Center and published in the University of Texas at Austin British Studies Distinguished Lectures series in 1995. It is reprinted by permission of the series editor, Roger Louis.

Howard Woolmer's *A Checklist of The Hogarth Press: 1917–1946* (Revere, Penn., 1986) is the standard bibliography of the Press, and J. H. Willis, Jr's *Leonard and Virginia as Publishers: The Hogarth Press, 1917–41* (Charlottesville, Va., 1992) a useful history. Leonard Woolf's autobiographical accounts of the Press are to be found in *Beginning Again, Downhill All the Way* and *The Journey Not the Arrival Matters* (London, 1964, 1967, 1969) as well as his *Letters*, ed. Frederic Spotts (New York, 1989). Virginia Woolfs's *Letters*, ed. Nigel Nicolson and Joanne Trautmann (London, 6 vols., 1975–80) and *Diary*, ed. Anne Olivier Bell (London, 5 vols., 1977–84) are the primary sources for the Woolfs on the Press. John Lehmann's last account of his Hogarth Press experiences is given in *Thrown to the Woolves* (London, 1978). (Lehmann's correspondence about Woolf's *The Journey Not the Arrival Matters* is in the Victoria College Library, Toronto.) Richard Kennedy's *A Boy at the Hogarth Press* (Harmondsworth, Middlesex, 1978) is an amusing account by an office boy in 1928 but written forty years afterwards. The archives of the Hogarth Press can be found at the Universities of Reading and Sussex. Forster's and Cavafy's correspondence is at King's College, Cambridge. Anthony Powell's reminiscences of Duckworth and Company appear in *Messengers of Day*, Vol. 2 of *To Keep the Ball Rolling* (London, 1978). Recent American currency values are derived from Dolf Mootham's 1990 Central Statistical Office figures in Jonathan Gathorne-Hardy's *The Interior Castle: A Life of Gerald Brenan* (London, 1992), p. 611. Examples of the differences between Virginia Woolf's English and American texts can be found in Blackwell's Shakespeare Head Press editions of Virginia Woolf's works, particularly *To the Lighthouse*, ed. Susan Dick (Oxford, 1992).

NOTES TO CHAPTER 8: WITTGENSTEIN IN BLOOMSBURY

The opening address at the 1994 International Wittgenstein Symposium in Kirchberg am Wechsel, Austria, this lecture was published in *The British Tradition in 20th Century Philosophy: Proceedings of the 17th Annual Wittgenstein Symposium*, ed. Jaakko Hintikka and Klaus Puhl (Vienna, 1995), pp. 60–84. It is reprinted, slightly revised and expanded, by permission of Verlag Hölder-Pichler-Tempsky.

1. Janik and Toulmin, for example, who discuss in detail the historical backgrounds of Wittgenstein's Vienna simply accept Keynes's picture as the best account of Wittgenstein's Cambridge circle (p. 277).
2. For Moore's influence on Bloomsbury and the controversies surrounding it, see my *Victorian Bloomsbury*, pp. 214–38.
3. In addition to being an industrialist, Wittgenstein's father was an economist as well, and this may have been a further basis for Wittgenstein's and Keynes's friendship.
4. References are usually to the Ogden Ramsey translation of the *Tractatus*, as this was the version Bloomsbury would have known.
5. For a discussion of Strachey's papers see my *Victorian Bloomsbury*, pp. 256–7 and *Edwardian Bloomsbury*, pp. 308–10.
6. Ramsey's paper was published under the title 'Epilogue' at the end of *The Foundations of Mathematics*.
7. The poem originally appeared in Blunt, Fedden and Redgrave's *The Venture* in 1930. Two years later it was revised and reprinted in Sherard Vines's *Whips and Scorpions: Specimens of Modern Satiric Verse, 1914–1931*.
8. Wittgenstein had been something of an aesthete himself as a young man according to David Pinsent's diary which records Wittgenstein's horror of Philistines and his serving tea in porcelain beakers because the crockery was too ugly.
9. Conversation with Dr Benedict Richards, 22 July 1994.
10. In his revised edition *Recollections of Wittgenstein*, Rhees omitted the confusion but still described Leslie Stephen peculiarly as a distinguished writer on 'social affairs', philosophy and history (p. 186).
11. Weininger appears after Kraus and Loos, before Spengler and Sraffa, which suggests his main impact on Wittgenstein came in the early 1930s. Weininger may have given Wittgenstein the idea in his ethics lecture that if one could write a book which was really about ethics it would 'with an explosion destroy all other books in the world' (p. 7). What made Weininger great, Wittgenstein also told Moore enigmatically in 1931, was his 'enormous mistake' (*Cambridge Letters*, p. 250).
12. See Virginia Woolf, *Women & Fiction: The Manuscript Versions of 'A Room of One's Own'*, p. 207.

Bibliography to Chapter 8

Bell, Clive, *Art*, ed. J. B. Bullen, Oxford, 1987.
——, *Old Friends: Personal Recollections*, London, 1956.
Bell, Julian, 'An Epistle on the Subject of the Ethical and Aesthetic Beliefs of Herr Ludwig Wittgenstein', *The Venture*, Feb 1930, pp. 208–15; revised for *Whips and Scorpions: Specimens of Modern Satiric Verse, 1914–1931*, ed. Sherard Vines, n.p., 1932, pp. 21–30.
Black, Max, *A Companion to Wittgenstein's Tractatus*, Ithaca, N.Y., 1964.
Braithwaite, R. B., Interview, 9 June 1966.
——, 'Keynes as a Philosopher', *Essays on John Maynard Keynes*, ed. Milo Keynes, Cambridge, 1975, pp. 237–46.
Delany, Paul, *The Neo-Pagans: Rupert Brooke and the Ordeal of Youth*, New York, 1987.
Engelmann, Paul, *Letters from Ludwig Wittgenstein with a Memoir*, Oxford, 1967.
Forster, E. M., *Howards End*, ed. Oliver Stallybrass, London, 1973.
——, 'What I Believe', *Two Cheers for Democracy*, ed. Oliver Stallybrass, London, 1972, pp. 65–73.
Fry, Roger, 'An Essay in Aesthetics', *Vision and Design*, ed. J. H. Bullen, London, 1981, pp. 12–27.
Geach, Peter, *Mental Acts: Their Contexts and Their Objects*, London, 1957.
Grant, Duncan, Interview, 23 Aug 1968.
Howarth, T. E. B., *Cambridge Between Two Wars*, London, 1978.
Janik, Allan and Stephen Toulmin, *Wittgenstein's Vienna*, New York, 1973.
Keynes, John Maynard, *The Collected Writings*, ed. Donald Moggridge et al., 30 vols., London, 1971–89.
Kraus, Karl, *In These Great Times: A Karl Kraus Reader*, ed. Harry Zohn, Manchester, 1984.
Levy, Paul, *G. E. Moore and the Cambridge Apostles*, London, 1979.
Malcolm, Norman, *Ludwig Wittgenstein: A Memoir*, London, 1958.
McGuinness, Brian, 'The Mysticism of the Tractatus', *Philosophical Review*, LXXV (1966), 305–28.
——, *Wittgenstein, A Life: Young Ludwig*, London, 1988.
Moggridge, D. E., *Maynard Keynes: An Economist's Biography*, London, 1992.
Monk, Ray, *Ludwig Wittgenstein: The Duty of Genius*, London, 1991.
Moore, G. E., *Principia Ethica*, Cambridge, 1965.
——, 'Wittgenstein's Lectures in 1930–33', *Philosophical Papers*, New York, 1962.
Partridge, Frances, *Memories*, London, 1981.
——, Unpublished letter, 16 Oct 1968.
Passmore, John, *A Hundred Years of Philosophy*, 2nd ed., London, 1966.
Pinsent, David, Diary Extracts, Trinity College, Cambridge.
Ramsey, F. P., *The Foundations of Mathematics and Other Logical Essays*, ed. R. B. Braithwaite, London, 1965.
Read, Herbert, *English Prose Style*, New York, 1952.
Regan, Tom, *Bloomsbury's Prophet: G. E. Moore and the Development of His Moral Philosophy*, Philadelphia, 1986.

Rhees, Rush, ed. *Ludwig Wittgenstein: Personal Recollections*, Totowa, N.J., 1981; revised, Oxford, 1984.
Richards, Benedict, Interview, 22 July 1994.
Richards, I. A., *Selected Letters*, ed. John Constable, Oxford, 1990.
Rosenbaum, S. P., *Edwardian Bloomsbury: The Early Literary History of the Bloomsbury Group*, London, 1994.
——, 'Keynes, Lawrence and Cambridge Revisited', *The Cambridge Quarterly*, XI (1982), 252–64. (See pp. 68–83.)
——, *Victorian Bloomsbury: The Early Literary History of the Bloomsbury Group*, London, 1987.
Sidgwick, Henry, *A Memoir by A. S. and E. M. S.*, London, 1906.
Skidelsky, Robert, *John Maynard Keynes, Vol. 2: The Economist as Saviour, 1920–1937*, London, 1992.
Strachey, Lytton, *Landmarks in French Literature*, London, 1964.
——, Papers, British Library.
——, *Queen Victoria*, London, 1921.
Tolstoy, Leo, *What is Art?* Indianapolis, Ind., 1960.
Von Wright, Georg Henrik, *Wittgenstein*, Oxford, 1982.
Wittgenstein, Ludwig, *The Blue and Brown Books*, Oxford, 1960.
——, *Cambridge Letters*, ed. Brian McGuinness and Georg Henrik von Wright, Oxford, 1995.
——, *Culture and Value*, ed. G. H. von Wright, Oxford, 1980.
——, 'A Lecture on Ethics', *Philosophical Review*, LXXIV (Jan 1965), 3–16.
——, *Notebooks: 1914–1916*, ed. G. H. von Wright and G. E. M. Anscombe, Oxford, 1961.
——, *On Certainty*, ed. G. E. M. Anscombe and G. H. von Wright, Oxford, 1969.
——, *Philosophical Investigations*, Oxford, 1958.
——, *Philosophical Remarks*, ed. Rush Rhees, Oxford, 1975.
——, *Remarks on Frazer's 'Golden Bough'*, ed. Rush Rhees, Retford, England, 1979.
——, *Tractatus Logico-Philosophicus*, intro. by Bertrand Russell, trans. C. K. Ogden and F. P. Ramsey, London, 1951; trans. D. F. Pears and B. F. McGuinness, London, 1963.
Woolf, Leonard, Interview, 27 Aug 1968.
——, *Sowing: An Autobiography of the Years 1880–1904*, London, 1960.
Woolf, Virginia, *The Complete Shorter Fiction*, ed. Susan Dick, 2nd ed., London, 1989.
——, Letters, III and IV, ed. Nigel Nicolson and Joanne Trautmann, London, 1977–8.
——, *Roger Fry*, London, 1940.
——, *A Room of One's Own*, London, 1929
——, *To the Lighthouse*, ed. Susan Dick, Oxford, 1992.
——, *The Waves*, ed. James M. Haule and Philip H. Smith, Jr, Oxford, 1993.
——, *Women & Fiction: The Manuscript Versions of 'A Room of One's Own'*, ed. S. P. Rosenbaum, Oxford, 1992.

Index of Names

Alain, 93, 94–5, 109; *Système des beaux-arts*, 97
Apostles, 3, 81, 115, 162, 166–70, 178, 179
Arden, Mary, 125–6, 137
Aristotle, 93, 109; *Poetics*, 94–6, 172
Arnold, Matthew, 109; 'Function of Criticism at the Present Time', 94
Arts and Crafts Movement, 151
Auden, W. H., 57, 147
Auerbach, Erich, 23; *Mimesis*, 192
Austen, Jane, 119, 126, 128, 135; *Mansfield Park*, 92; *Pride and Prejudice*, 137
Ayer, A. J., 162

Barrie, James, 49
Beerbohm, Max, 92
Beethoven, Ludwig van, 162, 174
Behn, Aphra, 126
Békássy, Ferenc, 167, 170
Bell, Anne Olivier Popham, 189
Bell, Clive, 2–3, 60, 63, 88, 91–2; *Art*, 91, 148, 161, 162, 171, 172–4, 177; *Civilisation*, 91–2; *Legend of Monte Della Sibilla*, 153; *Proust*, 160
Bell, Julian, 115, 116, 147, 162, 179, 189; 'Epistle on the Subject of the Ethical and Aesthetic Beliefs of Herr Ludwig Wittgenstein', 180–5
Bell, Quentin, 63, 78, 80, 111, 181, 189
Bell, Vanessa, 3, 140–1, 151, 153, 158–9, 161, 188–9
Belloc, Hilaire, 149
Bennett, Alan, *Beyond the Fringe*, 199; *Forty Years On*, 199
Bennett, Arnold, 6, 16–17, 91, 105, 106–7; *Old Wives' Tale*, 90, 92; *Our Women*, 204
Benson, E. F., 105
Bentham, Jeremy, 72, 165
Bergson, Henri, 2, 6, 19–20
Berkeley, George, 21

Bessborough, Lady, 137
Birrell, Francis, 77–8, 81, 82; *Letter to a Black Sheep*, 63
Black, Max, 175
Black, Naomi, 111
Blake, William, 38, 168
Bliss, Francis, 167, 170
Blunt, Anthony, 180
Bodley Head, 156
Brace, Donald, 112, 135
Bradbrook, M. C., 116–18
Bradley, A. C., 109; 'Poetry for Poetry's Sake', 88–9, 93
Bradley, F. H., 42–3, 195
Braithwaite, R. B., 72, 165, 180
British Museum, 91, 96, 103, 104, 123, 135
Broad, C. D., 175
Brontë, Charlotte, *Jane Eyre*, 126, 127, 137
Brontë, Emily, 92, 126, 135
Brontë sisters, 126
Brooke, Rupert, 167, 170, 188
Browning, Oscar, 137, 139
Burton, Robert, *Anatomy of Melancholy*, 40
Butcher, S. H., 96
Butler, Samuel, *Erewhon* 40; *Erewhon Revisited*, 40
Buttle, Myra, *Bitches Brew*, 57
Bywater, Ingram, 96

Campbell, Roy, *Georgiad*, 55–7, 194
Cannan, Gilbert, 54; *House of Prophecy*, 197; *Mendel*, 197; *Pugs and Peacocks*, 197; *Sembal*, 196
Cannan, Mrs Gilbert, 82
Cantor, Georg, 38
Cape, Jonathan, 148, 150, 154, 156
Carlyle, Thomas, 38
Carrington, Dora, 115, 143
Carroll, Lewis, *Alice's Adventures in Wonderland*, 40, 41; *Through the Looking Glass*, 40, 41–2

Index of Names

Carter, U. K. N., 114
Cary, Joyce, 57; *Arabella*, 198; *The Captive and the Free*, 198–9
Case, Janet, 66
Cavafy, C. P., 159
Cecil, Lady Robert, 66
Chastaing, Maxime, *La philosophie de Virginia Woolf*, 190
Chatto & Windus, 148, 156
Chekhov, Anton, 149
Chevalley, Abel, *Le roman anglais de notre temps*, 93
Churchill, Winston, 132, 139
Clark Lectureship, 86–7, 99, 202
Clark, R. & R., 144–5
Coleridge, Samuel Taylor, 131–2
Compton-Burnett, Ivy, *Brothers and Sisters*, 160
Conrad, Joseph, 38, 47, 193–4
Cornford, Frances, 146
Criterion, 137

Darwin, Charles, 21
Davies, Emily, 126, 127, 133, 138
Davies, W. H., 149
Day Lewis, C., 146, 147
De La Mare, Walter, 202
Defoe, Daniel, *Moll Flanders*, 10, 90, 92; *Robinson Crusoe*, 87–8, 93, 101
Derain, André, 164
Dick, Susan, 111
Dickens, Charles, 92, 100, 181
Dickinson, Goldsworthy Lowes, 4; *Greek View of Life*, 75
Dickinson, Violet, 66
Donne, John, 126
Dostoyevsky, Fyodor, 92
Doughty, Charles M., 149
Duckworth & Co., 149–50, 154, 158
Duckworth, George, 148–9
Duckworth, Gerald, 148–50

Eberhart, Richard, 147
Einstein, Alfred, 136
Eliot, George, 92, 119, 126, 135
Eliot, T. S., 47, 56, 63, 93–4, 109, 137, 146, 153, 159, 191, 195, 196; 'Mr. Apollinax', 42–5, 52, 54, 195; *Poems*, 143–4; *Sacred Wood*, 94; *Waste Land*, 45, 145, 176–7, 195; 'Whispers of Immortality', 191
Eliot, Vivien, 195
Empson, William, 120–1, 147
Epicurus, 181
Evening Standard, 124

Faber and Faber, 146, 156
Fedden, Robin, 181
Firbank, Ronald, 149
Fitzwilliam Museum, 110–11, 112
Flaubert, Gustave, 138
Fleishman, Avrom, 'Woolf and McTaggart', 192
Ford, Ford Madox, 105, 149
Forster, E. M., 14–15, 22, 60, 61, 62, 63, 65, 118, 158, 161, 162, 168, 171–2, 173, 177, 186; *Anonymity*, 86, 88, 104–5, 108–9, 166; 'Art for Art's Sake', 88; *Aspects of the Novel*, 67, 84–109, 115, 118, 135, 158, 202–4; *Commonplace Book*, 84, 87, 97, 100; 'Creator as Critic', 104; *Guide to Alexandria*, 176; *Howards End*, 62, 94, 171, 187; *Letter to Madam Blanchard*, 63; *Longest Journey*, 171; *Passage to India*, 86, 105, 172; 'Road to Colonus', 171; *Story of a Siren*, 144; 'What I Believe', 188
Forum, 119
France, Anatole, 92
Frazer, James, 187; *Golden Bough*, 161
Frege, Gottlob, 167
Freud, Sigmund, 8, 72, 123, 187; *Moses and Monotheism*, 157; *Works*, 146, 154, 159
Fry, Roger, 3, 4, 60, 88, 91, 97, 143, 146, 148, 150–1, 154, 161, 166, 172–4, 177, 179, 203; 'Essay in Aesthetics', 173; *Transformations*, 98; *Vision and Design*, 87–8, 101; *Woodcuts*, 153
Frye, Northrop, 40
Fuller, B. A. G., 43–4

Galsworthy, John, 6, 132, 149; *Forstye Saga*, 139
Garnett, Angelica, 111, 115

Index of Names

Garnett, David, 68–9, 72–3, 77–83, 189; *Flowers of the Forest*, 80, 82; *Great Friends*, 78–9, 82
Garnett, Edward, 149
Garnett, Richard, 82
Geach, Peter, 187
Gibbon, Edward, 38
Gide, André, 92, 96; *Les faux-monnayeurs*, 101; *School of Women*, 119
Girton College, 112, 113, 115–18, 119–20, 122–3, 126, 127, 133
Glyn, Elinor, 149
Gollancz, Victor, 156
Gorky, Maxim, 149; *Reminiscences of L. N. Tolstoi*, 144
Graham, J. W., 'Point of View in *The Waves*', 192–3
Grant, Duncan, 3, 62, 78, 81, 82, 153, 161, 162
Graves, Robert, 144, 198
Gray, Thomas, *Elegy in a Country Churchyard*, 38

Hall, Radclyffe, *Well of Loneliness*, 116–18, 128, 140
Hamilton, Clayton, *Materials and Methods of Fiction*, 93
Harcourt, Brace, 135, 140, 145, 158
Hardy, G. H., 76
Hardy, Thomas, 96, 176
Harrison, Jane Ellen, 123, 136
Hartley, L. P., 105
Heinemann, William, 145, 150, 154
Heretics Society, 115, 184
Hogarth Press, 29, 63, 86, 97, 115, 116, 118, 135, 137, 142–60, 178, 183, 187, 205
Housman, A. E., 176
Hudson, W. H., 149
Hulme, T. E., 194
Hume, David, 21, 46
Huxley, Aldous, 56; *Crome Yellow*, 51–4, 195–6, 197
Hynes, Samuel, 'Whole Contention between Mr. Bennett and Mrs. Woolf', 204

Ibsen, Henrik, 149

Isherwood, Christopher, 62, 160

Jakobson, Roman, 'Two Aspects of Language', 200
James, Henry, 90, 92, 93, 99–101, 106–7, 109, 149, 172; *Ambassadors*, 100; *Turn of the Screw*, 203; 'Younger Generation', 203
James, William, 6, 8, 158
Janik, Allan, *Wittgenstein's Vienna*, 207
Jeffers, Robinson, 146
Johnstone, J. K., *The Bloomsbury Group*, 190
Jones, David, *In Parenthesis*, 198
Jonson, Ben, 126
Jourdain, Philip, *The Philosophy of Mr. B*rtr*nd R*ss*ll*, 40–2, 52, 54
Joyce, James, 8, 10, 92, 158; *Ulysses*, 23, 35–6, 143, 160, 176, 191
Juvenal, 138

Kant, Immanuel, 5, 97, 173
Keats, John, 138
Kelmscott Press, 152
Kennedy, Richard, 159
Keynes, John Maynard, 60–1, 115, 146, 161, 162, 163, 164–72, 177–81, 185, 188, 201–2; *Economic Consequences of the Peace*, 177–8; 'Melchior', 74; 'My Early Beliefs', 2, 68–83, 165–6, 206; *Short View of Russia*, 178; *Treatise on Probability*, 175, 178
Keynes, John Neville, 166
Keynes, Lydia Lopokova, 115, 162, 178
King's College, Cambridge, 11, 112, 115, 167, 179
Kipling, Rudyard, 132
Koteliansky, S. S., 77
Kraus, Karl, 176

Lawrence, D. H., 45–51, 52, 63, 81, 92, 132, 149, 153, 169, 176, 201–2; 'Blind Man', 46, 49–51, 197; 'Crown', 47; *Lady Chatterley's Lover*, 132; Letters, 77, 82, 196; *Prussian Officer*, 74; *Rainbow*, 47;

Sons and Lovers, 47, 74; *Studies in Classic American Literature*, 105; *Tresspasser*, 74; *White Peacock*, 74; *Women in Love*, 45–7, 51, 75–6, 196
Leach, Henry Goddard, 119
Leaska, Mitchell, *Virginia Woolf's Lighthouse*, 192
Leavis, F. R., 118, 164, 185; 'Keynes, Lawrence and Cambridge', 68, 70–1, 78, 80
Leavis, Q. D., 118
Lee, Vernon, 138
Lehmann, John, 64, 147–8, 155, 159; *Thrown to the Woolves*, 142
Lehmann, Rosamond, *Dusty Answer*, 116; *Letter to a Sister*, 63
Lewis, Sinclair, 176
Lewis, Wyndham, *Apes of God*, 160
Life and Letters, 129, 136
Location Register of Twentieth-Century English Literary Manuscripts and Letters, 110
Locke, John, 6, 8, 21, 35, 38
London and National Society for Women's Service, 112
Lubbock, Percy, 92, 93, 99, 109, 202; *Craft of Fiction*, 99–100
Lucian, 44
Lucretius, 5

MacCarthy, Desmond, 2, 60, 129, 132, 136–7, 161, 166, 177, 184
Malcolm, Norman, 164
Malleson, Constance, *Coming Back*, 196
Mallock, W. H., *New Republic*, 40
Manchester Guardian, 177
Mansfield, Katherine, 50, 153, 159; *Prelude*, 143, 156
Martineau, Harriet, 138
Marx, Karl, 72, 78, 165, 182
Masefield, John, 115
Matson, Norman, 92
Mauron, Charles, 97, 203; *Nature of Beauty in Art and Literature*, 97–9
McGuiness, Brian, 164
McTaggart, J. McT. E., 3, 4, 5, 6, 13, 192

Melville, Herman, 92
Memoir Club, 68, 78, 82
Meredith, George, 1, 90, 92, 96; *Diana of the Crossways*, 138
Mill, John Stuart, 21
Milosz, Czeslaw, *Seizure of Power*, 199
Milton, John, 38, 111, 123–5, 126, 138, 181; *Lycidas*, 133
Monks House Papers, 110–12
Moore, G. E., 1–36, 39, 68, 72–7, 80, 95, 154, 162, 164–9, 171, 176, 178, 179, 181, 185, 187, 199, 206; 'Nature and Reality of Objects of Perception', 11; *Principia Ethica*, 2–4, 21, 27, 28, 69–72, 74, 77, 164–6, 167, 184, 191, 190–3; 'Refutation of Idealism', 5, 6, 31; Reply to My Critics', 4
Moore, George, 4
Montaigne, Michel de, 187
Morrell, Ottoline, 43–4, 45–7, 51, 53, 66, 75–7, 78, 80, 82, 167, 169, 196; *Ottoline at Garsington*, 75
Morris, William, 151
Mortimer, Raymond, 156
Muir, Edwin, 144; *Structure of the Novel*, 105
Murasaki, Lady, 119
Murray, Gilbert, 38
Murry, Middleton, 156

Napoleon Bonaparte, 138
Neilson, William Allan, 120
Neo-Pagans, 188
New Signatures, 147
New Statesman and Nation, 185
New Writing, 147
Newcastle, Duchess of, 126
Newnham, College, 113, 115, 116, 118, 119, 122–3
Nicolson, Harold, 121
Nietzsche, F. W., 101
Nightingale, Florence, 133, 139; *Cassandra*, 138
Nobel Prize, 193
Nonesuch Press, 152
Norton, Harry, 167
Noyes, Alfred, 55, 198

Index of Names

ODTAA Society, 115
Ogden, C. K., 176, 184
Olivier family, 188
Olivier, Noel, 188–9
Omega Workshops, 150–3, 154, 172
Osborne, Dorothy, 126, 137

Parthenon, 11
Partridge, Frances, 162–3, 184
Partridge, Ralph, 154
Pascal, Blaise, 183
Pascal, Fania, 163, 183
Pastons, 125
Peacock, Thomas Love, 40, 51
Phare, E. E., 113–14, 116, 120
Pinsent, David, 169–70, 206
Plomer, William, *Turbott Wolfe*, 145–6
Pound, Ezra, 35–6, 105
Powell, Anthony, 57, 149
Proust, Marcel, 92, 100–1, 160; *À la recherche du temps perdu*, 23, 35–6

Quiller-Couch, Arthur, 133, 139

Rabelais, François, 181
Radcliffe, Ann, 135
Raine, Kathleen, 116–17
Raleigh, Walter, *English Novel*, 93
Ramsey, F. P., 176, 179–82, 185–6
Random House UK, 148
Ransom, John Crowe, 144
Rantavaara, Irma, *Virginia Woolf and Bloomsbury*, 190
Read, Herbert, 144; *English Prose Style*, 176
Redgrave, Michael, 181
Rhees, Goronwy, 188
Rhees, Rush, 186, 206
Richards, Benedict, 188–9
Richards, I. A., 105, 184; *Principles of Literary Criticism*, 88, 98
Richardson, Dorothy, 10, 149
Richardson, Samuel, 92
Riding, Laura, 156–7
Rilke, Rainer Maria, 159
Rivers, W. H. R., 55
Robins, Elizabeth, *Votes for Women*, 62
Robinson, Edward Arlington, 146

Ross, Michael L., 46, 51
Rossetti, Dante Gabriel, 131
Roth, Philip, *Portnoy's Complaint*, 58
Russell, Bertrand, 2–3, 4, 5, 16, 19–20, 36, 37–59, 63, 69, 73, 75–6, 80, 81, 164, 166–7, 169, 171, 175, 185, 193–200; *Collected Stories*, 39; *Conquest of Happiness*, 56; 'Danger to Civilization', 48; 'Free Man's Worship', 39, 193–4; *History of Western Philosophy*, 193; *Human Knowledge*, 193; *Marriage and Morals*, 56, 193; 'My Mental Development', 193; *Mysticism and Logic*, 43, 164; Nightmares of *Eminent Persons*, 40; 'On Denoting', 40, 43; 'Perplexities of John Forstice', 40; *Portraits from Memory*, 71; 'Prelate and the Commissar', 41; *Principia Mathematica*, 199; *Principles of Social Reconstruction*, 47–8, 54, 81; *Problems of Philosophy*, 164; *Satan in the Suburbs*, 40; *Sceptical Essays*, 193; 'What I Believe', 179; *Why I Am Not a Christian*, 44
Rylands, George, 115, 118, 158, 180

Sackville-West, Vita, 4, 112, 115, 117, 119, 121, 146; *Edwardians*, 146, 157
Sand, George, 119
Sappho, 119
Sassoon, Siegfried, *Memoirs of an Infantry Officer*, 54–5, 198
Schoenman, Ralph, 199
Scott, Walter, *Antiquary*, 92; *Waverley*, 38
Scrutiny, 84, 117
Shakespeare, William, 21, 125, 130–2, 136, 156; *Antony and Cleopatra*, 126, 128, 133, 139; *Othello*, 19; Sonnets, 38
Shaw, George Bernard, 56, 195
Shelley, Percy Bysshe, 38, 139
Sheppard, J. T., 81
Shove, Gerald, 168
Sidgwick, Henry, 123, 167
Smith, Barbara Leigh, 127, 138
Smyth, Ethel, 112, 156

Spender, Stephen, 147
Spengler, Oswald, 161, 187
Spinoza, Baruch, 178
Spotts, Frederic, 110
Sitwell family, 149
Stallybrass, Oliver, 86
Stein, Gertrude, 146; *Composition as Explanation*, 155; *Making of Americans*, 155, 160
Stendhal, 35
Stephen family, 167, 169
Stephen, Julia, 23
Stephen, Leslie, 3–4, 6, 20–3, 87, 149, 166, 186; *English Thought in the Eighteenth Century*, 21; *Science of Ethics*, 21
Stephen, Thoby, 2, 10, 32
Sterne, Laurence, 8, 92; *Tristram Shandy*, 10, 38–9, 40, 84, 90
Stone, I. F., 199
Stoppard, Tom, *Jumpers*, 199–200
Strachey family, 167, 169
Strachey, James, 146, 167, 187, 189
Strachey, Lytton, 60, 62–3, 65, 67, 81, 102, 115, 148, 154, 161, 164, 166–70, 171, 172–3, 176, 179, 184, 185–7; *Elizabeth and Essex*, 187; *Eminent Victorians*, 177; *Queen Victoria*, 187
Strachey, Pernel, 113
Strachey, Philippa, 112
Strindberg, August, 138, 149
Sunday Times, 129
Svevo, Italo, 159
Swados, Harvey, *Celebration*, 199
Swift, Jonathan, *Gulliver's Travels*, 40
Sydney Turner, Saxon, 3, 162, 167–8

Tenniel, John, 41–2
Tennyson, Alfred, 131
Thackeray, William Makepeace, 111, 138
Thersites, 114
Times Literary Supplement, 144
Tolstoy, Leo, 144, 173–4; *War and Peace*, 92, 100, 133; *What Is Art?*, 173–4
Toulmin, Stephen, *Wittgenstein's Vienna*, 207

Trevelyan, G. M., 125
Trinity College, Cambridge, 112, 163, 166, 179–81
Tupper, Martin, 156
Turcon, Sheila, 199

Valéry, Paul, 119–20
Vaughan, Madge, 66
Vaughan Williams, Ralph, 151
Verrall, A. W., 123
Voltaire, 181, 182
Von Wright, Georg Henrik, 163

Wales, Prince of, 139
Walpole, Horace, 65
Waugh, Evelyn, 149
Weaver, Harriet Shaw, 143
Webb, Beatrice, 142
Webb, Sidney, 142
Weininger, Otto, *Sex and Character*, 186–7, 206
Wellesley, Dorothy, *Matrix*, 137, 146
Wells, H. G., 6, 92, 93, 100, 106–7, 109, 195; *Boon*, 100
West, Rebecca, 136–7; *Letter to a Grandfather*, 63
Wiener, Norbert, 58
Wilson, Edmund, 105
Whitehead, Alfred North, 166
Whitman, Walt, 38
Wilde, Oscar, 173
Willis, Jr., J. H., 142, 155–6
Winchilsea, Countess of, 126
Wittgenstein, Ludwig, 47, 161–89, 206–8; 'Lecture on Ethics', 172, 184–5; *On Certainty*, 164; *Philosophical Investigations*, 161, 166, 186, 187; *Tractatus Logico-Philosophicus*, 161, 162, 164, 165–6, 170–80, 187
Wollstonecraft, Mary, 137; *Vindication of the Rights of Woman*, 111
Woolf, Cecil, 143
Woolf, Leonard, 60, 63, 65, 71–2, 86, 97, 110–12, 115, 118, 121, 135, 137, 142–60, 161, 162, 165, 166, 173, 177, 178–9, 205; *Co-operation and the Future of Industry*, 157–8;

Journey Not the Arrival Matters, 148, 187; *Sowing*, 2–4; 'Three Jews', 143; *Wise Virgins*, 67

Woolf, Virginia, 1–36, 58, 60, 61–4, 65, 66, 67, 86–9, 90–1, 92, 93, 97, 102, 104, 105, 106–7, 110–41, 142–60, 161, 162, 168, 171, 173, 174, 177, 179, 184, 186–7, 188, 190–3, 205; *Between the Acts*, 36; 'Blue and Green', 7; *Captain's Death Bed*, 62; *Common Reader*, 102, 119; *Complete Shorter Fiction*, 111; *Flush*, 112; 'How Should One Read a Book?', 118; *Jacob's Room*, 9–14, 17, 36, 62, 63–4, 150, 176–7, 191; *Kew Gardens*, 143–4; *Letter to a Young Poet*, 63–4; *Life as We Have Known It*, 118; 'Mark on the Wall', 7–9, 143, 187; 'Middlebrow', 8; 'Modern Fiction', 6, 9, 10; *Monday or Tuesday*, 9, 36; *Mr. Bennett and Mrs. Brown*, 106, 146; *Mrs. Dalloway*, 14–20, 23, 26, 36, 101, 150, 158, 160, 171, 186, 191–2; 'Narrow Bridge of Art', 30; *Night and Day*, 9, 15, 26, 36; *On Being Ill*, 152–3; *Orlando*, 28–9, 30, 111, 118, 146; 'Phases of Fiction', 106–7, 118–19, 134–5, 158; 'Poetry, Fiction and the Future', 119; '*Robinson Crusoe*', 87–9, 93, 101; *Room of One's Own*, 12, 29, 65, 107–9, 110–41, 158, 187, 204–5; 'Sketch of the Past', 134; 'Slater's Pins Have No Points', 119; 'A Society', 116, 136; *Three Guineas*, 28, 64, 65, 116, 118, 119, 150; *To the Lighthouse*, 8, 20–8, 36, 111, 122, 158, 171, 179, 186, 192; 'Unwritten Novel', 7, 9; *Voyage Out*, 3, 9, 20, 36, 191; *Waves*, 8, 28–36, 111, 118–19, 122, 134, 140, 171–2, 184, 192–3; 'Women and Fiction', 110, 118–21; *Women & Fiction*, 110–41, 204–5; *Years*, 17, 28, 36

Woolmer, Howard, 142

Wright, Andrew, 198

Yeats, William Butler, 58, 146, 176, 198; *Fighting the Waves*, 35–6

Zeno, 38, 175